THOMAS CARLYLE

A Bibliography of English-Language Criticism
1824–1974

THOMAS CARLYLE

A BIBLIOGRAPHY OF
ENGLISH-LANGUAGE
CRITICISM
1824–1974

Rodger L. Tarr

Published for the Bibliographical Society
of the University of Virginia

by the University Press of Virginia
Charlottesville

THE UNIVERSITY PRESS OF VIRGINIA
Copyright © 1976 by the Rector and Visitors
of the University of Virginia

First published 1976

Library of Congress Cataloging in Publication Data

Tarr, Rodger L
    Thomas Carlyle: a bibliography of English-language
criticism, 1824–1974

    Bibliography: p.
    Includes indexes.
    1. Carlyle, Thomas, 1795–1881—Bibliography.
Z8147.T37 [PR4433]   016.824′8   76–10837
ISBN 0–8139–0695–4

Printed in the United States of America

For
    Beth
        Ashley
            and Sara Louise

PREFACE

Here hast thou, O Reader! the-from stone-printed
effigies of Thomas Carlyle, the thunderwordoversetter
of Herr Johann Wolfgang von Goethe.

In June of 1833, in this stylistically imitative language, William
Maginn, then editor of FRASER'S MAGAZINE, formally introduced
Thomas Carlyle to the London literati. Of course, what Maginn could
not have realized at the time is that in his prelude to the serial publication of SARTOR RESARTUS he had the distinction of introducing an
individual who subsequently became one of the most dominant figures
in Victorian letters. Although Carlyle's writings had received some
attention previously, it is here that the diverse history of Carlylean
criticism properly begins--a history pregnant with allusion, protected
by discipleship, and punctuated with misunderstanding. As the pro-
claimed authority on matters of life as divergent as transcendentalism
and horseshoes, the first of which precipitated Carlylean consternation
and the last of which evoked Carlylean pride, Carlyle commanded the
respect of his apologists, the disquietude of the perplexed, and the
disgust of the iconoclasts, a critical heritage that has only perceptibly
altered under the microscope of twentieth century scholarship. Yet
even though the nature of the man Carlyle is presently undergoing re-
evaluation as the result of the continuing Duke-Edinburgh Edition of
THE COLLECTED LETTERS OF THOMAS AND JANE WELSH CARLYLE,
which provides and will provide authority to subsequent critical impressions, there remains the question of Carlyle's English critics, who
loom large upon the horizon but who have yet to be fully and systemat-
ically documented. Aside from specialized and select bibliographies
of Carlyle scholarship--most recently Carlisle Moore's chapter in THE
ROMANTIC POETS AND ESSAYISTS (1957, rev. 1966), Charles Richard
Sanders's in the NCBEL (1969), my A BIBLIOGRAPHY OF ENGLISH
LANGUAGE ARTICLES ON THOMAS CARLYLE, 1900-1965 (1972), and
G. B. Tennyson's in VICTORIAN PROSE: A GUIDE TO RESEARCH
(1973)--each of which suffers from imposed limitations, we are still
dependent upon Isaac Watson Dyer's A BIBLIOGRAPHY OF THOMAS
CARLYLE'S WRITINGS AND ANA (1928), which though a monument
to its time is hopelessly inaccurate and incomplete, as well as out-of-
date.

At best, then, Carlylean bibliography at present is a potpourri of well-intentioned but eclectic compilations that do little justice to Carlyle's critical heritage, especially in the nineteenth century. Dyer remains the yardstick for this conclusion. In the past we have been lulled into the false security that his section on criticism has provided us with all we need to know, in spite of the fact that he admits to selectivity in his Preface, and in spite of the fact that his known pro-Carlyle bias holds even his selection open to suspect. Since virtually all of Dyer's journal entries lack authors, exact titles, volume numbers, dates, and/or inclusive pagination, his listings become enticingly debilitating as one searches for accurate and meaningful reference. Some examples will illustrate the point. In his first entry under CANADIAN MONTHLY, the following appears: "v. I, 273. Glimmerings of C. C. M. Sinclair" (p. 496). Ignoring the fact that the entry is incomplete, one would logically assume from the chronological placement that the reference is to volume one of the CANADIAN MONTHLY, which began publication in 1872, when in fact the article actually appeared in the CANADIAN MAGAZINE and should read in full: C. M. Sinclair, "Glimmerings of Sartor Resartus," CANADIAN MAGAZINE, I (June, 1893), 273-276. Four equally perplexing entries are given for the UNIVERSITY QUARTERLY: "v. 2, 214. Imitation of T. C. H. Ballou, 2nd. / v. 4, 1861, 69-78. C's Philosophy. H. O. Newcomb. / v. 42, 389. T. C. G. H. Emerson. / v. 46, 141. T. C. W. E. Gibbs" (p. 531). Only the second item appeared in the UNIVERSITY QUARTERLY REVIEW, while the other three, and one missed, were published in the UNIVERSALIST QUARTERLY REVIEW, which is a totally separate publication, the former issued in New Haven and the latter in Boston. The same confusion holds true for the four entries under the CONGREGATIONAL MAGAZINE (p. 498), the first two of which did indeed appear in that journal, while the last two were published in the CONGREGATIONALIST. Both have London imprints, but both are distinct publications. Bibliographical sleuthing becomes even more difficult when journals that are listed do not exist-- witness, for example, the entry for CURRENT THOUGHT (p. 501), of which I can find no trace; or the entry entitled BIOGRAPHY (p. 494), which is in fact the BIOGRAPH AND REVIEW; or the ENGLISH HISTORICAL MAGAZINE (p. 504), which properly is the ENGLISH ILLUSTRATED MAGAZINE; or the entry under SATURDAY REVIEW (p. 526) for 1840, a major review of CHARTISM, which actually appeared in the ATHENAEUM; the SATURDAY REVIEW did not begin publication until 1855. Errors of this magnitude abound, but are illustrative of the mistakes that permeate Dyer's critical section, which in turn are compounded by less egregious compilation errors that test the patience of the bibliographer and confound the consulting scholar. Dyer's accuracy, if not his comprehensiveness, does improve somewhat in his listing of books on Carlyle, although here again we are confronted with an inconsistent method of description and dating seemingly done at random. Nevertheless, it would be disingenuous not to acknowledge here Dyer's contribution. As a professed student of Carlyle, he preserved for scholarly posterity materials that otherwise might have been lost. His work is marked by sincerity and dedication, and his comment that the "work of a bibliographer is a modest one" (p. x) reflects not only his humility but a proclivity for understatement. Carlyle studies, and for that matter nineteenth century scholarship in general, owes him a debt, especially the subsequent bibliographical undertakings, including this one, and the foreign language and primary bibliographies that must follow.

The intention of this bibliography is to be comprehensive, listing in standard format the response of the English critics to Carlyle from the earliest found review in 1824 to the present. In claiming comprehensiveness, however, one immediately acknowledges that no bibliography is definitive, and that invariably there will be items missed. Considering the 150 years covered, inclusiveness is compounded, especially in the nineteenth century where sources are prolific but where access is often limited. The method used was to examine physically journals that might reasonably contain material. This approach was to insure both accuracy and scope. In the nineteenth century, for example, nearly 500 periodicals were consulted, ranging from the American humorist magazine DIOGENES HYS LANTERNE to the more conservative British WESTMINSTER REVIEW, and 264 contained material. Therefore, in addition to supplementing, correcting, and updating Dyer, perhaps the major contribution of this work lies in the discovery of new material, especially in the nineteenth century. Of the 2200 entries up to the publication of Dyer in 1928 (the number swells appreciably when reprinted material is considered), more than 1200 are fresh entries that have hitherto escaped permanent record. Of the 1200, approximately one-third appeared during Carlyle's lifetime, which together with the corrected and supplemented material provides for the first time a decisive picture of Carlyle at the hands of his contemporaries. The entries cover the spectrum from major reviews to minor notices, from significant biographical essays to slight but noteworthy anecdotal pieces, from considered critical responses to absurd evaluations, and from seminal studies to utterly worthless books. What becomes clear is that the storm that Carlyle created among his contemporaries is not unlike the disparate reactions of the twentieth century mind. To Ralph Waldo Emerson he was a "genius," to D. R. M. Wilkinson "second-rate"; to Edgar Allan Poe he was an "ass," to Logan Pearsall Smith a "Victorian Rembrandt" (see entries 149, 2964, 154, and 2426). It is to the refining of these conclusions that this bibliography is dedicated.

The chronological format employed is designed to facilitate specific reference, which has the advantage of avoiding cumulative and often cumbersome alphabetical listing, while at the same time permitting isolation of any given year or sequence of years. Author and subject indexes are provided to aid reference, and in each case the numbers listed correspond to the entries in the bibliography proper. Every effort has been made to identify anonymous authors, and here acknowledgment must be given to the WELLESLEY INDEX and to Jules P. Seigel's THOMAS CARLYLE AND THE PERIODICAL PRESS: A STUDY IN ATTITUDES (unpublished dissertation, Maryland, 1965), which made the task an easier one. Further, it is incumbent upon a bibliographer to point out what has not been included. No attempt has been made to index exhaustively British newspapers, except the London TIMES, for to do so is certainly desirable but surely at once impossible, exemplified by the TIMES itself which yielded nearly 200 entries. However, where feasible pertinent items have been included, such as one of the earliest reviews of SARTOR RESARTUS in the London SUN in 1834. The same situation applies to American newspapers, except the NEW YORK TIMES which has been indexed, although a number of significant items that appeared during Carlyle's lifetime have been listed, with credit to Howard D. Widger's THOMAS CARLYLE IN AMERICA: HIS REPUTATION AND INFLUENCE (unpublished dissertation, Illinois, 1945). Twentieth century reviews of works on Carlyle also have not been included, except in the case of review-essays or those that contribute directly to Carlyle scholarship. A difficult decision had to be made concerning references to Carlyle in primary works, autobiographies, biographies, and memoirs, especially those in the nineteenth century. Because of the voluminous quantity of such sources practicality dictated select exclusion. In the case of primary material, therefore, it is not noted that Sandy Mackaye in Kingsley's ALTON LOCKE is Carlyle, that Dr. Pessimist Anticant in Trollope's THE WARDEN is Carlyle, or that Carlyle plays an important role, for example, in Ruskin's UNTO THIS LAST and Arnold's CULTURE AND ANARCHY. Such literary allusion, although expressly significant, is deemed beyond the scope of this work. As for the passing references to Carlyle that proliferate autobiographies and memoirs, exclusion, except in justified circumstance, became a utilitarian necessity. The same general decision applies to biographies of nineteenth century figures, for there is hardly an index that does not contain a reference to Carlyle. Except for these parameters, comprehensiveness was the desired goal.

Needless to say this work owes an immeasurable debt to countless individuals, but especially to the reference librarians of the following institutions, who during the past five years have graciously and unsparingly made the materials in their archives available to me: American Antiquarian Society, Auburn University, Bodleian Library,

Boston Athenaeum Library, Boston Public Library, Bristol Public Library, British Library, British Museum, Brooklyn Public Library, California State Libraries (Sacramento and Sutro), Carnegie Library, Catholic University, Cincinnati Public Library, Cleveland Public Library, Colgate University, Columbia University, Congregational Library, Connecticut State Library, Cornell University, Creighton University, Dartmouth College, Denver University, Detroit Public Library, Drew University, Duke University, Dumfries County Library, Edinburgh Public Library, English Literary Society of Korea, Florida State University, Forbes Library, Franklin and Marshall College, Gettysberg College, Hamilton and Kirkland College, Harvard University, Haverford College, Historical Society of Pennsylvania, Honnold Library, Huntington Library, Illinois State University, Indiana University, John Crerar Library, Kansas City Public Library, Kansas State Historical Society, Library of Congress, Los Angeles Public Library, Manchester Public Library, Massachusetts State Library, McGill University, Mechanic's Institute, Miami University, Michigan State University, Milwaukee Public Library, Minneapolis Public Library, Mitchell Library, National Library of Scotland, New York State Library (Albany), Newberry Library, Northwestern University, Notre Dame University, Oberlin College, Office of the Hamilton Spectator, Ohio State University, Pennsylvania State University, Princeton University, Purdue University, Rutgers University, San Francisco Public Library, Seattle Public Library, Southern Illinois University, St. Louis Public Library, Stanford University, Syracuse University, Trinity College, Tulane University, Tuskegee Institute, University of Arizona, University of Arkansas, University of California (Berkeley), University of California (Los Angeles), University of Chicago, University of Edinburgh, University of Florida, University of Illinois, University of Iowa, University of Kansas, University of Michigan, University of Minnesota, University of Nebraska, University of North Carolina, University of South Carolina, University of Southern California, University of Texas, University of Tokyo, University of Washington, University of Wisconsin, Vancouver Public Library, Washington University, Wesleyan University, and Yale University.

To the faithful graduate assistants, who have come and gone but who worked tirelessly while at hand, my acknowledgment. To Miss Sandy Whiteley, former Senior Reference Librarian of Yale University, whose special efforts are reflected herein, my gratitude. And to my wife, who while working in Carlylean "well-doing" withstood the library dust and combatted the rigors of compilation, and whose imprint justly rests on this work, my dedication. Finally, acknowledgment is rightly given to the American Philosophical Society, the University of Edinburgh, and Illinois State University for respective grants that aided in the execution and completion of the bibliography.

CONTENTS

THE NINETEENTH CENTURY

1824

1   Anon. "Schiller's Life and Writings," TIMES (January 1, 1824), 3.

2   ____. "[Wilhelm Meister]," BLACKWOOD'S EDINBURGH MAGAZINE,
     XVI (August, 1824), 242.

3   [De Quincey, Thomas]. "Wilhelm Meister's Apprenticeship," LONDON
     MAGAZINE, X (September, 1824), 189-197, 291-307.

4   Q. "Wilhelm Meister's Apprenticeship, A Novel," EXAMINER, no.
     858 (July 11, 1824), 451-452.

1825

5   [Jeffrey, Francis]. "Wilhelm Meister's Apprenticeship, A Novel,"
     EDINBURGH REVIEW, XLII (August, 1825), 409-449.

1826

6   Anon. "[Carlyle's Style]," DUMFRIES MONTHLY MAGAZINE, II
     (May, 1826), 419.

7   [Lockhart, John G.]. "[Wilhelm Meister]," QUARTERLY REVIEW,
     XXXIV (June, 1826), 136.

1827

8   Q. "German Romance," EXAMINER, no. 992 (February 4, 1827), 69-70.

1829

9   Anon. "[Carlyle Letter]," ESSAYS AND TRANSACTIONS OF THE
     HIGHLAND SOCIETY, VII (1829), 290-291.

10   ____. "The Foreign Reviews," ATHENAEUM, no. 63 (January 7,
     1829), 1-2.

11   ____. "[Wilhelm Meister]," NORTH AMERICAN REVIEW, XXVIII
     (April, 1829), 549.

12   ____. "Goethe's Wilhelm Meister," SOUTHERN REVIEW, III (May,

1829), 353-385.

13 _____. "The Foreign Review," ATHENAEUM, no. 91 (July 22, 1829), 456.

14 [Willis, Nathaniel P.]. "[Wilhelm Meister]," AMERICAN MONTHLY MAGAZINE, I (June, 1829), 160.

1830

15 [Willis, Nathaniel P.]. "[Wilhelm Meister]," AMERICAN MONTHLY MAGAZINE, II (September, 1830), 430.

1831

16 Walker, Timothy. "Defense of Mechanical Philosophy," NORTH AMER-ICAN REVIEW, XXXIII (July, 1831), 126-136.

17 [Wilson, John]. "[Carlyle on Burns]," BLACKWOOD'S EDINBURGH MAGAZINE, XXX (September, 1831), 484.

1832

18 [Peabody, W. B. O.]. "[Carlyle on Burns]," NORTH AMERICAN RE-VIEW, XXXIV (January, 1832), 102.

19 [Wilson, John]. "[Genius of Carlyle]," BLACKWOOD'S EDINBURGH MAGAZINE, XXXI (April, 1832), 694.

1833

20 Anon. "Life of Friedrich Schiller," AMERICAN QUARTERLY REVIEW, XIII (March, 1833), 60-93.

21 Cunningham, Allan. "Thomas Carlyle," ATHENAEUM, no. 321 (Dec-ember 28, 1833), 893.

22 Edinburgh Evening Post. "Mr. Carlyle," TIMES (September 18, 1833), 3.

23 [Maginn, William]. "Thomas Carlyle," FRASER'S MAGAZINE, VII (June, 1833), 706.

24 N[orton], A[ndrews]. "Recent Publications Concerning Goethe, "

4

SELECT JOURNAL OF FOREIGN PERIODICAL LITERATURE, I (April, 1833), 250-293.

1834

25   Anon. "['Richter']," SELECT JOURNAL OF FOREIGN PERIODICAL LITERATURE, I (January, 1834), 124-125.

26   ____ . "Life of Friedrich Schiller," AMERICAN QUARTERLY OBSERV-ER, II (January, 1834), 172-174.

27   ____ . "Life of Friedrich Schiller," NEW ENGLAND MAGAZINE, VI (February, 1834), 165-166.

28   ____ . "[The Life of Friedrich Schiller]," KNICKERBOCKER MAGA-ZINE, III (April, 1834), 309-310.

29   ____ . "[Sartor Resartus]," SUN (April 1, 1834), 2.

30   [Calvert, George?]. "The Life of Friedrich Schiller," NORTH AMERI-CAN REVIEW, XXXIX (July, 1834), 1-30.

31   Hedge, Frederick H. "The Life of Friedrich Schiller," CHRISTIAN EXAMINER, XVI (July, 1834), 365-392.

1835

32   Anon. "['Edward Irving']," ATHENAEUM, no. 375 (January 3, 1835), 15.

33   ____ . "[Sartor Resartus]," ATHENAEUM, no. 424 (December 12, 1835), 931.

34   [Everett, Alexander H.]. "Thomas Carlyle," NORTH AMERICAN REVIEW, XLI (October, 1835), 454-482.

1836

35   F[rothingham], N[athaniel] L. "Sartor Resartus," CHRISTIAN EXAM-INER, XXI (September, 1836), 74-84.

1837

5

36   Anon. "Carlyle's Sartor Resartus," SOUTHERN LITERARY JOURNAL,
      n.s. I (March, 1837), 1-8.

37   ____. "[London Lectures]," ATHENAEUM, no. 491 (March 25, 1837),
      218.

38   ____. "The Life of Friedrich Schiller," KNICKERBOCKER MAGA-
      ZINE, IX (April, 1837), 425.

39   ____. "Sartor Resartus," KNICKERBOCKER MAGAZINE, IX (April,
      1837), 432.

40   ____. "Mr. Thomas Carlisle's Lectures," SPECTATOR, X (May 6,
      1837), 421-422.

41   ____. "Lectures on German Literature," TIMES (May 9, 1837), 6.

42   ____. "The French Revolution," LITERARY GAZETTE, no. 1062 (May
      27, 1837), 330-332.

43   ____. "The French Revolution," MONTHLY REVIEW, n.s. II (August,
      1837), 543-548.

44   ____. "The French Revolution," MONTHLY REPOSITORY, n.s. XI
      (September, 1837), 219-220.

45   ____. "The French Revolution," EXAMINER, nos. 1546-1548 (Sept-
      ember 17-October 1, 1837), 596-598, 629-630.

46   ____. "Histories of the French Revolution," SOUTHERN ROSE, VI
      (November 25, 1837), 101-102.

47   A. [John S. Mill]. "The French Revolution," LONDON AND WEST-
      MINSTER REVIEW, XXVII (July, 1837), 17-53.

48   B[owen], F[rancis]. "[Carlyle as Transcendentalist]," CHRISTIAN EX-
      AMINER, XXIII (November, 1837), 186.

49   [Morgan, Lady Sydney]. "The French Revolution," ATHENAEUM, no.
      499 (May 20, 1837), 353-355. Rpt. Albert Mordell, NOTORIOUS
      LITERARY ATTACKS. New York: Boni and Liberight, 1926.

50   [Palfrey, J. G.]. "Miss Martineau's Society in America," NORTH

AMERICAN REVIEW, XLV (October, 1837), 418-460.

51 [Thackeray, William M.]. "The French Revolution," TIMES (August 3, 1837), 6. Rpt. SULTAN STORK AND OTHER STORIES. London: George Redway, 1887.

52 [Wilson, John]. "[The French Revolution]," BLACKWOOD'S EDIN-BURGH MAGAZINE, XLII (November, 1837), 592-593.

1838

53 Anon. "The French Revolution," CHRISTIAN EXAMINER, XXIII (January, 1838), 386-387.

54 ____. "Life of Schiller," CHARLESTON MERCURY (January 11, 1838), 4.

55 ____. "Carlyle's History of the French Revolution," SOUTHERN ROSE, VI (January 20, 1838), 174.

56 ____. "Carlyleana," CHRISTIAN REGISTER, XVII (March, 1838), 46.

57 ____. "Carlyleiana," CHRISTIAN REGISTER, XVII (March, 1838), 50.

58 ____. "The French Revolution," AMERICAN MONTHLY MAGAZINE, V (March, 1838), 290.

59 ____. "Carlyle's History of the French Revolution," NEW YORKER, IV (March 10, 1838), 813.

60 ____. "The French Revolution," CHARLESTON MERCURY (March 14, 1838), 3.

61 ____. "Protestant Nonconformity," SOUTHERN ROSE, VI (April 14, 1838), 271.

62 ____. "Carlyle vs. Scott," BOSTON EVENING TRANSCRIPT, (April 20, 1838), 1.

63 ____. "Mr. Carlyle's New Lectures," EXAMINER, no. 1577 (April 22, 1838), 246.

64   ____. "Mr. Carlyle's Lectures," TIMES (April 30, May 1, 22, 1838), 4, 5, 6.

65   ____. "Mr. Carlyle's Lectures," EXAMINER, nos. 1579-1585 (May 6-June 17, 1838), 278-279, 294, 310, 324, 340, 358, 373-374.

66   ____. "Walter Scott," SOUTHERN ROSE, VI (May 26, 1838), 309-310.

67   ____. "[Critical and Miscellaneous Essays]," CHRISTIAN REGISTER, XVII (July, 1838), 111.

68   ____. "Mr. Carlyle, the English Reviewer," SOUTHERN LITERARY JOURNAL, n.s. IV (August, 1838), 160.

69   ____. "Sartor Resartus," METROPOLITAN MAGAZINE, XXIII (September, 1838), 1-5.

70   ____. "Carlyle's Sartor Resartus," MONTHLY REVIEW, CXLVII (September, 1838), 54-66.

71   ____. "[Sartor Resartus]," TAIT'S EDINBURGH MAGAZINE, V (September, 1838), 611-612.

72   An Auditor. "Mr. Carlyle's Lectures," TIMES (May 2, 1838), 6.

73   [Anstey, T. Chisholm]. "Carlyle's Works," DUBLIN REVIEW, V (October, 1838), 349-376.

74   B[artol], C. A. "The French Revolution," CHRISTIAN EXAMINER, XXIV (July, 1838), 345-362.

75   [Channing, W. H.]. "The French Revolution," BOSTON QUARTERLY REVIEW, I (October, 1838), 407-417.

76   C[larke], J[ames] F. "Thomas Carlyle: The German Scholar," WESTERN MESSENGER, IV (February, 1838), 417-423.

77   Ellis, George E. "[Carlyle and Swedenborg]," CHRISTIAN EXAMINER, XXIV (March, 1838), 28.

78   J., J. J. [Isaac Jewett]. "Thomas Carlyle," HESPERIAN, II (November, 1838), 5-20.

79   Quilibet [pseud.]. "Innovations in English Style," SOUTHERN LITER-
      ARY MESSENGER, IV (May, 1838), 322-327.

1839

80   Anon. "Carlyle," NEW YORKER, VI (January, 1839), 244.

81   _____. "Mr. Carlyle's Lectures on the Revolutions of Modern Europe,"
      MORNING CHRONICLE (May 8, 10, 1839), 3, 3. See also CHRISTIAN
      REGISTER, XVIII (July, 1839), 106.

82   _____. "Mr. Carlyle's Lectures on the Revolutions of Modern Europe,"
      TIMES (May 10, 1839), 5.

83   _____. "The Lectures of Mr. Carlyle on the Revolutions of Modern
      Europe," EXAMINER, nos. 1632-1634 (May 12-May 26, 1839), 293-294,
      326.

84   _____. "Germanic Infections: Dr. Channing," KNICKERBOCKER MAG-
      AZINE, XIV (July, 1839), 90-92.

85   _____. "The French Revolution," NEW YORK REVIEW, V (July, 1839),
      109-135.

86   _____. "Critical and Miscellaneous Essays," LITERARY EXAMINER AND
      WESTERN MONTHLY REVIEW, I (December, 1839), 459-464.

87   [Bancroft, George]. "Specimens of Foreign Standard Literature,"
      CHRISTIAN EXAMINER, XXVI (July, 1839), 360-376.

88   [Henry, C. S.?]. "Writings of Thomas Carlyle," NEW YORK REVIEW,
      IV (January, 1839), 179-208. See also NEW YORKER, VI (January,
      1839), 244.

89   [Prescott, William H.]. "[Carlyle on the French Revolution]," NORTH
      AMERICAN REVIEW, XLIX (October, 1839), 342.

90   [Sterling, John]. "Carlyle's Works," LONDON AND WESTMINSTER
      REVIEW, XXXIII (October, 1839), 1-68. Rpt. ESSAYS AND TALES.
      London: J. W. Parker, 1848.

1840

91   Anon. "Chartism," BRITISH AND FOREIGN REVIEW, XI (1840), 1-31.
Rpt. AMERICAN ECLECTIC, I (January, 1841), 41-63.

92   ____. "Chartism," NEW MONTHLY MAGAZINE, LVIII (1840), 293.

93   ____. "Chartism," MONTHLY CHRONICLE, V (February, 1840), 97-
107.

94   ____. "Carlyle's Chartism," TAIT'S EDINBURGH MAGAZINE, VII
(February, 1840), 115-120.

95   ____. "Chartism," MONTHLY MAGAZINE, XCI (February, 1840),
196-204.

96   ____. "Wilhelm Meister," MONTHLY MAGAZINE, XCI (February,
1840), 222-223.

97   ____. "Carlyle on Chartism," MONTHLY REVIEW, XLI (February,
1840), 243-253.

98   ____. "[Lectures on Heroes and the Heroic]," EXAMINER, no. 1684
(May 10, 1840), 292.

99   ____. "Carlyle-ism," KNICKERBOCKER MAGAZINE, XV (June,
1840), 525-528.

100   ____. "Carlyle's Chartism," DEMOCRATIC REVIEW, VIII (July, 1840),
13-30.

101   ____. "Chartism and 'The Laboring Classes,'" CHRISTIAN EXAMINER,
XXIX (September, 1840), 119-124.

102   ____. "Carlyle-iana," IRIS, I (November, 1840), 48.

103   ____. "The French Revolution," LITTELL'S MUSEUM OF FOREIGN
LITERATURE, XL (December, 1840), 385-394.

104   Appollodorus [George Gilfillan]. "Carlyle and the French Revolution,"
DUMFRIESSHIRE AND GALLOWAY HERALD AND ADVERTISER, VI (Oct-
ober 15, 1840), 3.

105   [Brownson, Orestes A.]. "Norton and the Transcendentalists," BOSTON

QUARTERLY REVIEW, III (July, 1840), 265-323.

106   ____. "Chartism," BOSTON QUARTERLY REVIEW, III (July, 1840), 358-395.

107   M[azzini], J[oseph]. "The French Revolution," MONTHLY CHRONICLE, V (January, 1840), 71-84. Rpt. ESSAYS. London: Walter Scott, 1887.

108   [Merivale, Herman]. "Carlyle on the French Revolution," EDINBURGH REVIEW, LXXI (July, 1840), 411-445.

109   [Morgan, Lady Sydney]. "Chartism," ATHENAEUM, no. 637 (January 11, 1840), 27-29.

110   N. "Chartism," WESTERN MESSENGER, VIII (June-August, 1840), 87-90, 108-115, 162-168.

111   [Porter, O.]. "Hints for a Critical Estimate of the Writings of Thomas Carlyle," YALE LITERARY MAGAZINE, V (August, 1840), 478-482.

112   [Sewell, William]. "Carlyle's Works," QUARTERLY REVIEW, LXVI (September, 1840), 446-503.

1841

113   Anon. "Chartism," BRITISH AND FOREIGN REVIEW, XII (1841), 303-335. Rpt. AMERICAN ECLECTIC, III (March, 1842), 205-230.

114   ____. "Carlyleism," CLASSIC; OR, COLLEGE MONTHLY, I (January 1, 1841), 335.

115   ____. "Heroes and Heroism," BOSTON DAILY ADVERTISER (April 8, 1841), 2.

116   ____. "Heroes and Hero-Worship," BOSTON EVENING TRANSCRIPT (April 20, 1841), 2.

117   ____. "Specimens of German Romance," BOSTON DAILY ADVERTISER (May 15, 1841), 2.

118   ____. "Carlyle's Lectures on Heroes and Hero-Worship," TAIT'S EDINBURGH MAGAZINE, VIII (June, 1841), 379-383.

119   . "The French Revolution," BOSTON DAILY ADVERTISER (June 23, 1841), 2.

120   . "Carlyle's Heroes and Hero-Worship," NEW YORK REVIEW, IX (July, 1841), 266.

121   . "Carlyle's Specimens of German Romance," NEW YORK RE-VIEW, IX (July, 1841), 266-267.

122   [Barrett, Joseph H.]. "Heroes and Hero-Worship," MONTHLY REVIEW CLV (May, 1841), 1-21.

123   D. "Unpublished Lectures," ARCTURUS, I (May, 1841), 354-362.

124   [Fuller, Margaret]. "Heroes and Hero-Worship," DIAL, II (July, 1841), 131-133.

125   [Grant, James]. PORTRAITS OF PUBLIC CHARACTERS. 2 vols. London: Saunders and Otley, 1841.

126   H., J. A. "T. Carlyle on Hero-Worship," MONTHLY MAGAZINE, XCIII (April, 1841), 391-412.

127   J. "Thomas Carlyle," ARCTURUS, II (June, 1841), 41-49.

128   . "German Romance," ARCTURUS, II (June, 1841), 65-66.

1842

129   Anon. "The French Revolution," AMERICAN BIBLICAL REPOSITORY, n.s. VII (January, 1842), 233-234.

130   . "Chartism," ECLECTIC REVIEW, LXXV (April, 1842), 429-451.

131   "J---" [pseud.]. "The Clothes Philosophy of Carlyle," YALE LITER-ARY MAGAZINE, VII (August, 1842), 378-382.

132   "N" [pseud.]. "Stray Thoughts on Carlyle," YALE LITERARY MAGA-ZINE, VII (February, 1842), 170-177.

133   Richardson, Merrill. "The Religious Sentiments of Thomas Carlyle," AMERICAN BIBLICAL REPOSITORY, n.s. VIII (October, 1842), 382-405.

134   [Thomson, William]. "Heroes and Hero-Worship," CHRISTIAN REMEM-
BRANCER, III (March, 1842), 341-353.

1843

135   Anon. "Past and Present," MAGAZINE OF DOMESTIC ECONOMY
AND FAMILY REVIEW, n.s. I (January, 1843), 561-564.

136   _____. "Thomas Carlyle and His Writings," CHAMBERS'S EDINBURGH
JOURNAL, XII (February 18, 1843), 37-38.

137   _____. "Past and Present," EXAMINER, no. 1839 (April, 1843), 259-
261.

138   _____. "Past and Present," MONTHLY REVIEW, CLXI (May, 1843),
190-203.

139   _____. "Carlyle on Heroes," BOSTON EVENING TRANSCRIPT, (May
10, 1843), 2.

140   _____. "Past and Present," GRAHAM'S MAGAZINE, XXIII (June,
1843), 58.

141   _____. "Thomas Carlyle's Past and Present," TAIT'S EDINBURGH MAG-
AZINE, X (June, 1843), 341-348.

142   _____. "Past and Present," BOSTON EVENING TRANSCRIPT, (June
20, 1843), 2.

143   _____. "Carlyle and Macaulay," DARTMOUTH, V (September, 1843),
30-35.

144   _____. "Past and Present," TIMES (October 6, 1843), 3-4.

145   Brownson, Orestes A. "The Present State of Society," DEMOCRATIC
REVIEW, XIII (July, 1843), 17-38.

146   Copcott, Francis. "Byron: Collected from the Various Writings of
Thomas Carlyle," KNICKERBOCKER MAGAZINE, XXI (March, 1843),
199-212.

147   D[eLeon], E. "Carlyle's Miscellanies," MAGNOLIA; OR, SOUTHERN

APPALACHIAN, n.s. II (February, 1843), 96-100.

148   E., R. B. THOUGHTS ON THOMAS CARLYLE; OR, A COMMENTARY ON "PAST AND PRESENT," London: Ward, 1843.

149   [Emerson, Ralph W.]. "Past and Present," DIAL, IV (July, 1843), 96-102.

150   Foster, J. K. "On Thomas Carlyle's Writings," CONGREGATIONAL MAGAZINE, XXVI (March, 1843), 262-264.

151   Maurice, F[rederick D.]. "On the Tendency of Mr. Carlyle's Writings," CHRISTIAN REMEMBRANCER, VI (October, 1843), 451-461.

152   [Morgan, Lady Sydney]. "Past and Present," ATHENAEUM, nos. 811-812 (May 13-May 20, 1843), 453-454, 480-481.

153   P., T. W. "'Epistle to Thomas Carlyle,'" KNICKERBOCKER MAGAZINE, XXII (July, 1843), 62-65.

154   Poe, Edgar A. "William Ellery Channing," GRAHAM'S MAGAZINE, XXIII (August, 1843), 113-117.

155   [Renouf, Peter L.]. "Carlyle's Past and Present," DUBLIN REVIEW, XV (August, 1843), 182-200.

156   [Smith, William H.]. "Past and Present," BLACKWOOD'S EDINBURGH MAGAZINE, LIV (July, 1843), 121-138.

157   [Thomson, William]. "Carlyle's Heroes and Hero-Worship," CHRISTIAN REMEMBRANCER, VI (August, 1843), 121-143.

1844

158   Anon. "Advice to Young Men," CHAMBERS'S EDINBURGH JOURNAL, n.s. I (April 13, 1844), 239. Rpt. LITTELL'S LIVING AGE, CCCXLVI (May, 1934), 214-216.

159   _____. "[Carlyle's Introduction to Emerson's Essays]," EXAMINER, no. 1922 (November 30, 1844), 757.

160   _____. "Thomas Carlyle," LITTELL'S LIVING AGE, III (December 7, 1844), 346.

161   Horne, Richard H. A NEW SPIRIT OF THE AGE. 2 vols. London: Smith,
       Elder, 1844. Rpt. LITERARY ANECDOTES OF THE NINETEENTH CEN-
       TURY. London: Hodder and Stoughton, 1896.

162   [Mazzini, Joseph]. "The Works of Thomas Carlyle," BRITISH AND FOR-
       EIGN REVIEW, XVI (1844), 262-293. Rpt. ECLECTIC MAGAZINE, II
       (May, 1844), 1-15; and ESSAYS. London: Walter Scott, 1887.

163   [Richardson, Merrill]. "Carlyle's Past and Present," NEW ENGLANDER,
       II (January, 1844), 25-39.

164   Smith, J. T. "Carlyle's Past and Present," AMERICAN BIBLICAL RE-
       POSITORY, XII (October, 1844), 317-352.

165   [Thackeray, William M.]. "[Carlyle, Dickens, and Christmas]," FRA-
       SER'S MAGAZINE, XXIX (February, 1844), 169.

                                    1845

166   Anon. "Carlyle's Preface to Emerson's Essays," BROADWAY JOURNAL,
       I (January 11, 1845), 29-30.

167   _____. "The Works of Thomas Carlyle," ECLECTIC REVIEW, LXXXI
       (April, 1845), 377-399.

168   _____. "Carlyle's Schiller," BOSTON EVENING TRANSCRIPT (Nov-
       ember 7, 1845), 2.

169   _____. "The Life of Schiller," NEW YORK EVENING POST (November
       8, 1845), 2.

170   _____. "The Life of Friedrich Schiller," NEW YORK TRIBUNE (Nov-
       ember 8, 1845), 2.

171   _____. "Heroes and Hero-Worship," CHARLESTON MERCURY (Novem-
       ber 10, 1845), 4.

172   _____. "Carlyle's Life of Schiller," AMERICAN WHIG REVIEW, II
       (December, 1845), 668.

173   _____. "Life of Schiller," RICHMOND ENQUIRER (December 1, 1845),
       2.

174 _____. "The Life of Friedrich Schiller," BROADWAY JOURNAL, II (December 6, 1845), 336-337.

175 _____. "Oliver Cromwell," PHILADELPHIA UNITED STATES GAZETTE AND NORTH AMERICAN (December 12, 29, 1845), 1, 2.

176 _____. "Oliver Cromwell," BOSTON DAILY ADVERTISER (December 12, 29, 1845), 1, 1.

177 _____. "Oliver Cromwell's Letters and Speeches," CRITIC, n.s. II (December 13, 1845), 653-656, 694-695.

178 _____. "Oliver Cromwell's Letters and Speeches," EXAMINER, no. 1976 (December 13, 1845), 787-789.

179 _____. "Letters and Speeches of Oliver Cromwell," BOSTON EVENING TRANSCRIPT (December 14, 16, 1845), 2, 1.

180 [Fuller, Margaret.]. "The Letters and Speeches of Oliver Cromwell," NEW YORK TRIBUNE (December 19, 1845), 1. See also LIFE WITHOUT AND LIFE WITHIN. Boston: Brown, Taggard, and Chase, n.d. [1859].

181 Gilfillan, George. A GALLERY OF LITERARY PORTRAITS. Edinburgh: William Tait, 1845. See also MODERN LITERATURE AND LITERARY MEN. New York: D. Appleton, 1856.

182 [Heraud, Abraham]. "Oliver Cromwell's Letters and Speeches," ATHENAEUM, nos. 945-947 (December 6-December 20, 1845), 1165-1167, 1193-1195, 1218-1219.

183 Hudson, T. B. "Thomas Carlyle," OBERLIN QUARTERLY REVIEW, I (August, 1845), 56-75.

184 N., C. S. [H. Ballou]. "Another Chapter from Carlyle the Younger," UNIVERSALIST QUARTERLY REVIEW, II (April, 1845), 214-217.

185 [Vaughn, Robert]. "German Philosophy and Christian Theology," BRITISH QUARTERLY REVIEW, II (November 1, 1845), 297-336.

1846

186 Anon. "Carlyle's Oliver Cromwell," KNIGHT'S PENNY MAGAZINE,

XV (1846), 81-96.

187   _____ . "Oliver Cromwell's Letters and Speeches," DOUGHLAS JER-
ROLD'S SHILLING MAGAZINE, III (1846), 182-184.

188   _____ . "Mr. Carlyle's Oliver Cromwell's Letters and Speeches," TAIT'S
EDINBURGH MAGAZINE, XIII (January, 1846), 38-50.

189   _____ . "Letters and Speeches of Oliver Cromwell," KNICKERBOCKER
MAGAZINE, XXVII (January, 1846), 75.

190   _____ . "Life of Friedrich Schiller," METHODIST QUARTERLY REVIEW,
XXVIII (January, 1846), 155-156.

191   _____ . "Life of Friedrich Schiller," SOUTHERN QUARTERLY REVIEW,
IX (January, 1846), 282.

192   _____ . "Letters and Speeches of Oliver Cromwell," BOSTON DAILY AD-
VERTISER (January 21, 1846), 2.

193   _____ . "Carlyle's Cromwell," CHARLESTON COURIER (January 27,
1846), 2.

194   _____ . "Oliver Cromwell," CHARLESTON MERCURY (January 27, 1846),
3.

195   _____ . "Oliver Cromwell," RICHMOND ENQUIRER (January 31, 1846), 1.

196   _____ . "Oliver Cromwell Vindicated by Thomas Carlyle," CHAMBERS'S
EDINBURGH JOURNAL, n.s. V (January-February, 1846), 8-11, 23-26,
130-133.

197   _____ . "[Oliver Cromwell]," PETERSON'S MAGAZINE, IX (February,
1846), 72.

198   _____ . "Life of Schiller," AMERICAN WHIG REVIEW, III (February,
1846), 224.

199   _____ . "Carlyle's Cromwell," DUBLIN UNIVERSITY MAGAZINE, XXVII
(February, 1846), 228-245.

200   _____ . "Life of Schiller," CHARLESTON MERCURY (February 3, 1846),
4.

201   ____. "[Carlyle on Labor]," NEW QUARTERLY REVIEW, VII (April, 1846), 137.

202   ____. "Carlyle's Letters and Speeches of Oliver Cromwell," METRO-POLITAN MAGAZINE, XLI (April, 1846), 293-311.

203   ____. "Oliver Cromwell," AMERICAN WHIG REVIEW, III (April, 1846), 396-414.

204   ____. "The Letters and Speeches of Oliver Cromwell," TIMES (April 17, May 4, 1846), 6, 8.

205   ____. "Oliver Cromwell's Letters and Speeches," LITTELL'S LIVING AGE, VIII (March 7, 1846), 457-462.

206   ____. "Cromwell and His Times," DEMOCRATIC REVIEW, XVIII (May, 1846), 336-343.

207   ____. "Thomas Carlyle," ALBION, n.s. V (May 23, 1846), 246-248.

208   ____. "Supplement to the First Edition of Oliver Cromwell's Letters and Speeches," ATHENAEUM, no. 973 (June 20, 1846), 623-624.

209   ____. "Thomas Carlyle," LITTELL'S LIVING AGE, IX (June 27, 1846), 585-593.

210   ____. "Oliver Cromwell's Letters and Speeches," SOUTHERN QUAR-TERLY REVIEW, X (October, 1846), 257-292.

211   ____. "Heroes and Hero-Worship," DEMOCRATIC REVIEW, XIX (Dec-ember, 1846), 490.

212   ____. "The French Revolution," DEMOCRATIC REVIEW, XIX (Decem-ber, 1846), 491.

213   [Felton, C. C.]. "Carlyle's Letters of Cromwell," NORTH AMERICAN REVIEW, LXII (April, 1846), 380-429.

214   [Grolly, George]. "The Great Irish Insurrection," DUBLIN REVIEW, XXI (September, 1846), 65-131.

215   L., W. P. [Edwin P. Whipple?]. "Oliver Cromwell--Puritanism," CHRISTIAN EXAMINER, XL (May, 1846), 440-459.

216 [Moncrieff, James]. "Critical and Miscellaneous Essays, Heroes and Hero-Worship, and Oliver Cromwell's Letters and Speeches," NORTH BRITISH REVIEW, IV (February, 1846), 505-536. Rpt. ECLECTIC MAGAZINE, VII (April, 1846), 452-470.

217 [Mozley, James B.]. "Oliver Cromwell's Letters and Speeches," CHRISTIAN REMEMBRANCER, XI (April, 1846), 243-315. Rpt. ESSAYS HISTORICAL AND THEOLOGICAL. Oxford: Rivington, 1878.

218 Poe, Edgar A. "Marginalia," DEMOCRATIC REVIEW, XVIII (April, 1846), 268-272.

219 [Richardson, Merrill]. "Carlyle's Cromwell," NEW ENGLANDER, IV (April, 1846), 211-228.

220 [Tayler, John J.]. "Oliver Cromwell's Letters and Speeches," PROSPECTIVE REVIEW, II (February, 1846), 119-158.

221 [Vaughan, Robert]. "Oliver Cromwell's Letters and Speeches," BRITISH QUARTERLY REVIEW, III (February 1, 1846), 50-95.

1847

222 Anon. "The French Revolution," GRAHAM'S MAGAZINE, XXX (January, 1847), 83.

223 _____. "[Carlyle and Germanism]," NORTH BRITISH REVIEW, VI (February, 1847), 325-329. See also CHRISTIAN REGISTER, XXVI (May, 1847), 73.

224 _____. "[Carlyle's Appearance and Conversation]," NEW YORK TRIBUNE (February 19, 1847), 1.

225 _____. "To Poets--A Letter from Carlyle," NEW YORK TRIBUNE (February 24, 1847), 2. Rpt. LITERARY WORLD, I (March 6, 1847), 110-111.

226 _____. "Past and Present and Chartism," GRAHAM'S MAGAZINE, XXX (June, 1847), 379.

227 [Bain, Alexander]. "Oliver Cromwell's Letters and Speeches," WESTMINSTER REVIEW, XLVI (January, 1847), 432-473.

228 [Donaldson, John W.]. "Pantagruelism," QUARTERLY REVIEW, LXXXI

(June, 1847), 106-130.

229   Fuller, [Margaret] Miss. "A Picture of Thomas Carlyle," LITTELL'S LIV-ING AGE, XXI (March, 1847), 605.

230   Lester, John W. CRITICISMS. London: Longman, Brown, 1847.

231   [Smith, William H.]. "Cromwell," BLACKWOOD'S EDINBURGH MAG-AZINE, LXI (April, 1847), 393-423. Rpt. LITTELL'S LIVING AGE, XIII (May 29, 1847), 385-403.

232   Summerfield, Charles [Alfred A. Arrington]. DUELS AND DUELLING IN THE SOUTH-WEST. New York: W. H. Graham, 1847.

233   Tholuck, Prof. "The Influence of German Theology and Philosophy on England," BIBLICAL REVIEW, III (February, 1847), 95-102.

234   _____. "Carlyle's Heroes and Hero-Worship," BIBLICAL REVIEW, III (March, 1847), 183-186.

235   Thoreau, Henry D. "Thomas Carlyle and His Works," GRAHAM'S MAG-AZINE, XXX (March-April, 1847), 145-152, 238-245. Rpt. A YANKEE IN CANADA. Boston: Ticknor and Fields, 1866.

1848

236   Anon. "Thomas Carlyle on Ragged Schools," CRITIC, n.s. VII (January 29, 1848), 74-75. Rpt. CHRISTIAN REGISTER, XXVII (March, 1848), 37.

237   _____. "The Cromwell Letters," ELEPHANT, I (February, 1848), 28.

238   _____. "Carlyle's Works," SOUTHERN QUARTERLY REVIEW, XIV (July, 1848), 77-101.

239   _____. "Sartor Resartus," DEMOCRATIC REVIEW, XXIII (August, 1848), 139-149.

240   _____. "Carlyle and Macaulay," SOUTHERN LITERARY MESSENGER, XIV (August, 1848), 476-480.

241   _____. "Headley's The Life of Oliver Cromwell," SOUTHERN QUARTER-

LY REVIEW, XIV (October, 1848), 506-538.

242   Lowell, James R. A FABLE FOR CRITICS. New York: G. P. Putnam, 1848.

243   M[ill, John S.]. "England and Ireland," EXAMINER, no. 2102 (May 13, 1848), 307-308.

244   Richardson, David L. LITERARY CHIT-CHAT. London: James Madden, 1848.

245   Whipple, Edwin P. ESSAYS AND REVIEWS. 2 vols. New York: D. Appleton, 1848-1849.

246   Wright, Elizur. "Thomas Carlyle," CHRISTIAN REGISTER, XXVII (November, 1848), 182.

1849

247   Anon. "New Translation of Dante," LITERARY WORLD, IV (June 16, 1849), 509-510.

248   [Barrett, Joseph H.]. "Sartor Resartus," AMERICAN WHIG REVIEW, IX (February, 1849), 121-134.

249   _____. "Carlyle's Heroes," AMERICAN WHIG REVIEW, IX (April, 1849), 339-344.

250   [Greg, William R.]. "[Carlyle and Mary Barton]," EDINBURGH REVIEW, LXXXIX (April, 1849), 423.

251   [Lewes, George H.]. "Thomas Carlyle," BRITISH QUARTERLY REVIEW, X (August 1, 1849), 1-45. Rpt. ECLECTIC MAGAZINE, XVIII (November, 1849), 285-309.

252   Moore, T. V. "Thomas Carlyle," METHODIST QUARTERLY REVIEW, XXXI (January-April, 1849), 119-139, 217-240.

253   Poe, Edgar A. "Marginalia," SOUTHERN LITERARY MESSENGER, XV (June-July, 1849), 338, 416.

254   Powell, Thomas. THE LIVING AUTHORS OF ENGLAND. New York:

D. Appleton, 1849. Rpt. PICTURES OF THE LIVING AUTHORS OF BRITAIN. London: Partridge and Oakey, 1851.

1850

255   Anon. "Carlyle on the Negro Question," BOSTON EVENING TRANS-CRIPT (January 30, 1850), 2.

256   _____. "Carlyle on the Negro Question," BOSTON LIBERATOR (February 8, 15, 1850), 23, 26.

257   _____. "Latter-Day Pamphlets," PHILADELPHIA UNITED STATES GAZETTE AND NORTH AMERICAN (February 14, April 29, May 31, June 17, 1850), 6, 2, 2, 1.

258   _____. "The Scoffer and the Servile," BOSTON LIBERATOR (February 15, 1850), 26.

259   _____. "Mr. Carlyle and the West Indies Negro Question," BOSTON LIBERATOR (February 22, 1850), 31.

260   _____. "The Nigger Question," CHARLESTON MERCURY (February 22, 1850), 2.

261   _____. "Latter-Day Pamphlets," BOSTON EVENING TRAVELLER (March 2, April 19, May 6, 1850), 2, 2, 2.

262   _____. "Latter-Day Pamphlets," BOSTON EVENING TRANSCRIPT (March 2, 4, April 25, May 17, 1850), 2, 2, 2, 2.

263   _____. "Latter-Day Pamphlets," BOSTON HERALD (March 2, 4, April 2, 6, May 15, 1850), 2, 2, 2, 2, 2.

264   _____. "Latter-Day Pamphlets," BOSTON DAILY ADVERTISER (March 2, 5, April 6, 1850), 2, 2, 2.

265   _____. "Latter-Day Pamphlets," NEW YORK EVENING POST (March 4, 1850), 1.

266   _____. "Latter-Day Pamphlets," PHILADELPHIA EVENING BULLETIN (March 6, April 2, 3, 17, 1850), 1, 1, 2, 2.

267   _____. "Carlyle Made Easy," PUNCH, XVIII (March 16, 1850), 110.

268 _____. "Carlyle's Pamphlet," LITERARY WORLD, VI (March 16, 1850), 275-276.

269 _____. "Emerson's Queer Movements in Literature," NEW YORK HER-ALD (March 24, 1850), 2.

270 _____. "Latter-Day Pamphlets," INDEPENDENT, II (March-August, 1850), 48, 68, 92, 104, 139.

271 _____. "Carlyle's Seventy-Four," CHRISTIAN REGISTER, XXIX (April, 1850), 66.

272 _____. "Latter-Day Pamphlets," CHRISTIAN OBSERVATORY, IV (April, 1850), 189-191.

273 _____. "Carlylism," RAMBLER, V (April, 1850), 354-366.

274 _____. "Rivalry Among the Book Sellers," NEW YORK HERALD (April 1, 1850), 2.

275 _____. "Carlyleism," LITERARY WORLD, VI (April 6, 1850), 351.

276 _____. "[Carlyle on Bores]," NEW YORK EVENING POST (April 9, 1850), 2.

277 _____. "[Latter-Day Pamphlets]," NEW YORK TRIBUNE (April 15, May 1, 1850), 6, 6.

278 _____. "Latter-Day Pamphlets," BOSTON LIBERATOR (April 19, 1850), 63.

279 _____. "Latter-Day Pamphlets," CHARLESTON COURIER (April 22, 1850), 1.

280 _____. "[Latter-Day Pamphlets]," BOSTON LIBERATOR (April 26, 1850), 68.

281 _____. "Carlyle on Bores," BALTIMORE SUN (April 29, 1850), 2.

282 _____. "Punch's Police: A Very Melancholy Case," LITERARY WORLD, VI (April 20, 1850), 402-403. See also PUNCH, XVIII (May, 1850), 107. Rpt. LITTELL'S LIVING AGE, XXV (May 25, 1850), 372.

283   ____ . "Latter-Day Pamphlets," ELIZA COOK'S JOURNAL, II (April 30, 1850), 398-399.

284   ____ . "Carlyle and Carlylese," CHRISTIAN REGISTER, XXIX (May, 1850), 78.

285   ____ . "Latter-Day Pamphlets," AMERICAN WHIG REVIEW, XI (May, 1850), 550-551.

286   ____ . "[Latter-Day Pamphlets]," LEADER, I (May 4, 1850), 130.

287   ____ . "Latter-Day Pamphlets," CHARLESTON MERCURY (May 17, 1850), 1.

288   ____ . "Latter-Day Pamphlets," PETERSON'S MAGAZINE, XVII-XVIII (May-November, 1850), 23, 135, 215.

289   ____ . "Carlyle's Latter-Day Pamphlets," SARTAIN'S UNION MAGAZINE, VI (June, 1850), 436.

290   ____ . "Carlyle on West India Emancipation," DE BOW'S REVIEW, VIII (June, 1850), 527-538.

291   ____ . "Latter-Day Pamphlets," EXAMINER, no. 2213 (June 29, 1850), 404-406.

292   ____ . "Carlyle's Latter-Day Pamphlets," PALLADIUM, I (July, 1850), 3-16.

293   ____ . "[Latter-Day Pamphlets]," METHODIST QUARTERLY REVIEW, XXXII (July, 1850), 484.

294   ____ . "Carlyle's Latter-Day Pamphlets," CHRISTIAN OBSERVER, L (July, 1850), 488-496.

295   ____ . "Latter-Day Pamphlets," SOUTHERN QUARTERLY REVIEW, XVII (July, 1850), 509.

296   ____ . "Carlyle's Latter-Day Pamphlets," CHAMBERS'S EDINBURGH JOURNAL, n.s. XIV (July 13, 1850), 26-28.

297   ____ . "[Latter-Day Pamphlets]," HARPER'S MAGAZINE, I (August-

September, 1850), 430, 571.

298 _____. "Memoranda About Thomas Carlyle," ECLECTIC MAGAZINE, XXI (September, 1850), 141-142. Rpt. FRIEND'S INTELLIGENCER, X (1854), 9-10.

299 _____. "Latter-Day Pamphlets," HOLDEN'S DOLLAR MAGAZINE, VI (September, 1850), 565.

300 _____. "Carlyleiana," LITERARY WORLD, VII (September 7, 1850), 186-187.

301 _____. "Carlyle's Latter-Day Pamphlets," ECLECTIC REVIEW, CII (October, 1850), 385-409.

302 _____. "Thomas Carlyle," ELIZA COOK'S JOURNAL, III (October 12, 1850), 369-371.

303 _____. "[Latter-Day Pamphlets and David Copperfield]," FRASER'S MAGAZINE, XLII (December, 1850), 707-710.

304 _____. "Carlyle's Latter-Day Pamphlets," TIMES (December 25, 31, 1850), 3, 7.

305 [Aytoun, William E.]. "Latter-Day Pamphlets," BLACKWOOD'S EDINBURGH MAGAZINE, LXVII (June, 1850), 641-658.

306 C., E. W. "Latter-Day Pamphlets," CRITIC, n.s. IX (February 15-March 15-July 15, 1850), 96-97, 145-146, 356-357.

307 Caliban [James H. Stirling]. "Letters on Carlyle," TRUTH-SEEKER, I (April-August, 1850), 94-101, 148-163, 245-249.

308 Carlylian [James Hannay]. BLACKWOOD VERSUS CARLYLE: A VINDICATION. London: Effingham Wilson, 1850.

309 [Cooke, John E.]. "Thomas Carlyle and His Latter-Day Pamphlets," SOUTHERN LITERARY MESSENGER, XVI (June, 1850), 330-340.

310 D. [John S. Mill]. "The Negro Question," FRASER'S MAGAZINE, XLI (January, 1850), 25-31. Rpt. LITTELL'S LIVING AGE, XXIV (March 9, 1850), 465-469.

311   [Dixon, Hepworth]. "Latter-Day Pamphlets," ATHENAEUM, nos. 1162-
        1191 (February 2-August 24, 1850), 126-127, 704-705, 894-895.

312   Ellsworth, Erastus W. "'To Mr. Carlyle,'" SARTAIN'S UNION MAGA-
        ZINE, VII (November, 1850), 267.

313   [Field, H M.]. "Writings and Opinions of Thomas Carlyle," NEW
        ENGLANDER, VIII (February, 1850), 46-66.

314   Frank, Parson. "Thomas Carlyle," PEOPLE'S AND HOWITT'S JOURNAL,
        X (January, 1850), 239-243. Rpt. ECLECTIC MAGAZINE, XXII (Feb-
        ruary, 1850), 199-205.

315   Giles, Henry. LECTURES AND ESSAYS. 2 vols. Boston: Ticknor,
        Reed and Fields, 1850.

316   Gilfillan, George. "Thomas Carlyle," HARPER'S MAGAZINE, I (Oct-
        ober, 1850), 586-588.

317   [Guy, W. A.]. "Thomas Carlyle and John Howard," FRASER'S MAG-
        AZINE, XLI (April, 1850), 406-410. Rpt. LITTELL'S LIVING AGE,
        XXV (May 25, 1850), 369-371.

318   H., G. F. "Latter-Day Pamphlets," SOUTHERN QUARTERLY REVIEW,
        XVIII (November, 1850), 313-356.

319   Headley, J. T. MISCELLANIES. New York: Barker and Scribner, 1850.

320   [Hervey, T. K.]. "Latter-Day Pamphlets," ATHENAEUM, no. 1166
        (March 2, 1850), 227-228.

321   Hunt, Leigh. AUTOBIOGRAPHY. 3 vols. London: Smith, Elder, 1850.

322   M., W. "Carlyle's New Treatise," CHRISTIAN REGISTER, XXIX
        (March, 1850), 46.

323   [Masson, David]. "Carlyle's Latter-Day Pamphlets," NORTH BRITISH
        REVIEW, XIV (November, 1850), 1-40.

324   [O'Hagan, John]. "Carlyle's Works," DUBLIN REVIEW, XXIX (Sept-
        ember, 1850), 169-206.

325   P., N. E. "The Present Time," TRUTH-SEEKER, I (April, 1850), 101-105.

326   Pease, Elizabeth. "A Letter to the Liberator," BOSTON LIBERATOR
      (February 8, 1850), 23.

327   Poe, Edgar A. "[Carlyle's Style]," GRAHAM'S MAGAZINE, XXXVI
      (January, 1850), 49.

328   _____. "Margaret Fuller," INTERNATIONAL MONTHLY MAGAZINE,
      I (August 5, 1850), 162-165.

329   [Spring-Rice, Thomas]. "[Latter-Day Pamphlets]," EDINBURGH REVIEW,
      XCI (April, 1850), 492-493.

330   [Wicksteed, Charles]. "Mr. Carlyle's Latter-Day Pamphlets," PROS-
      PECTIVE REVIEW, VI (May, 1850), 212-229.

331   Wright, Elizur. PERFORATIONS IN THE "LATTER-DAY PAMPHLETS"
      BY ONE OF THE 'EIGHTEEN MILLIONS OF BORES.' Boston: Phillips,
      Sampson, 1850.

1851

332   Anon. "Thomas Carlyle," HOGG'S WEEKLY INSTRUCTOR, VII (1851),
      81-86. Rpt. ECLECTIC MAGAZINE, XXVII (December, 1852), 516-526.

333   _____. "[Latter-Day Pamphlets]," TIMES (January 13, 1851), 4.

334   _____. "'The Beetle,'" LITERARY WORLD, VIII (February 1, 1851), 94.

335   _____. "Originals of Carlyle's Cromwell Correspondence," LITERARY
      WORLD, VIII (April 26, 1851), 340.

336   _____. "[Carlyle and Election Addresses]," TIMES (June 21, 1851), 4.

337   _____. "[Life of John Sterling]," PRINCETON REVIEW, XXIII (Octo-
      ber, 1851), 712.

338   _____. "The Life of John Sterling," CRITIC, n.s. X (October 15-Nov-
      ber 1, 1851), 478-480, 507-509.

339   _____. "Carlyle's Life of John Sterling," EXAMINER, nos. 2281-2282
      (October 18-October 25, 1851), 659-661, 677-678. Rpt. LITTELL'S LIV-
      ING AGE, XXXI (December 20, 1851), 543-550.

340 _____. "Carlyle's Life of Sterling," TAIT'S EDINBURGH MAGAZINE, XVIII (November, 1851), 699-707.

341 _____. "The Life of John Sterling," TIMES (November 1, 1851), 7. Rpt. ESSAYS FROM THE 'LONDON TIMES.' 2nd sers. New York: D. Appleton, 1852.

342 _____. "Carlyle's Life of Sterling," INTERNATIONAL MONTHLY MAGAZINE, IV (November 1, 1851), 599-602.

343 _____. "Carlyle's Life of Sterling," LITERARY WORLD, IX (November 1-8, 1851), 341-342, 363-365.

344 _____. "Carlyle's Life of Sterling," LEADER, II (November 8, 1851), 1066-1067.

345 [Brimley, George]. "Carlyle's Life of John Sterling," SPECTATOR, XXIV (October 25, 1851), 1023-1024. Rpt. ESSAYS. Cambridge: Macmillan, 1858.

346 [Dixon, Hepworth]. "The Life of John Sterling," ATHENAEUM, no. 1251 (October 18, 1851), 1088-1090. Rpt. ECLECTIC MAGAZINE, XXIV (December, 1851), 546-551.

347 [Gilfillan, George]. "Life of John Sterling," ECLECTIC REVIEW, CIV (December, 1851), 717-729. Rpt. LITTELL'S LIVING AGE, XXXII (January 31, 1852), 219-223; and A THIRD GALLERY OF LITERARY PORTRAITS. Edinburgh: James Hogg, 1854.

348 Paul, Lucian [Francis Espinasse]. "Thomas Carlyle," CRITIC, n.s. X (June 14, 1851), 276-278. Rpt. LITERARY WORLD, IX (August 23, 1851), 150-152; and LITTELL'S LIVING AGE, XXX (September 13, 1851), 550-552.

1852

349 Anon. "Carlyle's Life of Sterling," SHARPE'S LONDON MAGAZINE, XV (1852), 52-55.

350 _____. "Carlyle's Life of Sterling," DEMOCRATIC REVIEW, XXX (January, 1852), 67-75.

351 _____. "Carlyle's Life of John Sterling," CHRISTIAN REMEMBRANCER,

XXIII (January, 1852), 153-185.

352 _____ . "Latter-Day Pamphlets," ENGLISH REVIEW, XVI (January, 1852), 331-351.

353 _____ . "John Sterling and His Biographers," DUBLIN UNIVERSITY MAG-AZINE, XXXIX (February, 1852), 185-199.

354 _____ . "Carlyle's Life of John Sterling," BRITISH QUARTERLY REVIEW, XV (February 1, 1852), 240-253. Rpt. LITTELL'S LIVING AGE, XXXIII (April 3, 1852), 1-6.

355 _____ . "[Life of John Sterling]," LEADER, III (February 7, 1852), 133.

356 _____ . "Carlyle's Life of Sterling," CHRISTIAN OBSERVER, LII (April, 1852), 262-276. Rpt. LITTELL'S LIVING AGE, XXXIII (June 5, 1852), 470-476.

357 _____ . "Styles, American and Foreign: Carlyle and His Imitators," AMERICAN WHIG REVIEW, XV (April, 1852), 349-356.

358 _____ . "Thomas Carlyle," CRITIC, n.s. XI (May 1, 1852), 249.

359 _____ . "John Sterling and Thomas Carlyle," NATIONAL MAGAZINE, I (July, 1852), 20-25.

360 _____ . "Letter[s] from Thomas Carlyle," DIOGENES HYS LANTERNE, II (August 14-21, 1852), 55, 67.

361 _____ . "Poems," DIOGENES HYS LANTERNE, II (August 28, 1852), 77.

362 _____ . "[Frederick the Great]," PRINCETON REVIEW, XXIV (October, 1852), 717.

363 _____ . "The Critic Abroad," CRITIC, n.s. XI (November 1, 1852), 571-572.

364 Bartlett, David W. LONDON BY DAY AND NIGHT. New York: Derby and Miller, 1852.

365 Brown, W. B. "Personal Sketches of Distinguished Men," NEW YORK TIMES (November 3, 1852), 5.

366   [Eliot, George]. "Carlyle's Life of John Sterling," WESTMINSTER RE-
       VIEW, LVII (January, 1852), 247-251. Rpt. ESSAYS OF GEORGE ELIOT.
       Ed. Thomas Pinney. New York: Columbia University Press, 1963.

367   Fuller, Margaret. MEMOIRS. 2 vols. Boston: Phillips, Sampson, 1852.

368   [McNicoll, Thomas]. "The Writings of Thomas Carlyle," WESLEYAN
       METHODIST MAGAZINE, LXXV (May-October, 1852), 489-493, 696-
       702, 802-805, 999-1008. Rpt. CRITICAL ESSAY ON THE WRITINGS
       OF THOMAS CARLYLE. London: Whittaker, 1853; and ESSAYS ON ENG-
       LISH LITERATURE. London: Basil Montagu Pickering, 1861.

369   [Newman, Francis W.]. "The Life of John Sterling," PROSPECTIVE RE-
       VIEW, VIII (February, 1852), 1-15.

370   Richardson, David L. LITERARY RECREATIONS. London: Thacker, 1852.

371   [Ross, John (John Dix)]. LIONS: LIVING AND DEAD. London: Part-
       ridge and Oakey, 1852.

372   [Tullock, John]. "Life of John Sterling," NORTH BRITISH REVIEW, XVI
       (February, 1852), 359-389.

                                 1853

373   Anon. "Writings of Thomas Carlyle," CHAMBERS'S REPOSITORY OF
       TRACTS, V (1853), 1-32.

374   _____. "Thomas Carlyle, As Described and Reviewed by a French Critic,"
       ELIZA COOK'S JOURNAL, VIII (January 1, 1853), 154-156.

375   _____. "[Notice of 'Dr. Johnson' and 'Nigger Question' Pamphlets],"
       CRITIC, n.s. XII (July 15, 1853), 377.

376   _____. "[John A. Carlyle]," DUBLIN UNIVERSITY MAGAZINE, XLII
       (September, 1853), 253-275.

377   Ficulnus [pseud.]. "Passage in Carlyle," NOTES AND QUERIES, sers.
       I, VII (March 19, 1853), 285.

378   Kennard, Kate. "Sonnet After Carlyle. A Versification of a Sentence
       in Sartor Resartus," GODEY'S LADY'S BOOK, XLVI (January, 1853), 32.

379   Ware, Motley [John E. Cooke]. "Unpublished MSS from the Portfolio of
       the Most Celebrated Authors," LITERARY WORLD, XII (February 26,
       1853), 172.

1854

380   Anon. "[Death of Margaret Aitken Carlyle]," LEADER, V (January,
       1854), 10.

381   _____. "Mrs. Carlyle," CRITIC, n.s. XIII (January 16, 1854), 52.

382   _____. "Letter from Carlyle," MONTHLY RELIGIOUS MAGAZINE,
       XI (April, 1854), 191-192.

383   _____. "Thomas Carlyle," BIOGRAPHICAL MAGAZINE, XXX (June,
       1854), 241-256.

384   Whittier, John G. LITERARY RECREATIONS AND MISCELLANIES.
       Boston: Ticknor and Fields, 1854.

1855

385   Anon. "Passages Selected from the Writings of Thomas Carlyle," RAM-
       BLER, n.s. IV (July, 1855), 471-472.

386   _____. "[Latter-Day Pamphlets]," ECLECTIC REVIEW, XVII (September,
       1855), 351-371.

387   _____. "Bayne's Christian Life," CHRISTIAN REVIEW, XX (October,
       1855), 602-608.

388   _____. "[Misses Lowe]," ATHENAEUM, no. 1562 (November 3, 1855),
       1275.

389   Ballantyne, Thomas. PROPHECY FOR 1855. London: Chapman and Hall,
       1855.

390   _____. PASSAGES SELECTED FROM THE WRITINGS OF THOMAS
       CARLYLE, WITH A BIOGRAPHICAL MEMOIR. London: Chapman and
       Hall, 1855.

391   Bayne, Peter. THE CHRISTIAN LIFE. Edinburgh: James Hogg, 1855.

392   [Eliot, George]. "Thomas Carlyle," LEADER, VI (October 27, 1855), 1034-1035.

393   [Smith, Goldwin]. "Carlyle's and Guizot's Cromwell," LITTELL'S LIV-ING AGE, XLIV (February 17, 1855), 429-434.

1856

394   Anon. "Passages Selected from the Writings of Thomas Carlyle," NEW QUARTERLY REVIEW, V (April, 1856), 203-206.

395   Chambers, Robert. CHAMBERS'S CYCLOPAEDIA OF ENGLISH LITER-ATURE. 2 vols. Philadelphia: J. B. Lippincott, 1856-1859.

396   Emerson, Ralph W. ENGLISH TRAITS. Boston: Phillips, Sampson, 1856.

397   Gilfillan, George. THE HISTORY OF A MAN. London: Arthur Hall, 1856.

398   [Lushington, Vernon]. "Carlyle," OXFORD AND CAMBRIDGE MAGA-ZINE, I (April-December, 1856), 193-211, 292-310, 336-352, 697-712, 743-771.

399   [Martineau, James]. "Personal Influences on Our Present Theology: Newman--Coleridge--Carlyle," NATIONAL REVIEW, III (October, 1856), 449-494. Rpt. ESSAYS, PHILOSOPHICAL AND THEOLOGICAL. London: Trubner, 1866.

400   Monkshood [Francis Jacox]. "Thomas Carlyle," BENTLEY'S MISCEL-LANY, XL (1856), 538-550. Rpt. ECLECTIC MAGAZINE, XL (February, 1857), 184-191.

401   Wallace, Horace B. LITERARY CRITICISMS AND OTHER PAPERS. Phila-delphia: Parry and McMillan, 1856.

1857

402   Anon. "The French Revolution," CRITIC, n.s. XVI (January 15-February 16, 1857), 39, 76.

403   _____. "Oliver Cromwell's Letters and Speeches," CRITIC, n.s. XVI (March 16-May 15, 1857), 126, 220.

404 _____. "Oliver Cromwell's Letters and Speeches," LONDON QUAR-
TERLY REVIEW, VIII (April, 1857), 561.

405 _____. "[French Revolution and Cromwell]," NOTES AND QUERIES,
sers. 2, III (April 11, 1857), 300.

406 _____. "[Carlyle Letter to Edward Everett]," HISTORICAL MAGAZINE,
I (June, 1857), 143-144.

407 _____. "[John Sterling]," NOTES AND QUERIES, sers. 2, III (June
20, 1857), 500.

408 _____. "[Critical and Miscellaneous Essays]," NOTES AND QUERIES,
sers. 2, IV (July 25-October 24, 1857), 80, 339.

409 Clapp, Theodore. AUTOBIOGRAPHICAL SKETCHES AND RECOLLEC-
TIONS. Boston: Phillips, Sampson, 1857.

410 Fitzhugh, George. CANNIBALS ALL! OR, SLAVES WITHOUT MASTERS.
Richmond, Virginia: A. Morris, 1857.

411 Jones, William A. CHARACTERS AND CRITICISMS. 2 vols. New
York: I. Y. Westervelt, 1857.

412 [Phillips, George S.]. "Thomas Carlyle," ATLANTIC MONTHLY, I
(December, 1857), 185-196.

413 [Venables, G. S.]. "Carlyle's Cromwell," SATURDAY REVIEW, III
(June 20, 1857), 574-575.

1858

414 Anon. "Of Mr. Carlyle--His Style," SHARPE'S LONDON MAGAZINE,
XXVIII (1858), 66-69.

415 _____. "[Critical and Miscellaneous Essays]," NOTES AND QUERIES,
sers. 2, V (January 23, 1858), 80.

416 _____. "[Sartor Resartus and Heroes]," NOTES AND QUERIES, sers. 2,
V (February 20, 1858), 160.

417 _____. "[Translations from the German]," NOTES AND QUERIES, sers.
2, VI (August 21, 1858), 140.

418   ____. "Frederick the Great," ATHENAEUM, nos. 1612-1613 (September 18-September 25, 1858), 351-354, 388-390.

419   ____. "Carlyle's Life of Frederick the Great," NATIONAL REVIEW, VII (October, 1858), 247-279. Rpt. LITTELL'S LIVING AGE, LIX (November 6, 1858), 403-421; and ECLECTIC MAGAZINE, XLVI (January, 1859), 49-61.

420   ____. "Carlyle's Frederick the Great," LEADER, IX (October, 1858), 1091.

421   ____. "Frederick the Great," BOSTON EVENING TRANSCRIPT (October 2, 19-November 2, 6, 13, 1858), 2, 2, 2, 2, 1.

422   ____. "Carlyle's New Work," NEW YORK TIMES (October 14, 1858), 2.

423   ____. "Carlyle's Life of Frederick the Great," CRITIC, n.s. XVII (October 9, 1858), 654-656, 680-681.

424   ____. "Carlyle's Frederick the Great," TIMES (October 12, 19, 26, 1858), 4, 10, 10.

425   ____. "[Frederick the Great]," NEW YORK TIMES (October 14, November 5, 1858), 2, 2.

426   ____. "Carlyle's Frederick the Great," CHARLESTON COURIER (October 21, November 10, 19, 1858), 2, 2, 1.

427   ____. "Carlyle's Frederick the Great," NEW YORK TIMES (November 5, 1858), 2.

428   ____. "Frederick the Great," PHILADELPHIA EVENING BULLETIN (November 6, 1858), 1.

429   ____. "History of Frederick the Great," ALBION, XXXVI (November 6-13, 1858), 537, 549.

430   ____. "Frederick the Great," PHILADELPHIA PRESS (November 8, 1858), 1.

431   ____. "Frederick the Great," RUSSELL'S MAGAZINE, IV (December,

1858), 276-281.

432 ____. "Frederick the Great," GENTLEMAN'S MAGAZINE, n.s. V (December, 1858), 570-579.

433 ____. "Carlyle's History of Frederick the Great," TAIT'S EDINBURGH MAGAZINE, XXV (December, 1858), 743-748.

434 ____. "Thomas Carlyle," BALLOU'S PICTORIAL DRAWING-ROOM COMPANION, XV (December 11, 1858), 380.

435 ____. "[Translations from the German and Wilhelm Meister]," NOTES AND QUERIES, sers. 2, VI (December 11, 1858), 491.

436 ____. "Frederick the Great," CHARLESTON MERCURY (December 24, 1858), 2.

437 [Acton, John E., Lord]. "Frederick the Great," RAMBLER, n.s. X (December, 1858), 429-431.

438 Forster, John. HISTORICAL AND BIOGRAPHICAL ESSAYS. London: John Murray, 1858.

439 [Guernsey, Alfred H.]. "Carlyle's Frederick the Great," HARPER'S MAGAZINE, XVIII (December, 1858), 86-95.

440 L[ewes], G[eorge] H. "Carlyle's Frederick the Great," FRASER'S MAG-AZINE, LVIII (December, 1858), 631-649.

441 Nathaniel, Sir [pseud.]. "Carlyle's History of Frederick the Great," NEW MONTHLY MAGAZINE, CXIV (November, 1858), 253-271.

442 [Stephen, James F.]. "Mr. Carlyle," SATURDAY REVIEW, V (June 19, 1858), 638-640. Rpt. LITTELL'S LIVING AGE, LVIII (July 31, 1858), 323-327; and ESSAYS. London: Smith, Elder, 1862.

443 [Venables, G. S.]. "Carlyle's History of Frederick the Great," SATUR-DAY REVIEW, VI (October 23-November 6, 1858), 398-399, 423-425, 450-451.

444 Ware, Motley [John E. Cooke]. "Thomas Carlyle: From 'Still Latter-Day Pamphlets,'" SOUTHERN LITERARY MESSENGER, XXVII (November,

1858), 335-337.

1859

445   Anon. "Carlyle and His Writings," MELIORA, I (1859), 338-351.

446   _____. "Thomas Carlyle's Frederick the Great," NATIONAL MAGA-ZINE, V (January, 1859), 12-20.

447   _____. "Frederick the Great," DUBLIN UNIVERSITY MAGAZINE, LIII (January, 1859), 12-31.

448   _____. "Carlyle's History of Frederick the Great," TAIT'S EDINBURGH MAGAZINE, XXVI (January, 1859), 41-45.

449   _____. "Frederick the Great," PETERSON'S MAGAZINE, XXXV (January, 1859), 88.

450   _____. "Frederick the Great," METHODIST QUARTERLY REVIEW, XLI (January, 1859), 161.

451   _____. "Carlyle's Frederick the Great," BRITISH QUARTERLY REVIEW, XXIX (January I, 1859), 239-292.

452   _____. "Carlyle's History of Frederick the Great," CHAMBERS'S JOURNAL, XXXI (January 22-29, 1859), 51-55, 73-77.

453   _____. "Thomas Carlyle and the Nieces of Robert Burns," NEW YORK TIMES (January 26, 1859), 2.

454   [Bucker, Lothar]. "Carlyle's History of Frederick the Second," WESTMINSTER REVIEW, LXXI (January, 1859), 174-208.

455   [Gilfillan, George]. "Carlyle's Frederick the Great," SCOTTISH REVIEW, IX (January, 1859), 36-46.

456   [Hale, Edward E.]. "Carlyle's Frederick," CHRISTIAN EXAMINER, LXVI (January, 1859), 78-89.

457   [Hamley, Edward B.]. "Carlyle: Mirage Philosophy, and History of Frederick," BLACKWOOD'S EDINBURGH MAGAZINE, LXXXV (February, 1859), 127-154. Rpt. THOMAS CARLYLE. Edinburgh: William Blackwood,

1881.

458   [Hutton, Richard H.?]. "The Religion of the Working Class," NATION-
AL REVIEW, VIII (January, 1859), 167-197.

459   [Kelton, Mrs.]. "Carlyle's Frederick the Great," NORTH BRITISH RE-
VIEW, XXX (February, 1859), 22-43.

460   Milburn, William H. TEN YEARS OF PREACHER-LIFE. New York:
Derby and Jackson, 1859.

461   [Pollock, William F.]. "Carlyle's Frederick the Great," QUARTERLY
REVIEW, CV (April, 1859), 275-304.

462   [Russell, Charles W.]. "Carlyle's Frederick the Great," DUBLIN RE-
VIEW, XLVII (September, 1859), 132-168.

463   [Stigand, William]. "Carlyle's Frederick the Great," EDINBURGH RE-
VIEW, CX (October, 1859), 376-410.

464   Tiffany, O. "Carlyle's Life of Frederick the Great," NORTH AMERICAN
REVIEW, LXXXVIII (April, 1859), 503-547.

1860

465   Anon. "Thomas Carlyle," BENTLEY'S MISCELLANY, XLVIII (1860),
471-478.

466   _____. "Life of Friedrich Schiller," LONDON QUARTERLY REVIEW,
XIV (April, 1860), 109-148.

467   _____. "Critical and Miscellaneous Essays," ATLANTIC MONTHLY, V
(June, 1860), 756.

468   _____. "Critical and Miscellaneous Essays," KNICKERBOCKER MAG-
AZINE, LVI (July, 1860), 85.

469   _____. "Carlyle's Critical and Miscellaneous Essays," CHRISTIAN RE-
VIEW, XXV (October, 1860), 690.

470   [Fitzhugh, George]. "Frederick the Great," DE BOW'S REVIEW, XXIX
(August, 1860), 151-167.

471   [Peabody, A. P.]. "Critical and Miscellaneous Essays," NORTH AMER-
ICAN REVIEW, XCI (July, 1860), 274.

1861

472   Anon. "Frederick the Great," NEW MONTHLY MAGAZINE, CXXI
(1861), 364-378.

473   ____. "Frederick the Great," CALCUTTA REVIEW, XXXVI (March,
1861), 74-80.

474   ____. "Euphuism," QUARTERLY REVIEW, CIX (April, 1861), 350-383.

475   ____. "A Hard-Working Age," ECLECTIC MAGAZINE, LIII (May,
1861), 24-26.

476   Battershall, W. W. "Carlyle and His Religion," LADIES' REPOSITORY,
XXI (1861), 678-681.

477   Buckton, T. J. "Carlyle's Cromwell," NOTES AND QUERIES, sers. 2,
XI (June 15, 1861), 467.

478   Collier, William F. A HISTORY OF ENGLISH LITERATURE. London:
Thomas Nelson, 1861.

479   [Hood, Edwin P.]. "Thomas Carlyle and His Critics," ECLECTIC REVIEW,
CXIV (July, 1861), 25-57.

480   ____. "Thomas Carlyle on Modern Sociology," ECLECTIC REVIEW,
CXIV (September, 1861), 316-351.

481   [Hutton, Richard H.?]. "Politics and Faith," NATIONAL REVIEW, XII
(April, 1861), 432-457.

482   Landreth, P. STUDIES AND SKETCHES IN MODERN LITERATURE. Edinburgh: William Oliphant, 1861.

483   Newcomb, H. O. "Carlyle's Philosophy," UNIVERSITY QUARTERLY
REVIEW, IV (July, 1861), 69-78.

484   Smiles, Samuel. BRIEF BIOGRAPHIES. Boston: Ticknor and Fields, 1861.

1862

485   Anon. "Mr. Carlyle's Third Volume," CRITIC, n.s. XXIV (May 10, 1862), 458-461.

486   ____. "Carlyle's Frederick the Great," LONDON REVIEW, IV (June 7, 1862), 527-528.

487   ____. "Carlyle's Last Volume," DUBLIN UNIVERSITY MAGAZINE, LX (July, 1862), 110-128.

488   ____. "Carlyle's Frederick the Great," TIMES (August 14, 1862), 6. Rpt. ALBION, XL (September 6-13, 1862), 429, 441-442.

489   ____. "[Frederick the Great]," NEW YORK TIMES (September 29, 1862), 2.

490   ____. "[Frederick the Great]," WESTMINSTER REVIEW, LXXVIII (October, 1862), 561-563.

491   ____. "Frederick the Great," CHRISTIAN REVIEW, XXVII (October, 1862), 680.

492   ____. "Frederick the Great," AMERICAN PRESBYTERIAN REVIEW, IV (October, 1862), 747.

493   ____. "Frederick the Great," ATLANTIC MONTHLY, X (November, 1862), 642-643.

494   ____. "Frederick the Great," PETERSON'S MAGAZINE, XLII (December, 1862), 479.

495   [Abraham, G. W.]. "Frederick the Great," DUBLIN REVIEW, LI (May, 1862), 404-428.

496   Dillard, A. W. "Thomas Carlyle--His Philosophy and Style," SOUTHERN LITERARY MESSENGER, XXXIV (May, 1862), 290-296.

497   [Guernsey, Alfred H.]. "Carlyle's Frederick the Great," HARPER'S MAGAZINE, XXV (September, 1862), 523-532.

498   [Hood, Edwin P.]. "Carlyle's Frederick the Great," ECLECTIC REVIEW, CXV (June, 1862), 499-523.

499   L., S. "The Third Volume of Mr. Carlyle's Frederick," WELDON'S

REGISTER, 2nd sers. (August, 1862), 14-20.

500   [Lewes, George H., and Frederick Greenwood]. "[Frederick the Great]," CORNHILL MAGAZINE, VI (July, 1862), 107-109.

501   Lucas, Samuel. SECULARIA. London: John Murray, 1862.

502   R., K. "Leigh Hunt's Poetry," MACMILLAN'S MAGAZINE, VI (July, 1862), 238-248.

503   [St. John, Horace]. "Frederick the Great," ATHENAEUM, no. 1801 (May 3, 1862), 585-588.

1863

504   Anon. "Thomas Carlyle on the American War," NEW YORK TRIBUNE (August 12, 1863), 8. See also NEW YORK EVENING POST (August 12, 1863), 2.

505   _____. "Thomas Carlyle and Black Quashes," CHICAGO TRIBUNE (August 18, 1863), 2.

506   _____. "Macaulay and Carlyle in America," RICHMOND RECORD (August 20, 1863), 86.

507   _____. "Ill Ass (Anglicus) in a Noose," BOSTON LIBERATOR (September 4, 1863), 143. See also NATIONAL ANTI-SLAVERY STANDARD (September 12, 1863), 3.

508   _____. "The English Literati on the War," RICHMOND RECORD (October 15, 1863), 169.

509   Guernsey, Alfred H. "Carlyle's Table Talk," HARPER'S MAGAZINE, XXVI (January, 1863), 221-226.

510   H[arte], F. B[ret]. "'Peter of the North' to Thomas Carlyle," SAN FRANCISCO EVENING BULLETIN (September 8, 1863), 3.

511   [Wasson, David A.]. "A Letter to Thomas Carlyle," ATLANTIC MONTHLY, XII (October, 1863), 497-504.

1864

512   Anon. "Frederick the Great," EXAMINER, nos. 2928-2930 (March 12-26, 1864), 167, 196-197.

513   _____. "Mr. Carlyle's History of Frederick the Great," TIMES (March 23, 1864), 6.

514   _____. "Carlyle's Frederick the Great," LONDON REVIEW, VIII (April 2, 1864), 366-367.

515   _____. "Carlyle's Frederick," ECLECTIC REVIEW, CXIX (June, 1864), 703-714.

516   _____. "[Carlyle and William Roupell]," DUBLIN UNIVERSITY MAG-AZINE, LXIV (July, 1864), 56-64.

517   _____. "[Frederick the Great]," WESTMINSTER REVIEW, LXXXII (July, 1864), 228-229.

518   _____. "[Frederick the Great]," NEW YORK TIMES (July 18, 1864), 3.

519   _____. "Frederick the Great," PETERSON'S MAGAZINE, XLVI (September, 1864), 217.

520   _____. "Frederick the Great," AMERICAN PRESBYTERIAN REVIEW, n.s. II (October, 1864), 676-677.

521   [Clarke, James F.]. "The Two Carlyles, or Carlyle Past and Present," CHRISTIAN EXAMINER, LXXVII (September, 1864), 206-231.

522   [Doran, John]. "Frederick the Great," ATHENAEUM, no. 1898 (March 12, 1864), 369-371.

523   Kebbel, Thomas E. ESSAYS UPON HISTORY AND POLITICS. London: Chapman and Hall, 1864.

524   [Lowell, James R.]. "The History of Frederick the Second," NORTH AMERICAN REVIEW, XCIX (October, 1864), 628.

525   [Stephen, James F.]. "Carlyle's Frederick the Great," SATURDAY REVIEW, XVII (April 2, 1864), 414-415.

526   _____. "A French View of Mr. Carlyle," SATURDAY REVIEW, XVII (June 4, 1864), 690-691.

527 _____. "Carlyle's Frederick the Great," FRASER'S MAGAZINE, LXIX (May, 1864), 539-550. Rpt. ECLECTIC MAGAZINE, LXII (July, 1864), 321-331.

1865

528 Anon. "Carlyle on Natural History as a Branch of Education," FRIENDS' INTELLIGENCER, XXII (1865), 670-671.

529 _____. "Frederick the Great," EXAMINER, nos. 2982-2985 (March 25-April 15, 1865), 182-183, 213-214, 228-229.

530 _____. "Carlyle's Frederick the Great," BOSTON EVENING TRANS-SCRIPT (April 15, 1865), 2.

531 _____. "Carlyle's Frederick the Great," LONDON REVIEW, X (April 15-22, 1865), 409-410, 436-437.

532 _____. "Carlyle's History of Frederick the Great," TIMES (April 18, 1865), 4.

533 _____. "Thomas Carlyle," AUTOGRAPHIC MIRROR, III (July, 1865), 6-7, 12-13.

534 _____. "[Frederick the Great]," WESTMINSTER REVIEW, LXXXIV (July, 1865), 265-267.

535 _____. "The Dante Festival," LONDON QUARTERLY REVIEW, XXV (October, 1865), 1-31.

536 _____. "Mr. Carlyle's Last Chapter in the Book of Kings," ECLECTIC REVIEW, CXXII (October, 1865), 299-324.

537 _____. "Frederick the Great," PHILADELPHIA UNITED STATES GAZ-ETTE AND NORTH AMERICAN (October 2, November 15, 1865), 1, 1.

538 _____. "Mr. Carlyle on Natural History," TIMES (October 10, 1865), 9.

539 _____. "Frederick the Great," ST. LOUIS POST DISPATCH (November 15, 1865), 1.

540 _____. "Frederick the Great," PHILADELPHIA PRESS (November 21,

1865), 2.

541   _____. "Frederick the Great," BALTIMORE SUN (November 30, 1865), 2.

542   Blair, David. CARLYLISM AND CHRISTIANITY. Melbourne: W. B. Stephens, 1865.

543   [Doran, John]. "Frederick the Great," ATHENAEUM, no. 1952 (March 25, 1865), 413-414.

544   [Hamley, Edward B.]. "Carlyle's Frederick the Great," BLACKWOOD'S EDINBURGH MAGAZINE, XCVIII (July, 1865), 38-56. Rpt. THOMAS CARLYLE. Edinburgh: William Blackwood, 1881.

545   [James, Henry, Jr.]. "Carlyle's Translation of Wilhelm Meister," NORTH AMERICAN REVIEW, CI (July, 1865), 281-285.

546   James, Henry. "Carlyle," NATION, I (July 6, 1885), 20-21.

547   Japp, Alexander H. THREE GREAT TEACHERS OF OUR OWN TIMES. London: Smith, Elder, 1865.

548   [Lancaster, Henry H.]. "Frederick the Great," NORTH BRITISH REVIEW, XLIII (September, 1865), 79-126. Rpt. ESSAYS AND REVIEWS. Edinburgh: Edmonston and Douglas, 1876.

549   Masson, David. RECENT BRITISH PHILOSOPHY. London: Macmillan, 1865.

550   [Merivale, Herman]. "Thomas Carlyle's Frederick the Great," QUARTERLY REVIEW, CXVIII (July, 1865), 224-254.

551   [Rands, William B.]. HENRY HOLBEACH: STUDENT IN LIFE AND PHILOSOPHY. 2 vols. London: Alexander Strahan, 1865.

552   [Stephen, James F.]. "Carlyle's Frederick the Great," SATURDAY REVIEW, XIX (April 22, 1865), 476-478.

553   _____. "Mr. Carlyle," FRASER'S MAGAZINE, LXXII (December, 1865), 778-810. Rpt. LITTELL'S LIVING AGE, LXXXVIII (March 7, 1866), 737-763.

1866

554   Anon. "Carlyle's <u>Frederick</u>," HARPER'S WEEKLY, X (January, 1866), 3.

555   _____. "Thomas Carlyle: Mr. Henry James Lectures," NEW YORK TIMES (January 16, 1866), 8. Rpt. ALBION, XLIV (January 20, 1866), 34.

556   _____. "Three Cynical Observers: Gulliver--Candide--Teufelsdröckh," DUBLIN UNIVERSITY MAGAZINE, LXVII (January-February, 1866), 64-75.

557   _____. "Frederick the Great," AMERICAN PRESBYTERIAN REVIEW, n.s. IV (January-April, 1866), 184, 343-344.

558   _____. "Mr. Thomas Carlyle," TIMES (March 14, 1866), 12.

559   _____. "[Carlyle at Edinburgh University]," TIMES (April 4, 1866), 8.

560   _____. "Installation of Mr. Carlyle as Rector," TIMES (April 4, 1866), 10.

561   _____. "Mr. Carlyle's Religion," SPECTATOR, XXXIX (April 7, 1866), 377-379.

562   _____. "Mr. Carlyle at Edinburgh," SATURDAY REVIEW, XXI (April 7, 1866), 406-407.

563   _____. "[Inaugural Address]," NOTES AND QUERIES, sers. 3, IX (April 14, 1866), 310.

564   _____. "Lord Rector," PUNCH, L (April 14, 1866), 154-155.

565   _____. "On the Choice of Books," LONDON REVIEW, XII (April 21, 1866), 460.

566   _____. "The Late Mrs. Carlyle," TIMES (June 23, 1866), 12.

567   [Alden, Henry]. "[Inaugural Address]," HARPER'S MAGAZINE, XXXIII (June, 1866), 118-120.

568   Alexander, Patrick P. MILL AND CARLYLE. Edinburgh: William P.

Nimmo, 1866. See also CARLYLE REDIVIVUS. Glasgow: James Maclehose, 1881.

569   Hotten, John C. ON THE CHOICE OF BOOKS. London: John Camden Hotten, 1866. See Introductory Memoir that was enlarged by R. H. Shepherd in the 2nd edition (1869).

570   Lowell, James R. "Carlyle's Frederick the Great," NORTH AMERICAN REVIEW, CII (April, 1866), 419-445. Rpt. MY STUDY WINDOWS. Boston: J. R. Osgood, 1871.

571   Smith, Alexander. "Mr. Carlyle at Edinburgh," ARGOSY, I (May, 1866), 504-510. Rpt. HARPER'S MAGAZINE, XXXIII (August, 1866), 391-393; and LAST LEAVES. Edinburgh: William P. Nimmo, 1868.

1867

572   Anon. "[Carlyle and Ruskin on London Streets]," TIMES (June 3, 1867), 9.

573   _____. "Mr. Ruskin and Mr. Carlyle," SATURDAY REVIEW, XXIII (June 15, 1867), 748-749.

574   _____. "A New Latter-Day Pamphlet," SATURDAY REVIEW, XXIV (August 10, 1867), 176-177.

575   _____. "Carlyle's Frederick," NATION, V (August, 15, 1867), 128.

576   _____. "Shooting Niagara; and After?" NEW YORK TRIBUNE (August 16, 1867), 2.

577   _____. "Carlyle and Democracy," NEW YORK TRIBUNE (August 16, 1867), 4.

578   _____. "[Shooting Niagara]," BOSTON DAILY ADVERTISER (August 17, 1867), 1.

579   _____. "Shooting Niagara," BOSTON DAILY ADVERTISER (August 19, 1867), 2.

580   _____. "Shooting Niagara; and After?" NEW YORK WORLD (August 19, 1867), 4.

581 _____. "Shooting Niagara," CHICAGO TIMES (August 21, 1867), 2.

582 _____. "Carlyle's New Essay," CHICAGO TRIBUNE (August 21, 1867), 3.

583 _____. "Shooting Niagara," ST. LOUIS MISSOURI DEMOCRAT (August 26, 1867), 1, 3.

584 _____. "Carlyle and the Tribune (NY)," RICHMOND ENQUIRER (August 28, 1867), 2.

585 _____. "[Shooting Niagara]," PHILADELPHIA PUBLIC LEDGER (August 29, 1867), 2.

586 _____. "Shooting Niagara," CHARLESTON COURIER (September 4, 1867), 2.

587 _____. "Shooting Niagara," CHARLESTON NEWS (September 5, 1867), 2.

588 _____. "Carlyle vs. the Human Race," HARPER'S WEEKLY, XI (September 7, 1867), 562.

589 _____. "[Shooting Niagara; and After?]," SATURDAY REVIEW, XXIV (October 5, 1867), 430-431.

590 _____. "Mr. Carlyle's Singing Peers," SPECTATOR, XL (October 12, 1867), 1140-1141.

591 _____. "An Essay on Carlyleism," SAINT PAUL'S MONTHLY MAGA-ZINE, I (December, 1867), 292-305.

592 [Godkin, E. L.]. "Thomas Carlyle," NATION, V (September 5, 1867), 194-195.

593 _____. "Thomas Carlyle's Influence," NATION, V (September 19, 1867), 235-236.

594 Kirk, J. F. "Carlyle," NATION, V (September 5, 1867), 196.

595 _____. "Thomas Carlyle's Position," NATION, V (September 19, 1867), 237-238.

596   [Parsons, R.]. "Carlyle's Shooting Niagara," CATHOLIC WORLD,
       VI (October, 1867), 86-92.

597   Sherwood, J. D. "The Home of Thomas Carlyle," HOURS AT HOME,
       V (June, 1867), 113-116.

598   Whitman, Walt. "Democracy," GALAXY, IV (December, 1867), 919-
       933.

                                1868

599   Anon. "Thomas Carlyle," LEISURE HOUR, XVII (January 1, 1868),
       38-42.

600   _____. "Matthew Arnold versus Thomas Carlyle," SPECTATOR, XLI
       (July 4, 1868), 788-790. Rpt. LITTELL'S LIVING AGE, XCVIII (Sept-
       ember 5, 1868), 629-632.

601   _____. "Carlyle on Moral Philosophy," NEW YORK TIMES (August
       9, 1868), 2.

602   _____. "University of Edinburgh," TIMES (December 10, 1868), 7.

603   [Kirk, J. F.]. "Democracy, Carlyle, and Whitman," NEW ECLEC-
       TIC, I (February, 1868), 190-194.

604   Smith, Goldwin. THREE ENGLISH STATESMEN. London: Macmillan,
       1868.

605   [Stirling, James H.]. "The Poetical Works of Robert Browning,"
       NORTH BRITISH REVIEW, XLIX (December, 1868), 353-408.

                                1869

606   Anon. "Thomas Carlyle as a Practical Guide," PUTNAM'S MONTH-
       LY MAGAZINE, XIII (May, 1869), 519-532.

607   _____. "Thomas Carlyle on a 'Future State,'" NEW YORK TIMES
       (May 13, 1869), 5.

608   _____. "Carlyle, the Prophet," SPECTATOR, XLII (May 15, 1869),
       589-590.

609   _____. "Carlyle on Napoleon I," NEW YORK TIMES (May 23, 1869), 3.

610   _____. "Mr. Thomas Carlyle," TIMES (November 6, 1869), 9.

611   [Gladstone, William E.]. LIVING LIVES. THOMAS CARLYLE. London: Provost, n.d. [1869].

612   Greg, William R. LITERARY AND SOCIAL JUDGMENTS. 2nd ed. London: Trubner, 1869.

613   Robinson, Henry C. DAIRY, REMINISCENCE S AND CORRESPONDENCE. 3 vols. Boston: Fields, Osgood, 1869.

614   Russell, W. C. THE BOOK OF AUTHORS. London: Warne, n.d. [1869].

1870

615   Anon. "[Carlyle and Americans]," APPLETON'S JOURNAL, III (April 2, 1870), 386.

616   _____. "Thomas Carlyle," GRAPHIC, I (April 30, 1870), 515-516.

617   _____. "Carlyle and Disraeli," NEW MONTHLY MAGAZINE, CXLVII (July, 1870), 118-122.

618   _____. "[Carlyle on the War]," TIMES (October 25, 1870), 5.

619   _____. "Thomas Carlyle on the War," HARPER'S WEEKLY, XIV (November, 1870), 766.

620   _____. "[Carlyle on the War]," TIMES (November 18, 1870), 7.

621   Friswell, J. H. MODERN MEN OF LETTERS HONESTLY CRITICISED. London: Hodder and Stoughton, 1870.

622   [Morley, John]. "Carlyle," FORTNIGHTLY REVIEW, XIV (July, 1870), 1-22. Rpt. CRITICAL MISCELLANIES. London: Chapman and Hall, 1871; and LITERARY ESSAYS. London: Arthur L. Humphreys, 1906.

623   Seeley, John R. LECTURES AND ESSAYS. London: Macmillan, 1870.

1871

624   Anon. "Carlyle on 'Muslin Theology,'" RELIGIOUS MAGAZINE AND MONTHLY REVIEW, XLV (January, 1871), 99-100.

625   _____. "[Scribner's Edition of Works]," NEW YORK TIMES (April 24, 1871), 2.

626   _____. "[French Revolution]," NEW YORK TIMES (May 27, 1871), 2.

627   _____. "Napoleon III, A Prophecy by Mr. Carlyle," NEW YORK TIMES (September 4, 1871), 8.

628   _____. "Thomas Carlyle," APPLETON'S JOURNAL, VI (October 21, 1871), 465-467.

629   Boner, Charles. MEMOIRS AND LETTERS. 2 vols. Ed. R. M. Kettle. London: Richard Bentley, 1871.

630   Bouchier, Jonathan. "Macaulay and Carlyle," NOTES AND QUERIES, sers. 4, VII (June 17, 1871), 513-514.

631   Buchanan, Robert. "Mr. John Morley's Essays," CONTEMPORARY REVIEW, XVII (June, 1871), 319-337.

632   C., T. L. "The Philosopher of Chelsea," GENTLEMAN'S MAGAZINE, CCXXXI (July, 1871), 159-171.

633   [Dwinell, I. E.]. "Religion According to Carlyle," CONGREGATIONAL REVIEW, XI (September, 1871), 413-427.

634   Taine, Hippolyte A. HISTORY OF ENGLISH LITERATURE. 2 vols. Trans. H. Van Laun. Edinburgh: Edmonston and Douglas, 1871.

635   [Young, A.]. "Mr. Carlyle and Pere Bonhours," CATHOLIC WORLD, XIII (September, 1871), 820-825.

1872

636   Anon. "[Heroes and Hero-Worship]," NEW YORK TIMES (March 14, 1872), 2.

637   _____ . "Thomas Carlyle," ONCE A WEEK, XXVII (September 28, 1872), 275-277.

638   _____ . "'A Birthday in December,'" PUNCH, LXIII (December 14, 1872), 252.

639   Alcott, A. Bronson. CONCORD DAYS. Boston: Roberts Brothers, 1872.

640   Manning, J. M. HALF TRUTHS AND THE TRUTH. Boston: Lee and Shepherd, 1872.

641   Masson, David. "A Memoir of Mazzini," MACMILLAN'S MAGA-ZINE, XXV (April, 1872), 509-520.

642   Minto, William. A MANUAL OF ENGLISH PROSE LITERATURE. Edinburgh: William Blackwood, 1872.

643   [Mozley, James B.]. "Thomas Carlyle's Collected Works," QUARTER-LY REVIEW, CXXXII (April, 1872), 335-366. Rpt. LITTELL'S LIVING AGE, CXIII (June 15, 1872), 666-683; and ECLECTIC MAGAZINE, LXXIX (August, 1872), 129-148.

644   Routledge, James. "Thomas Carlyle," MOOKERJEE'S MAGAZINE, n.s. I (October, 1872), 217-231.

645   Sears, E. H. "Dr. Manning's Analysis of Carlyle," RELIGIOUS MAG-AZINE AND MONTHLY REVIEW, XLVII (March, 1872), 288.

646   _____ . "Carlyle and the Commonwealth," RELIGIOUS MAGAZINE AND MONTHLY REVIEW, XLVII (April, 1872), 501.

647   [Shepherd, Richard H.]. "Carlyle's Letters," ECHO, no. 1074 (May 21, 1872), 2.

648   Towle, George M. "Carlyle as a Historian," PENN MONTHLY, III (August, 1872), 439-447.

1873

649   Anon. "[Carlyle and Bismark]," NEW YORK TIMES (December 13, 1873), 3.

650   ____. "Mr. Carlyle," TIMES (December 30, 1873), 3.

651   Addis, John. "[Heroes and Hero-Worship]," NOTES AND QUERIES, sers. 4, XI (May 17, 1873), 401.

652   Clark, Daniel. A NEW CANADIAN WORK. Toronto: Flint, Morton, 1873.

653   Hodge, David. THOMAS CARLYLE: THE MAN AND THE TEACHER. Edinburgh: Menzies, n.d. [1873].

654   Maclise, Daniel. A GALLERY OF ILLUSTRIOUS LITERARY CHARAC-TERS (1830-1838). Ed. William Bates. London: Chatto and Windus, 1873.

655   Mill, John S. AUTOBIOGRAPHY. London: Longmans, Green, 1873.

1874

656   Anon. "Mr. Carlyle on Capital and Labour," TIMES (January 28, 1874), 10.

657   ____. "Mr. Carlyle on Capital and Labor," NEW YORK TIMES (February 13, 1874), 2.

658   ____. "[Works]," NOTES AND QUERIES, sers. 5, I (April 11, 1874), 298-300.

659   ____. "Mr. Thomas Carlyle," ATHENAEUM, no. 2424 (April 11, 1874), 495. Rpt. TIMES (April 13, 1874), 12.

660   [Baynes, T. Spencer]. "Hall's Modern English," EDINBURGH REVIEW, CXL (July, 1874), 143-167.

661   Blair, David. "Varia--The Quarterly Review on Carlyle," NOTES AND QUERIES, sers. 5, I (May 30, 1874), 427-428.

662   [Courthope, William J.]. "Modern Culture," QUARTERLY REVIEW, CXXXVII (October, 1874), 389-415.

663   [Croskery, Thomas]. "Froude's Irish Parliament and Irish Rebellion," EDINBURGH REVIEW, CXXXIX (April, 1874), 468-506.

664   G., E. "Carlyle's New Order," OLD AND NEW, IX (February, 1874), 264.

665   [Hutton, Richard H.]. "Mr. Carlyle's Faith," SPECTATOR, XLVII (January 31, 1874), 137-138.

666   Minto, William. CHARACTERISTICS OF ENGLISH POETS FROM CHAUCER TO SHIRLEY. London: William Blackwood, 1874.

667   Mitchell, Ellen M. "Thomas Carlyle," ARTHUR'S ILLUSTRATED HOME MAGAZINE, XLII (May, 1874), 283-285.

668   Stephen, Leslie. HOURS IN A LIBRARY. sers. I. London: Smith, Elder, 1874.

669   Wilson, James G. "Thomas Carlyle," HARPER'S MAGAZINE, XLVIII (April, 1874), 726-729.

1875

670   Anon. THE NATIONAL PORTRAIT GALLERY. Part 16. London: Cassell, Petter and Galpin, 1875.

671   _____. "Great Britain Honors to Carlyle and Tennyson," NEW YORK TIMES :(January 29, 1875), 5.

672   _____. "[Carlyle Declines Order of Bath]," NEW YORK TIMES (January 30, 1875), 1. See also NEW YORK TIMES (February 13, 1875), 1.

673   _____. "Mr. Carlyle on Modern Liberalism," NEW YORK TIMES (March 15, 1875), 8.

674   _____. "Mr. Carlyle's Kings of Norway," EXAMINER, no. 3515 (June 12, 1875), 664-665.

675   _____. "Carlyle's Early Kings of Norway," SATURDAY REVIEW, XXXIX (June 12, 1875), 758-759.

676   _____. "Mr. Carlyle 'Interviewed,'" TIMES (June 28, 1875), 12.

677   _____. "The Early Kings of Norway," LITERARY WORLD, VI (July, 1875), 11.

678 ____. "Early Kings of Norway," METHODIST QUARTERLY REVIEW, LVII (July, 1875), 531.

679 ____. "A Visit to Carlyle," NEW YORK TIMES (July 30, 1875), 4.

680 ____. "[Carlyle's Gift to Harvard]," APPLETON'S JOURNAL, XIV (October 30, 1875), 567.

681 ____. "The Health of Mr. Carlyle," NEW YORK TIMES (November 6, 1875), 3.

682 ____. "Germany," TIMES (December 1, 1875), 5.

683 ____. "Mr. Thomas Carlyle," NEW YORK TIMES (December 5, 1875), 2.

684 ____. "Thomas Carlyle," TIMES (December 6, 1875), 10.

685 ____. "Harvard's Honor to Carlyle," NEW YORK TIMES (December 13, 1875), 5.

686 ____. "Mr. Carlyle," TIMES (December 17, 1875), 11.

687 ____. "Germany," TIMES (December 22, 1875), 5.

688 ____. "Carlyle's Early Kings of Norway," TIMES (December 23, 1875), 3-4.

689 A., E. E. "[The French Revolution]," NOTES AND QUERIES, sers. 5, IV (September 11, 1875), 206.

690 A Wandering Englishman [William G. Hamley]. "[Frederick the Great]," BLACKWOOD'S EDINBURGH MAGAZINE, CXVIII (November, 1875), 574-589.

691 Bowen, Clarence W. "Thomas Carlyle at Home," INDEPENDENT, XXVII (September 9, 1875), 6.

692 Browne, Junius H. "The Warlock of Windbags," GALAXY, XIX (January, 1875), 44-54.

693 Calvert, George H. ESSAYS AESTHETICAL. Boston: Lee and Shepard, 1875.

694   Cameron, T. W. "Notes on Carlyle," NEW MONTHLY MAGAZINE, CLVII (August, 1875), 201-209.

695   [Dasent, George W.]. "The Early Kings of Norway," EDINBURGH REVIEW, CXLII (July, 1875), 203-232.

696   Drummond, James. "Notes Upon Some Scottish Historical Portraits--John Knox and George Buchanan," PROCEEDINGS OF THE SOCIETY OF ANTIQUARIES OF SCOTLAND, XI (May 10, 1875), 237-264. Rpt. THE PORTRAITS OF JOHN KNOX AND GEORGE BUCHANAN. Edinburgh: privately printed, 1875.

697   Editor. "Thomas Carlyle," ECLECTIC MAGAZINE, LXXXIV (June, 1875), 761-763.

698   Fields, James T. "'Barry Cornwall' and Some of His Friends," HARPER'S MAGAZINE, LI (November, 1875), 777-796. Rpt. OLD ACQUAINTANCES. Boston: James R. Osgood, 1876.

699   [Gosse, Edmund]. "Early Kings of Norway," ATHENAEUM, no. 2476 (April 10, 1875), 481-482.

700   Hogg, David. LIFE OF ALLAN CUNNINGHAM. Dumfries: John Anderson, 1875.

701   Hood, Edwin P. THOMAS CARLYLE: PHILOSOPHIC THINKER, THEOLOGIAN, HISTORIAN AND POET. London: James Clarke, 1875.

702   McCrie, George. THE RELIGION OF OUR LITERATURE. London: Hodder and Stoughton, 1875.

1876

703   Anon. "Mr. Carlyle," DUBLIN REVIEW, LXXVIII (January, 1876), 97-122.

704   ____. "Mr. Carlyle's Birthday," NEW YORK TIMES (January 5, 1876), 2.

705   ____. "Mr. Thomas Carlyle on Teaching," NEW YORK TIMES (February 13, 1876), 2.

706   ____. "The Illustrious Sage of Chelsea," NEW YORK TIMES (October 15, 1876), 9.

707   ____. "The Carlyle Anthology," LITERARY WORLD, VII (December, 1876), 96.

708   ____. "Mr. Thomas Carlyle," NEW YORK TIMES (December 11, 1876), 8.

709   Bennett, D. M. THE WORLD'S SAGES, INFIDELS AND THINKERS. New York: D. M. Bennett, 1876.

710   Bouchier, Jonathan. "Burns," NOTES AND QUERIES, sers. 5, V (January 1, 1876), 8.

711   C., J. R. S. "Carlyle as a Poet," NOTES AND QUERIES, sers. 5, VI (July 22, 1876), 67-68.

712   Davey, Samuel J. DARWIN, CARLYLE AND DICKENS. London: James Clarke, n.d. [1876].

713   E., J. W. "Carlyle as Poet," NOTES AND QUERIES, sers. 5, VI (August 5, 1876), 110-111.

714   Gomme, G. Laurence. "Burns," NOTES AND QUERIES, sers. 5, VI (August 26, 1876), 177.

715   Guernsey, Alfred H. "Thomas Carlyle," APPLETON'S JOURNAL, XV (June 10-June 24, 1876), 754-757, 780-783, 805-808. Rpt. THOMAS CARLYLE: HIS LIFE--HIS BOOKS--HIS THEORIES. New York: D. Appleton, 1879.

716   Ma., Ch. El. "Carlyle as Poet," NOTES AND QUERIES. sers. 5, VI (September 30, 1876), 275.

717   [Smith, Goldwin]. "Carlyle's Early Kings of Norway," NATION, XXIII (September 21, 1876), 184-185.

718   Swinburne, Algernon C. NOTE OF AN ENGLISH REPUBLICAN ON THE MUSCOVITE CRUSADE. London: Chatto and Windus, 1876.

719   ____. "'Two Leaders,'" ATHENAEUM, no. 2515 (January 8, 1876), 54.

720   Ward, C. A. "Burns," NOTES AND QUERIES, sers. 5, V (May 6, 1876), 372.

721   Yeats, Edmund. "Thomas Carlyle at Cheyne Row," WORLD (November 22, 1876), 4-5. Rpt. CELEBRITIES AT HOME. London: Office of the World, 1877.

1877

722   Anon. "Mr. Carlyle on 'Darwinism,'" TIMES (January 17, 20, 1877), 5, 7.

723   _____. "Mr. Thomas Carlyle on the Gospel of Dirt," NEW YORK TIMES (January 30, 1877), 5.

724   _____. "[Barrett's Carlyle Anthology]," ATLANTIC MONTHLY, XXXIX (March, 1877), 380.

725   _____. "Mr. Carlyle," TIMES (April 6, 1877), 9.

726   _____. "Mr. Carlyle on the Situation [Russo-Turkish War] ," NEW YORK TIMES (May 6, 1877), 1. See also NEW YORK TIMES (May 7, 1877), 5.

727   _____. "[Frederick Martin's Biography]," ATHENAEUM, no. 2590 (June 16, 1877), 769.

728   _____. "German Influence in English Literature," NEW YORK TIMES (August 5, 1877), 4.

729   _____. "[Frederick Martin's Biography]," ATHENAEUM, no. 2600 (August 25, 1877), 235.

730   _____. "[Frederick Martin's Biography]," LITERARY WORLD, VIII (October, 1877), 83.

731   Beckwith, Frank A. "The Junior Prize Oration--Thomas Carlyle," YALE LITERARY MAGAZINE, XLII (April, 1877), 293-299.

732   Edgar, A. "Carlyle's Essays," NOTES AND QUERIES, sers. 5, VII (February 10, 1877), 117.

733   Gibson, T. H. "The Prophet of Chelsea," LONDON MAGAZINE OF

LIGHT LITERATURE, III (1877), 33-36.

734   Jabez [psued.]. "An Emendation on a Passage in Carlyle," NOTES AND QUERIES, sers. 5, VII (April 7, 1877), 266.

735   Martin, Frederick. "Thomas Carlyle: A Biography, with Autobiographical Notes," BIOGRAPHICAL MAGAZINE, I (June, 1877), 1-22.

736   _____. "The Biography of Mr. Carlyle," ATHENAEUM, no. 2603 (September 15, 1877), 337.

737   Martineau, Harriet. AUTOBIOGRAPHY. 2 vols. Ed. Maria W. Chapman. Boston: J. R. Osgood, 1877.

738   Moth [pseud.]. "Carlyle's Essays," NOTES AND QUERIES, sers. 5, VII (January 27, 1877), 68.

739   Perry, Thomas S. "German Influence in English Literature," ATLANTIC MONTHLY, XL (August, 1877), 129-147.

740   Proctor, Bryan W. [Barry Cornwall]. BRYAN WALLER PROCTOR: AN AUTOBIOGRAPHICAL FRAGMENT AND BIOGRAPHICAL NOTES. London: George Bell, 1877.

1878

741   Anon. "Carlyle on the Lord's Prayer," FRIEND'S INTELLIGENCER, XXXV (1878), 212.

742   _____. "[The Conway Biography]," NEW YORK TIMES (April 24, 1878), 4.

743   _____. "[Carlyle's Autobiography]," NEW YORK TIMES (September 30, 1878), 4.

744   _____. "[Carlyle's Life and His Contemporaries]," NEW YORK TIMES (November 7, 1878), 4.

745   Axon, William E. A. "Carlyle's Difficulties as an Author," NOTES AND QUERIES, sers. 5, X (August 3, 1878), 88.

746   Bayne, Peter. "Thomas Carlyle," LITERARY WORLD, XVIII (July 5-12, 1878), 8-11, 24-26. This and the following rpt. LESSONS FROM

MY MASTERS. London: James Clark, 1879.

747 _____. "Carlyle's Life of Sterling," LITERARY WORLD, XVIII (August 16, 1878), 104-106.

748 _____. "Carlyle on the Rise of the Hohenzollerns," LITERARY WORLD, XVIII (August 23, 1878), 120-122.

749 _____. "Carlyle on Hohenzollern Heroism," LITERARY WORLD, XVIII (August 30, 1878), 136-139.

750 _____. "Carlyle on the Seizure of Silesia and Frederick's Battles," LITERARY WORLD, XVIII (September 6, 1878), 152-155.

751 _____. "Frederick's Victories of Peace," LITERARY WORLD, XVIII (September 13, 1878), 168-171.

752 _____. "Carlyle on Voltaire," LITERARY WORLD, XVIII (September 20, 1878), 184-187.

753 Cochrane, Robert. THE TREASURY OF MODERN BIOGRAPHY. London: Hay and Mitchell, 1878.

754 Dowden, Edward. STUDIES IN LITERATURE, 1789-1877. London: Kegan Paul, 1878.

755 Guy, Robert. "Carlyle's Difficulties as an Author," NOTES AND QUERIES, sers. 5, X (August 24, 1878), 159.

756 Harrison, W. H. "Notes and Reminiscences," UNIVERSITY MAGAZINE, II (July, 1878), 56-67.

757 Hill, George B. DR. JOHNSON: HIS FRIENDS AND HIS CRITICS. London: Smith, Elder, 1878.

758 [Larkin, Henry]. EXTRA PHYSICS AND THE MYSTERY OF CREATION. London: Hodder and Stoughton, 1878.

759 Stewart, George. EVENINGS IN A LIBRARY. Toronto: Belford, 1878.

1879

760 Anon. "Stories About Carlyle," NEW YORK TIMES (March 17, 1879),

2.

761 _____. "Mr. Peter Bayne on Carlyle and Tennyson," SPECTATOR, LII (August 16, 1879), 1044-1046.

762 _____. "Carlyle on Future Punishment," NEW YORK TIMES (August 17, 1879), 8.

763 _____. "[Marriage of Mary Aitken and Alexander Carlyle]," NEW YORK TIMES (August 26, 1879), 1.

764 _____. "[Carlyle and Burns]," NEW YORK TIMES (September 29, 1879), 4.

765 _____. "Carlyle and Dyspepsia," NEW YORK TIMES (December 5, 1879), 4.

766 Allingham, William. "Some Fifty Years Ago," FRASER'S MAGAZINE, XCIX (June, 1879), 790-800.

767 Cochrane, Robert. GALLERY OF NOTABLE MEN AND WOMEN. Edinburgh: William P. Nimmo, 1879.

768 Courtney, William L. "Carlyle's Political Doctrines," FORTNIGHTLY REVIEW, XXXII (December, 1879), 817-828. Rpt. ECLECTIC MAGAZINE, XCIV (February, 1880), 242-249.

769 Gomme, Alice B. "Thackeray and Carlyle," NOTES AND QUERIES, sers. 5, XII (July 19, 1879), 45.

770 Spalding, John L. "Theories of Education and Life: Thomas Carlyle," AMERICAN CATHOLIC QUARTERLY, IV (January, 1879), 1-21.

771 T[hayer], W[illiam] R. "Biography of Thomas Carlyle," BIOGRAPH AND REVIEW, I (May, 1879), 295-298.

1880

772 Anon. "Thomas Carlyle," PHRENOLOGICAL MAGAZINE, I (1880), 289-292.

773 _____. "Carlyle's Change of Opinion [on America]," NEW YORK TIMES (March 8, 1880), 4.

774   ____. "Thomas Carlyle," CHAMBERS'S JOURNAL, LVII (October 16, 1880), 663-666. Rpt. LITTELL'S LIVING AGE, CXLVII (November 13, 1880), 438-442.

775   Bayne, Thomas. "Mr. Carlyle's 'Essay on Burns,'" NOTES AND QUER-IES, sers. 6, I (April 24, 1880), 336.

776   Crozier, John B. THE RELIGION OF THE FUTURE. London: C. Kegan Paul, 1880.

777   Japp, Alexander H. GERMAN LIFE AND LITERATURE. London: M. Japp, n.d. [1880].

778   Macrae, David. AMONGST THE DARKIES. Glasgow: J. S. Marr, 1880.

779   Potter, William J. "Buckle and Carlyle," SKETCHES AND REMINIS-CENCES OF THE RADICAL CLUB. Ed. Mrs. J. T. Sargent (Boston: J. R. Osgood, 1880), 251-258.

780   Seeley, John R. "Political Somnambulism," MACMILLAN'S MAGA-ZINE, XLIII (November, 1880), 28-44.

781   [Shinn, Chas. H.]. "Thomas Carlyle," CALIFORNIAN, II (November, 1880), 443-449.

1881

782   Anon. THE LIFE OF THOMAS CARLYLE. London: Haughton, n.d. [1881].

783   ____. "Thomas Carlyle," FRIEND'S INTELLIGENCER, XXXVIII (1881), 12.

784   ____. "Thomas Carlyle," ANNUAL REGISTER, II (1881), 99-101.

785   ____. "Squib Mottoes for Twelfth-Night Crackers: For Thomas Carlyle," PUNCH, LXXX (January 8, 1881), 11.

786   ____. "Carlyle's Lost Manuscript," NEW YORK TIMES (January 16, 1881), 10.

787   ____. "Mr. Carlyle," TIMES (January 31-February 1, 2, 3, 4, 5,

1881), 9, 10, 10, 10, 9, 10.

788 _____ . "Thomas Carlyle," HARPER'S WEEKLY, XXV (February, 1881), 117.

789 _____ . "Thomas Carlyle--Essayist, Biographer and Historian," BOSTON EVENING TRANSCRIPT (February 3, 1881), 6.

790 _____ . "Thomas Carlyle," BALTIMORE AMERICAN AND COMMERCIAL ADVERTISER (February 4, 1881), 1-2.

791 _____ . "Thomas Carlyle," CHICAGO INTER-OCEAN (February 4, 1881), 4.

792 _____ . "Thomas Carlyle," NEW YORK EVENING POST (February 4, 1881), 2.

793 _____ . "Death of Carlyle," BOSTON EVENING TRANSCRIPT (February 5, 1881), 1, 8.

794 _____ . "Thomas Carlyle," BOSTON EVENING TRANSCRIPT (February 5, 1881), 4.

795 _____ . "Thomas Carlyle," CHICAGO EVENING JOURNAL (February 5, 1881), 2.

796 _____ . "Carlyle," NEW YORK DAILY GRAPHIC (February 5, 1881), 722.

797 _____ . "Death of Carlyle," NEW YORK EVENING POST (February 5, 1881), 5.

798 _____ . "Thomas Carlyle," PALL MALL GAZETTE (February 5, 1881), 1.

799 _____ . "The Death of Thomas Carlyle," RICHMOND STATE (February 5, 1881), 1.

800 _____ . "Mr. Carlyle," ST. JAMES'S GAZETTE, II (February 5, 1881), 11-12.

801 _____ . "Thomas Carlyle," ST. LOUIS POST DISPATCH (February 5, 1881), 1.

802 _____. "[Sketch of Carlyle's Life]," BALTIMORE SUN (February 6, 1881), 1.

803 _____. "Thomas Carlyle's Rank," BOSTON HERALD (February 6, 1881), 7.

804 _____. "Death of Thomas Carlyle," CHICAGO TIMES (February 6, 1881), 2.

805 _____. "Carlyle," CHICAGO TIMES (February 6, 1881), 7.

806 _____. "Thomas Carlyle," CHICAGO TRIBUNE (February 6, 1881), 4.

807 _____. "Death of Thomas Carlyle," CHICAGO TRIBUNE (February 6, 1881), 5.

808 _____. "Death of Thomas Carlyle," NEW YORK TIMES (February 6, 1881), 1-2.

809 _____. "Sartor Resartus," NEW YORK TIMES (February 6, 1881), 6.

810 _____. "Thomas Carlyle," NEW YORK TRIBUNE (February 6, 1881), 2.

811 _____. "Thomas Carlyle," NEW YORK SUN (February 6, 1881), 4.

812 _____. "Thomas Carlyle," NEW YORK WORLD (February 6, 1881), 1-2.

813 _____. "Thomas Carlyle," RICHMOND DISPATCH (February 6, 1881), 3.

814 _____. "Death of Carlyle," ST. LOUIS REPUBLICAN (February 6, 1881), 2.

815 _____. "Thomas Carlyle," ST. LOUIS REPUBLICAN (February 6, 1881), 4.

816 _____. "Thomas Carlyle," BALTIMORE GAZETTE (February 7, 1881), 1-2.

817 _____. "Thomas Carlyle," BALTIMORE SUN (February 7, 1881), 1.

818 _____. "Thomas Carlyle," BOSTON DAILY ADVERTISER (February 7, 1881), 2.

819 _____. "[Smalley at Carlyle's Grave]," BOSTON DAILY ADVER-TISER (February 7, 1881), 1.

820 _____. "Thomas Carlyle," BOSTON EVENING STAR (February 7, 1881), 3.

821 _____. "Death of Carlyle," CHARLESTON NEWS AND COURIER (February 7, 1881), 1.

822 _____. "Thomas Carlyle," CHARLESTON NEWS AND COURIER (February 7, 1881), 2.

823 _____. "Thomas Carlyle," CHICAGO DAILY NEWS (February 7, 1881), 2.

824 _____. "Thomas Carlyle," PHILADELPHIA INQUIRER (February 7, 1881), 4.

825 _____. "Thomas Carlyle," PHILADELPHIA PRESS (February 7, 1881), 4.

826 _____. "Carlyle," PHILADELPHIA PUBLIC LEDGER (February 7, 1881), 2.

827 _____. "Thomas Carlyle," PHILADELPHIA RECORD (February 7, 1881), 2.

828 _____. "Thomas Carlyle," PHILADELPHIA UNITED STATES GAZ-ETTE AND NORTH AMERICAN (February 7, 1881), 1-2.

829 _____. "Death of Thomas Carlyle," RICHMOND WHIG (February 7, 1881), 1.

830 _____. "Carlyle," ST. LOUIS POST DISPATCH (February 7, 1881), 4.

831 _____. "Thomas Carlyle," SPRINGFIELD MASSACHUSETTS REPUB-LICAN (February 7, 1881), 4.

832 _____. "[Carlyle Eulogy]," TIMES (February 7, 1881), 9.

833 _____. "[Carlyle Just Before Death]," NEW YORK TIMES (February 8, 1881), 4.

834 _____. "The Late Mr. Carlyle," TIMES (February 8, 1881), 9.

835 _____. "The Closing Days of Carlyle," RICHMOND STATE (February 9, 1881), 3.

836 _____. "The Late Mr. Carlyle," EDINBURGH DAILY REVIEW (February 10, 1881), 6.

837 _____. "Carlyle and Conway," RICHMOND DISPATCH (February 10, 1881), 2.

838 _____. "The Late Mr. Carlyle," TIMES (February 11, 1881), 5.

839 _____. "Thomas Carlyle," LITERARY WORLD, XXIII (February 11, 1881), 91.

840 _____. "Carlyle," LITERARY WORLD, XII (February 12, 1881), 56-57.

841 _____. "'Thomas Carlyle,'" PUNCH, LXXX (February 12, 1881), 61.

842 _____. "Mr. Carlyle," SATURDAY REVIEW, LI (February 12, 1881), 199-200.

843 _____. "Thomas Carlyle," TABLET, XXV (February 12, 1881), 244-245.

844 _____. "Thomas Carlyle," AMERICAN, I (February 12, 1881), 281-282.

845 _____. "Thomas Carlyle's Place in the Century," AMERICAN, I (February 12, 1881), 287-288.

846 _____. "Professional Authorship," BOSTON HERALD (February 13, 1881), 4.

847 _____. "Emerson Upon Carlyle," NEW YORK TIMES (February 13, 1881), 7.

848   ____ . "Carlyle's Earliest Work," NEW YORK TIMES (February 13, 1881), 10.

849   ____ . "Whitman on Carlyle," ST. LOUIS GLOBE-DEMOCRAT (February 14, 1881), 3.

850   ____ . "[Froude and Carlyle's Papers]," NEW YORK TIMES (February 15, 1881), 5.

851   ____ . "Mr. Carlyle Impeached," RICHMOND CENTRAL PRESBY-TERIAN (February 16, 1881), 3.

852   ____ . "Thomas Carlyle," ILLUSTRATED LONDON NEWS, LXXVIII (February 19, 1881), 177, 180-182.

853   ____ . "[Carlyle, Emerson, and Early Publication]," NEW YORK TIMES (February 19, 1881), 4.

854   ____ . "Carlyle as Critic," NEW YORK TIMES (February 21, 1881), 3.

855   ____ . "[Carlyle on] Woman's Sphere of Usefulness," NEW YORK TIMES (February 21, 1881), 3.

856   ____ . "The Genius of Carlyle," NEW YORK TIMES (February 21, 1881), 3.

857   ____ . "The Late Mr. Carlyle," TIMES (February 22, 1881), 10.

858   ____ . "[French Revolution MS]," NEW YORK TIMES (February 23, 1881), 3.

859   ____ . "[Carlyle's Income]," NEW YORK TIMES (February 24, 1881), 4.

860   ____ . "Carlyle as a Political Power," NEW YORK TIMES (February 24, 1881), 5.

861   ____ . "[Statue and Bust of Carlyle]," TIMES (February 25, 1881), 8.

862   ____ . "Jane Welsh Carlyle," CHAMBERS'S JOURNAL, LVIII (February 26, 1881), 135-137.

863 _____ . "The Funeral of Carlyle," NEW YORK TIMES (February 27, 1881), 4.

864 _____ . "Carlyle as a Rejected Author," NEW YORK TIMES (February 27, 1881), 4.

865 _____ . "'Thomas Carlyle,'" NEW YORK TIMES (February 27, 1881), 4.

866 _____ . "[Lydia M. Child on Carlyle]," RICHMOND CENTRAL PRESBYTERIAN (March 2, 1881), 1.

867 _____ . "Reminiscences of Thomas Carlyle," TIMES (March 3, 7, 1881), 11, 5.

868 _____ . "Carlyle and His Friends," NEW YORK TIMES (March 8, 1881), 2.

869 _____ . "Carlyle's Reminiscences," LITERARY WORLD, XXIII (March 11, 1881), 145-147.

870 _____ . "Carlyle's Reminiscences," CRITIC (NY), I (March 12, 1881), 59-60.

871 _____ . "A Bibliography of Carlyle," LITERARY WORLD, XII (March 12, 1881), 101.

872 _____ . "Carlyle's Reminiscences," INQUIRER, nos. 2020-2024 (March 12-April 9, 1881), 162-163, 181-182, 195-198, 213-214, 232-234.

873 _____ . "Reminiscences," GRAPHIC, XXIII (March 12, 1881), 258.

874 _____ . "The Morose Side of Carlyle," SPECTATOR, LIV (March 12, 1881), 341-343.

875 _____ . "Carlyle's Reminiscences," SPECTATOR, LIV (March 12, 1881), 349-350. Rpt. ECLECTIC MAGAZINE, XCVI (May, 1881), 708-712.

876 _____ . "Reminiscences," ATHENAEUM, nos. 2785-2786 (March 12-19, 1881), 357-358, 387-389.

877   _____. "Mr. Newton on Thomas Carlyle as a Prophet," NEW YORK TIMES (March 14, 1881), 8.

878   _____. "[Carlyle's Egotism]," NEW YORK TIMES (March 15, 1881), 4.

879   _____. "Reminiscences," NOTES AND QUERIES, sers. 6, III (March 18, 1881), 220.

880   _____. "Thomas Carlyle," RICHMOND STANDARD (March 19, 1881), 2.

881   _____. "Carlyle's Reminiscences," SATURDAY REVIEW, LI (March 19, 1881), 370-372.

882   _____. "Carlyle as a Painter," SPECTATOR, LIV (March 19, 1881), 373-374.

883   _____. "Carlyle," LITERARY WORLD, XII (March 26, 1881), 123.

884   _____. "Works by Thomas Carlyle," LITERARY WORLD, XII (March 26, 1881), 111.

885   _____. "Carlyle's Reminiscences," LITERARY WORLD, XII (March 26, 1881), 113-114.

886   _____. "Carlyle's Message to This Age," NEW YORK TIMES (March 28, 1881), 8.

887   _____. "The Late Thomas Carlyle," TIMES (March 28, 1881), 6.

888   _____. "Reminiscences," CHURCHMAN, IV (April, 1881), 49-57.

889   _____. "Correspondence, Carlyle's Gift of Books on Cromwell and Frederick the Great to Harvard College," HARVARD UNIVERSITY BULLETIN, II (April, 1881), 166-168.

890   _____. "Carlyle's Reminiscences," MONTH, XLI (April, 1881), 457-464.

891   _____. "[Reminiscences]," BRITISH QUARTERLY REVIEW, LXXIII (April, 1881), 471-477.

892 _____ . "Memoirs of Carlyle," LITERARY WORLD, XXIII (April 1, 1881), 199-200.

893 _____ . "Mr. Carlyle," TIMES (April 2, 1881), 11.

894 _____ . "Carlyle in His Reminiscences," AMERICAN, I (April 2, 1881), 410-411.

895 _____ . "Carlyle and the Peace Society," NEW YORK TIMES (April 6, 1881), 2.

896 _____ . "[Carlyle's Will]," TIMES (April 9, 1881), 11.

897 _____ . "Carlyle's Preface to Emerson's Essays," LITERARY WORLD, XII (April 9, 1881), 132.

898 _____ . "Thomas Carlyle: The Man and His Books," and "Thomas Carlyle," ATHENAEUM, no. 2789 (April 9, 1881), 488-489.

899 _____ . "[Carlyle's Books Given to Harvard]," NEW YORK TIMES (April 10, 1881), 1.

900 _____ . "Carlyle's Querulousness," NEW YORK TIMES (April 10, 1881), 13.

901 _____ . "Dr. Lord on Carlyle," NEW YORK TIMES (April 15, 1881), 8.

902 _____ . "[Carlyle as Student and Teacher]," NEW YORK TIMES (April 18, 1881), 4.

903 _____ . "[Reminiscences]," NEW YORK TIMES (April 24, 1881), 1.

904 _____ . "Reminiscences," HARPER'S WEEKLY, XXV (May, 1881), 310.

905 _____ . "Reminiscences," LIPPINCOTT'S MAGAZINE, n.s. I (May, 1881), 525-526.

906 _____ . "[Froude, Mary Carlyle, and the Reminiscences]," NEW YORK TIMES (May 5, 1881), 1.

907 _____ . "[Controversy on Reminiscences]," NEW YORK TIMES (May 7, 1881), 4.

908 _____ . "Carlyle's Posthumous Book," NEW YORK TIMES (May 7, 1881), 5.

909 _____ . "[Mary Carlyle on Reminiscences]," NEW YORK TIMES (May 8, 1881), 1.

910 _____ . "[Froude-Mary Carlyle Dispute]," TIMES (May 9, 1881), 11.

911 _____ . "Carlyle's Manuscripts," NEW YORK TIMES (May 10, 1881), 2.

912 _____ . "The Best Biographical Policy," NEW YORK TIMES (May 11, 1881), 4.

913 _____ . "[Carlyle Memorials at Chelsea and Westminster Abbey]," NEW YORK TIMES (May 15, 1881), 1.

914 _____ . "'The Deaths of Thomas Carlyle and George Eliot,'" NEW YORK TIMES (May 22, 1881), 4.

915 _____ . "[Carlyle on Chatterton]," NEW YORK TIMES (May 31, 1881), 5.

916 _____ . "Carlyle's Will," ECLECTIC MAGAZINE, XCVI (June, 1881), 863.

917 _____ . "Carlyle's Reminiscences," ATLANTIC MONTHLY, XLVII (June, 1881), 863-866.

918 _____ . "Thomas Carlyle at Home," TIMES (June 2, 1881), 6.

919 _____ . "[Wylie's Carlyle and Shepherd's Bibliography]," NOTES AND QUERIES, sers. 6, III (June 4, 1881), 460.

920 _____ . "'Carlyle,'" NEW YORK TIMES (June 5, 1881), 4.

921 _____ . "Profits from Carlyle's Books," NEW YORK TIMES (June 19, 1881), 2.

922 _____ . "The Carlyle Memorial in Edinburgh, " TIMES (June 22, 1881), 12.

923 _____ . "Carlyle as a Nicknamer, " ST. JAMES MAGAZINE, XLI (July, 1881), 99-103.

924 _____ . "English Reviews [on Carlyle], " METHODIST QUARTERLY REVIEW, LXIII (July, 1881), 547-551.

925 _____ . "Reminiscences, " METHODIST QUARTERLY REVIEW, LXIII (July, 1881), 584-586.

926 _____ . "Thomas Carlyle, " TIMES (July 1, 1881), 5.

927 _____ . "Carlyle and His Parents, " NEW YORK TIMES (July 11, 1881), 3.

928 _____ . "The Philosophy of Carlyle, " LITERARY WORLD, XII (July 16, 1881), 241-242.

929 _____ . "Carlyle's Youth, " NEW YORK TIMES (August 5, 1881), 3.

930 _____ . "The Carlyles, Thomas and Jane, " ST. JAMES GAZETTE, III (August 6, 1881), 13-14.

931 _____ . "[Carlyle and Queen Victoria], " NEW YORK TIMES (August 14, 1881), 7.

932 _____ . "Conway's Thomas Carlyle, " BRITISH QUARTERLY REVIEW, LXXIV (October, 1881), 232-233.

933 _____ . "Carlyle on Ireland, " NEW YORK TIMES (October 4, 1881), 2.

934 _____ . "Stories of Carlyle, " NEW YORK TIMES (December 30, 1881), 2.

935 [Alden, Henry]. "[Carlyle and Mill], " HARPER'S MAGAZINE, LXII (April, 1881), 787-788.

936 _____ . "[Reminiscences], " HARPER'S MAGAZINE, LXII (May, 1881), 944-945.

937   A[llen], G[rant]. "The Carlyle Controversy," TEMPLE BAR, LXII
       (August, 1881), 516-526.

938   Anderson, A. "'At the Grave of Mrs. Carlyle,'" GOOD WORDS,
       XXII (1881), 231-233.

939   [Barbour, William M.]. "Thomas Carlyle," NEW ENGLANDER,
       XL (May, 1881), 396-404.

940   Bell, Charles D. "Thomas Carlyle," CHURCHMAN, IV (June,
       1881), 182-192.

941   B[ently], G[eorge]. "Carlyle's Reminiscences," TEMPLE BAR,
       LXII (May, 1881), 23-36.

942   _____. "Sincerity in Biography," TEMPLE BAR, LXII (July, 1881),
       329-336.

943   Binns, William. "Thomas Carlyle," INQUIRER, no. 2018 (Febru-
       ary 26, 1881), 132-134.

944   [Blaikie, William G. ?]. "[Eulogy of Carlyle]," CATHOLIC
       PRESBYTERIAN, V (March, 1881), 218-219.

945   Blunt, Gerald, and A. B. Mitford. "The Carlyle Memorial Fund,"
       TIMES (April 7, 1881), II.

946   Bower, George S. "An Incident in the Life of Thomas Carlyle,"
       NEW MONTHLY MAGAZINE, CLXIX (September, 1881), 238-240.

947   Brightwell, D. Barron. "Articles on Thomas Carlyle," NOTES
       AND QUERIES, sers. 6, IV (August 20, 1881), 145.

948   [Browne, Francis F.]. "Carlyle's Philosophy," DIAL, II (July, 1881),
       63-64.

949   [Brownell, William C.]. "Carlyle's Reminiscences," NATION,
       XXXII (March 17, 1881), 186-188.

950   Bryce, James. "Carlyle's Reminiscences, and Their Editor," NATION,
       XXXII (June 30, 1881), 454-456.

951   Buchanan, Robert. "Wylie's Life of Carlyle," CONTEMPORARY RE-

VIEW, XXXIX (May, 1881), 792-803.

952   Buchheim, C. A. "Mr. Carlyle," TIMES (February 18, 1881), 8.

953   C., J. [J. C. Manchester]. THOMAS CARLYLE: A STUDY. Manchester: John Heywood, 1881.

954   [Call, W. M. W.]. "Thomas Carlyle: His Life and Writings," WESTMINSTER REVIEW, CXV (April, 1881), 457-493.

955   Carlyle, Mary. "Mr. Carlyle's Reminiscences," TIMES (May 5, 7, 1881), 8, 12.

956   Chadwick, John W. "Thomas Carlyle," UNITARIAN REVIEW, XV (April, 1881), 289-309.

957   Coffey, Robert S. THOMAS CARLYLE AND SOME OF THE LESSONS OF HIS CAREER. Bradford: H. Gaskarth, n.d. [1881].

958   "Common Sense" [Abraham Hayward?]. "Carlyle--A Counter-Blast," TIMES (February 11, 1881), 4. See also NEW YORK TIMES (April 25, 1881), 2.

959   Conway, Moncure D. THOMAS CARLYLE: A MEMORIAL DISCOURSE. London: South Place Chapel, Finsbury, 1881.

960   _____. "By the Grave of Carlyle," HARPER'S WEEKLY (March, 1881), 166.

961   _____. "Thomas Carlyle," HARPER'S MAGAZINE, LXII (May, 1881), 888-912.

962   _____. THOMAS CARLYLE. New York: Harper, 1881.

963   Croker, D. "[Carlyle Letter to James Hannay]," ATHENAEUM, no. 2782 (February 19, 1881), 265-266.

964   D., G. B. "Thomas Carlyle: A Study in Comparative Criticism," INQUIRER, no. 2030 (May 21, 1881), 333-334.

965   [D., H. W.]. THE LIFE OF THOMAS CARLYLE. London: Ward, Lock, n.d. [1881].

966   Dale, R. W. "Thomas Carlyle," CONGREGATIONALIST, X (March-April, 1881), 208-217, 285-293.

967   _____. "Thomas Carlyle," INDEPENDENT, XXXIII (May 12, 1881), 5-6.

968   Davis, C. A. "Thomas Carlyle," SWORD AND THE TROWL, XVII (July, 1881), 336-343.

969   Dodds, James. "The Early Life of Thomas Carlyle," CHRISTIAN MONTHLY, IV (April, 1881), 216-221.

970   Dorling, William. "Carlyle as Painted by Himself," CHRISTIAN WORLD MAGAZINE, XVII (June, 1881), 401-413.

971   _____. "Thomas Carlyle's Father," SUNDAY MAGAZINE, XVII (August, 1881), 550-552.

972   Dowden, Edward. "Thomas Carlyle," ACADEMY, XIX (February 12, 1881), 117-118.

973   _____. "Carlyle's Lectures on the Periods of European Culture, From Homer to Goethe," NINETEENTH CENTURY, IX (May, 1881), 856-879. Rpt. LITTELL'S LIVING AGE, CXLIX (June 11, 1881), 643-658; LIBRARY MAGAZINE, VIII (October, 1881), 283-311; and TRANSCRIPTS AND STUDIES. London: Kegan Paul, 1887.

974   Dulcken, H. W. WORTHIES OF THE WORLD. London: Ward, Lock, n.d. [1881].

975   Emerson, Ralph W. "Impressions of Thomas Carlyle in 1848," SCRIBNER'S MONTHLY MAGAZINE, XXII (May, 1881), 89-92. See "Tribute to Thomas Carlyle," PROCEEDINGS OF THE MASSA- CHUSETTS HISTORICAL SOCIETY, XVIII (1880-1881), 324-328; and LECTURES AND BIOGRAPHICAL SKETCHES. Boston: Houghton Mifflin, 1883.

976   Fidelis [pseud.]. "In Memoriam--Thomas Carlyle," CANADIAN MONTHLY, XIX (March, 1881), 316-318.

977   Foster, W. E. "Special Reference Lists: Thomas Carlyle," LIBRARY JOURNAL, VI (March, 1881), 48-49.

978   [Fox-Bourne, H. R.]. "Mr. Carlyle," ATHENAEUM, no. 2781 (February 12, 1881), 232-235.

979   Francis, John C., and William H. Peet. "Carlyle on Music," NOTES AND QUERIES, sers. 6, III (March 5, 1881), 197.

980   Froude, James A. "Mr. Carlyle's Papers," TIMES (February 14, 1881), 8. Rpt. PALL MALL GAZETTE, XXXIII (February 14, 1881), 7.

981   _____. "The Late Thomas Carlyle," TIMES (February 25, 1881), 8.

982   _____. "Mr. Carlyle's Reminiscences," TIMES (May 6, 9, 1881), 10, 10.

983   _____. "The Early Life of Thomas Carlyle," NINETEENTH CENTURY, X (July, 1881), 1-42. Rpt. LITTELL'S LIVING AGE, CL (July 30, 1881), 259-284; ECLECTIC MAGAZINE, XCVII (September, 1881), 289-316; LIBRARY MAGAZINE, VIII (October, 1881), 491-540.

984   Gilfillan, George. SKETCHES, LITERARY AND THEOLOGICAL. Edinburgh: David Douglass, 1881.

985   [Godkin, E. L.]. "Carlyle's Political Influence," NATION, XXXII (April 28, 1881), 291-292.

986   _____. "A Blunder of Carlyle's," NOTES AND QUERIES, sers. 6, III (May 7, 1881), 364.

987   Gostwick, Joseph. "Thomas Carlyle," WESLEYAN METHODIST MAGAZINE, CIV (April, 1881), 257-263.

988   Graham, H. G. "The Two Carlyles," ATHENAEUM, no. 2794 (May 14, 1881), 654.

989   H. "The Late Mr. Carlyle," TIMES (February 22, 1881), 10.

990   Hale, Edward E. THOMAS CARLYLE. Boston: privately printed, 1881.

991   Harper. "Mr. Carlyle's Reminiscences," TIMES (March 24, 1881), 11.

992   _____. REMINISCENCES BY THOMAS CARLYLE. New York: Harper, 1881.

993   [Hayward, Abraham]. "Thomas Carlyle and His Reminiscences," QUARTERLY REVIEW, CLI (April, 1881), 385-428.

994   Higginson, Thomas W. "Carlyle's Laugh," ATLANTIC MONTHLY, XLVIII(October, 1881), 463-466. Rpt. CARLYLE'S LAUGH AND OTHER SURPRISES. Boston: Houghton Mifflin, 1909.

995   Howe, Julia W. "A Meeting with Thomas Carlyle," CRITIC (NY), I (April 9, 1881), 89-90.

996   Hutton, Richard H. "Thomas Carlyle," GOOD WORDS, XXII (1881), 282-288. Rpt. ECLECTIC MAGAZINE, XCVI (June, 1881), 749-756; and CRITICISMS ON CONTEMPORARY THOUGHT AND THINKERS. London: Macmillan, 1894.

997   _____. "Mr. Carlyle as a Political Power," SPECTATOR, LIV (February 12, 1881), 209-210.

998   _____. "Thomas Carlyle," SPECTATOR, LIV (February 12, 1881), 214-215. Rpt. ECLECTIC MAGAZINE, XCVI (April, 1881), 564-567.

999   Ireland, Alexander. "Thomas Carlyle and Leigh Hunt," ATHEN-AEUM, no. 2799 (June 18, 1881), 814-815.

1000   _____. "The Periodical Press on Carlyle: Books and Pamphlets on His Life and Works," NOTES AND QUERIES, sers. 6, IV (September 10, 1881), 201-203.

1001   James, Henry. "Some Personal Recollections of Carlyle," ATLANTIC MONTHLY, XLVII (May, 1881), 593-609. Rpt. THE LITERARY REMAINS OF THE LATE HENRY JAMES. Boston: J. R. Osgood, 1885.

1002   Jones, Philip L. "Thomas Carlyle," BAPTIST REVIEW, III (1881), 245-259.

1003   Keeling, Annie E. "The Reminiscences of Thomas Carlyle," WESLEYAN METHODIST MAGAZINE, CIV (July-September, 1881), 516-522, 677-681.

1004   Knighton, William. "Conversations with Carlyle," CONTEMPOR-
        ARY REVIEW, XXXIX (June, 1881), 904-920.

1005   Lang, Andrew. "Mr. Carlyle's Reminiscences," FRASER'S MAGA-
        ZINE, CIII (April, 1881), 515-528.

1006   Larkin, Henry. "Carlyle and Mrs. Carlyle: A Ten Years' Reminis-
        cence," BRITISH QUARTERLY REVIEW, LXXIV (July, 1881), 15-45.

1007   Le Sueur, W. D. "Carlyle and Comte," CANADIAN MONTHLY,
        XIX (June, 1881), 639-642.

1008   M., H. "Thomas Carlyle," NOTES AND QUERIES, sers. 6, IV
        (October 15, 1881), 307.

1009   [Macdonnell, James]. "Mr. Carlyle," TIMES (February 7, 1881),
        4. Rpt. LITTELL'S LIVING AGE, CXLVII (March 12, 1881), 692-
        703; LONDON QUARTERLY REVIEW, LVI (April, 1881), 189-200;
        and BIOGRAPHIES OF EMINENT PERSONS. London: Macmillan,
        1893.

1010   [Macleod, D.]. "Mr. Carlyle and Dr. Chalmers," GOOD WORDS,
        XXII (1881), 477-480. Rpt. LITTELL'S LIVING AGE, CL (August
        20, 1881), 499-502.

1011   Masson, David. "Carlyle's Edinburgh Life," MACMILLAN'S MAG-
        AZINE, XLV-XLVI (November, 1881-January, 1882), 64-80, 145-
        163, 234-256. Rpt. EDINBURGH SKETCHES AND MEMORIES.
        London: Adam and Charles Black, 1892.

1012   [McCarthy, Justin]. "Carlyle's Portrait of Himself," AMERICAN
        CATHOLIC QUARTERLY, VI (April, 1881), 249-279.

1013   Mead, Edwin D. THE PHILOSOPHY OF CARLYLE. Boston: Hough-
        ton Mifflin, 1881.

1014   Morison, James C. "Carlyle's Reminiscences," FORTNIGHTLY RE-
        VIEW, XXXV (April 1, 1881), 456-466. Rpt. ECLECTIC MAGA-
        ZINE, XCVI (June, 1881), 735-742.

1015   Morley, Henry. OF ENGLISH LITERATURE IN THE REIGN OF
        VICTORIA. Leipzig: B. Tauchnitz, 1881.

1016   Murray, Louisa. "A Defense of Carlyle's Reminiscences, Partly Written by Himself," CANADIAN MONTHLY, XX (August, 1881), 121-133.

1017   _____. "Thomas Carlyle and Edward Irving," CANADIAN MONTHLY, XX (September, 1881), 303-315.

1018   N., F., and J. R. Thorne. "Thomas Carlyle," NOTES AND QUERIES, sers. 6, IV (September 17, 1881), 226.

1019   Nicoll, Henry J. THOMAS CARLYLE. Edinburgh: Macniven and Wallace, 1881.

1020   Noel, Roden. "Carlyle and Genius," ACADEMY, XX (July 16, 1881), 52-53.

1021   [O'Conor, J. V.]. "Thomas Carlyle," CATHOLIC WORLD, XXXIII (April, 1881), 18-24.

1022   O[liphant], M. O. W. "Thomas Carlyle," MACMILLAN'S MAGAZINE, XLIII (April, 1881), 482-496. Rpt. LITTELL'S LIVING AGE, CXLIX (April 30, 1881), 307-319; APPLETON'S JOURNAL, XXV (June, 1881), 510-521; ECLECTIC MAGAZINE, XCVI (June, 1881), 721-734; and LIBRARY MAGAZINE, VIII (October, 1881), 187-214.

1023   _____. "Carlyle's Last Days," HARPER'S WEEKLY, XXV (April, 1881), 290.

1024   Ordish, T. F. "Carlyle as an Antiquary," ANTIQUARY, III (March, 1881), 124-126.

1025   Paul, C. Kegan. "The Irvings," ATHENAEUM, no. 2790 (April 16, 1881), 525-527.

1026   Putnam, Greyl. "Home Life of Thomas Carlyle," POTTER'S AMERICAN MONTHLY, XVI (May, 1881), 438-440.

1027   R., F. W. "The Late Mr. Carlyle," TIMES (February 12, 1881), III.

1028   [Reeve, Henry]. "Reminiscences of Thomas Carlyle," EDINBURGH REVIEW, XLIII (April, 1881), 469-497.

1029   Reid, Stuart J. THOMAS CARLYLE: HIS WORK AND WORTH. Manchester: Tubbs, Book and Chrystal, n.d. [1881].

1030   S., F. "Carlyle on Music," NOTES AND QUERIES, sers. 6, III
       (February 26, 1881), 167.

1031   [Saintsbury, George]. "The Literary Work of Thomas Carlyle,"
       SCRIBNER'S MONTHLY MAGAZINE, XXII (May, 1881), 92-106.

1032   Sarson, George. "George Eliot and Thomas Carlyle," MODERN
       REVIEW, II (April, 1881), 399-413.

1033   Scotch Preacher [James Wood]. THE STRAIT GATE AND OTHER
       DISCOURSES. Edinburgh: Andrew Eliot, 1881.

1034   Scribner. THE CARLYLE REMINISCENCES. New York: Charles
       Scribner, 1881.

1035   [Sedgwick, A. G.]. "Thomas Carlyle," NATION, XXXII (Feb-
       ruary 17, 1881), 109-110.

1036   Shairp, John C. ASPECTS OF POETRY. Oxford: Clarendon Press,
       1881.

1037   Shepherd, Richard H. THE BIBLIOGRAPHY OF CARLYLE. London:
       Elliot Stock, n.d. [1881].

1038   _____. "Thomas Carlyle," GENTLEMAN'S MAGAZINE, CCL
       (March, 1881), 361-370.

1039   _____. MEMOIRS OF THE LIFE AND WRITINGS OF THOMAS
       CARLYLE. 2 vols. London: W. H. Allen, 1881.

1040   [Stephen, Leslie]. "Thomas Carlyle," CORNHILL MAGAZINE,
       XLIII (March, 1881), 349-358. Rpt. ECLECTIC MAGAZINE,
       XCVI (June, 1881), 742-749.

1041   _____. "Carlyle's Ethics," CORNHILL MAGAZINE, XLIV (Dec-
       ember, 1881), 664-683. Rpt. LITTELL'S LIVING AGE, CLII (Jan-
       uary 14, 1882), 67-80; and HOURS IN THE LIBRARY. New ed.
       New York: G. P. Putnam, 1894.

1042   Sullivan, Margaret F. "Thomas Carlyle," DIAL, I (March, 1881),
       225-228.

1043   Swinburne, Algernon C. "'The Deaths of Thomas Carlyle and

George Eliot,'" ATHENAEUM, no. 2792 (April 30, 1881), 591.
Rpt. LITERARY WORLD, XII (May 21, 1881), 180.

1044   Symington, Andrew J. "Some Personal Reminiscences of Carlyle,"
independent (New York), XXXIII (May 19–June 23, 1881), 2-3,
3-4, 1, 2, 4-5, 3-4. Rpt. SOME PERSONAL REMINISCENCES OF
CARLYLE. Paisley: Alexander Gardner, 1886.

1045   Tabor, Mary C. "Young Mrs. Carlyle: A Life Study," GOOD
WORDS, XXII (1881), 688-693. Rpt. LIBRARY MAGAZINE OF
AMERICAN AND FOREIGN THOUGHT, IX (1883), 265-276.

1046   Taylor, Henry. "Carlyle's Reminiscences," NINETEENTH CEN-
TURY, IX (June, 1881), 1009-1025. Rpt. LITTELL'S LIVING AGE,
CL (July 9, 1881), 85-95.

1047   Tew, Edmund. "Dr. Southey and Thomas Carlyle," NOTES AND
QUERIES, sers. 6, III (April 9, 1881), 284-285. Rpt. LITTELL'S
LIVING AGE, CXLIX (May 28, 1881), 575-576.

1048   Thomas, David. THOMAS CARLYLE: "THE CEDAR IS FALLEN."
London: Wade, n.d. [1881].

1049   Thompson, R. E. "Thomas Carlyle," PENN MONTHLY, XII
(March, 1881), 199-229.

1050   Towle, George M. "Carlyle and His Home in Chelsea," BOSTON
DAILY ADVERTISER (February 7, 1881), 1.

1051   Tyndall, John. "Mr. Carlyle," TIMES (May 4, 1881), 13.

1052   W., G. "Carlyle's Reminiscences," CHURCHMAN'S SHILLING
MAGAZINE, XXIX (April, 1881), 132-140.

1053   Watkins, M. G. "Thomas Carlyle," NOTES AND QUERIES, sers.
6, III (April 16, 1881), 305.

1054   [Wedgwood, Julia]. "A Study of Carlyle," CONTEMPORARY RE-
VIEW, XXXIX (April, 1881), 584-609. Rpt. LITTELL'S LIVING
AGE, CXLIX (May 7, 1881), 361-376; and NINETEENTH CENTURY
TEACHERS. London: Hodder and Stoughton, 1909.

1055   _____. "Mr. Froude as a Biographer," CONTEMPORARY REVIEW,

XXXIX (May, 1881), 821-842.

1056   Whitman, Walt. "Death of Carlyle," CRITIC (NY), I (February
12, 1881), 30.

1057   ____. "The Dead Carlyle," LITERARY WORLD, XII (February
12, 1881), 57.

1058   Wilks, Mark. "Thomas Carlyle," INQUIRER, no. 2017 (February
19, 1881), 123-124.

1059   Williamson, C. N. "The Late Thomas Carlyle: A Biographical
and Critical Sketch," GRAPHIC, XXIII (February 12, 1881), 157-
164.

1060   Wilson, John. THOMAS CARLYLE: THE ICONOCLAST OF MOD-
ERN SHAMS. Paisley: Alexander Gardner, 1881.

1061   Witton, H. B. "Death of Thomas Carlyle," HAMILTON SPECTA-
TOR, XXXIV (February 7, 1881), 1-2.

1062   Wylie, William H. THOMAS CARLYLE: THE MAN AND HIS
BOOKS. London: Marshall Japp, 1881.

1063   Y. [James Bryce]. "Thomas Carlyle and George Eliot," NATION,
XXXII (March 24, 1881), 201-202.

1882

1064   Anon. "Letters from Carlyle," NEW YORK TIMES (March 6, 1882),
2.

1065   ____. "Carlyle's American Recognition," NEW YORK TIMES
(April 7, 1882), 4.

1066   ____. "Prophetic Misanthropy," SPECTATOR, LV (April 8,
1882), 462-463.

1067   ____. "Thomas Carlyle: A History of the First Forty Years of His
Life," ATHENAEUM, nos. 2841-2842 (April 8-April 15, 1882), 435-
436, 467-468.

1068   . "Froude's Life of Carlyle," SPECTATOR, LV (April 8-22, 1882), 468-469, 530-532.

1069   . "Froude's Life of Carlyle," NEW YORK TIMES (April 9, 1882), 10.

1070   . "Froude's Biography of Carlyle," AMERICAN, IV (April 22, 1882), 25-26.

1071   . "Thomas Carlyle," SATURDAY REVIEW, LIII (April 22-29, 1882), 499-500, 533-534.

1072   . "Carlyle's Gentle Side," NEW YORK TIMES (April 23, 1882), 3.

1073   . "Carlyle, Lamb, and Procter," NEW YORK TIMES (April 23, 1882), 11.

1074   . "Carlyle's First Forty Years," LITERARY WORLD, XIII (May 6, 1882), 141.

1075   . "Mr. Froude's Life of Carlyle," ALL THE YEAR ROUND, n.s. XXIX (May 20, 1882), 324-330.

1076   . "Emerson and Carlyle," NEW YORK TIMES (May 21, 1882), 2.

1077   . "A Portrait of Carlyle," TIMES (May 23, 1882), 5.

1078   . "Froude's Carlyle," CENTURY MAGAZINE, XXIV (June, 1882), 304-308.

1079   . "[Froude's Carlyle]," NOTES AND QUERIES, sers. 6, V (June 3, 1882), 438-439.

1080   . "Emerson to Carlyle," NEW YORK TIMES (June 9, 1882), 2.

1081   . "Froude's Carlyle," ATLANTIC MONTHLY, L (July, 1882), 127-135.

1082   . "Mr. Froude's Life of Carlyle," MODERN REVIEW, III (July, 1882), 645-651.

1083   . "Carlyle's Journey Through Ireland," SPECTATOR, LV (July 1, 1882), 867-868.

1084   . "Reminiscences of My Irish Journey," ATHENAEUM, no. 2853 (July 1, 1882), 7-8.

1085   . "Reminiscences of My Irish Journey in 1849," SATURDAY REVIEW, LIV (July 15, 1882), 87-88.

1086   . "[Carlyle's Irish Journey]," CRITIC (NY), II (July 15, 1882), 189.

1087   . "Carlyle's Grave," NEW YORK TIMES (July 24, 1882), 2.

1088   . "Mr. Froude's Life of Carlyle," TEMPLE BAR, LXV (August, 1882), 519-530.

1089   . "[John Welsh]," NEW YORK TIMES (August 21, 1882), 4.

1090   . "Carlyle's Early Years," MONTH, XLVI (September, 1882), 139-145.

1091   . "Miss Mitford, Carlyle, and Ruskin," NEW YORK TIMES (October 26, 1882), 2.

1092   . "A Tribute to Emerson," NEW YORK TIMES (October 27, 1882), 1.

1093   . "The Carlyle Statue," TIMES (October 27, 1882), 8.

1094   . "A French Critic on Carlyle," SATURDAY REVIEW, LIV (November 18, 1882), 660-661.

1095   . "Last Words of Thomas Carlyle on Trades Unions, Promoterism, and Signs of the Times," NOTES AND QUERIES, sers. 6, VI (December 9, 1882), 480.

1096   . "Carlyle's Nobler Side," NEW YORK TIMES (December 24, 1882), 8.

1097 Adams, Charles K. A MANUAL OF HISTORICAL LITERATURE.

New York: Harper, 1882.

1098   [Alden, Henry]. "[Froude's Life and Reminiscences]," HARPER'S MAGAZINE, LXV (October, 1882), 795-796.

1099   A[llingham], W[illiam]. "Carlyle in His Eightieth Year," ART JOURNAL, XXXIV (January, 1882), 7-8.

1100   Arden, Constance. "The Philosophy of Thomas Carlyle," JOURNAL OF SCIENCE, XIX (June, 1882), 313-322.

1101   Arnold, Frederick. "The Mills and Carlyle," LONDON SOCIETY, XLII (December, 1882), 591-601.

1102   [Brown, James]. "Thomas Carlyle's Apprenticeship," SCOTTISH REVIEW, I (November, 1882), 72-100. Rpt. LITTELL'S LIVING AGE, CLVI (January 6, 1883), 88-101.

1103   Burroughs, John. "Carlyle and Emerson," CRITIC (NY), II (May 20, 1882), 140-141.

1104   _____. "Froude's Estimate of Carlyle," CRITIC (NY), II (October 7, 1882), 277.

1105   [Cowell, Herbert]. "Carlyle's Life and Reminiscences," BLACK-WOOD'S EDINBURGH MAGAZINE, CXXXII (July, 1882), 18-35. Rpt. ECLECTIC MAGAZINE, XCIX (September, 1882), 289-303.

1106   [Dickens, Jane]. "Froude's Life of Carlyle," CATHOLIC WORLD, XXXV (July, 1882), 520-533.

1107   Fox-Bourne, H. R. "Carlyle and His Wife," GENTLEMAN'S MAGAZINE, CCLII (June, 1882), 685-705. Rpt. LITTELL'S LIVING AGE, CLIV (July 22, 1882), 167-179; and ECLECTIC MAGAZINE, XCIX (September, 1882), 289-303. See also GEN-TLEMAN'S MAGAZINE, CCLIV (May, 1883), 530-533.

1108   Froude, James A. THOMAS CARLYLE: A HISTORY OF THE FIRST FORTY YEARS OF HIS LIFE, 1795-1835. 2 vols. London: Longmans, Green, 1882.

1109   Gostwick, Joseph. GERMAN CULTURE AND CHRISTIANITY.

London: F. Norgate, 1882.

1110   Heaton, Mary M. "Reminiscences of My Irish Journey in 1849,"
        ACADEMY, XXII (August 12, 1882), 114.

1111   Hewlett, Henry G. "[Carlyle Letter to H. F. Chorley]," ATHE-
        NAEUM, no. 2875 (December 9, 1882), 772.

1112   Hughes, Thomas. MEMOIR OF DANIEL MACMILLAN. London:
        Macmillan, 1882.

1113   Ingleby, C. M. "Carlyle and Emerson," HIBERNIA, I (July,
        1882), 97-98.

1114   [Inglis, Henry]. "Some Early Letters of Mr. Carlyle," GLASGOW
        HERALD (February 16, 1882), 3.

1115   Ireland, Alexander. IN MEMORIAM. RALPH WALDO EMERSON.
        London: Simpkin, Marshall, 1882.

1116   Reily, William M. "Carlyle's Predilection for the Teutonic,"
        POTTER'S AMERICAN MONTHLY, XVIII (March, 1882), 335-
        338.

1117   Ritchie, Anne I. "Cheyne Walk, Chelsea," ART JOURNAL,
        XXXIV (November, 1882), 340-341.

1118   Scherr, Johannes. A HISTORY OF ENGLISH LITERATURE. London:
        Sampson Low, 1882.

1119   [Sedgwick, A. G.]. "Froude's Carlyle," NATION, XXXIV (June
        1, 1882), 465-466.

1120   Skinner, Charles M. "An Unpublished Letter from Carlyle,"
        CRITIC (NY), II (October 21, 1882), 278.

1121   Smith, Walter C. "Reminiscences of Carlyle and Leigh Hunt; Being
        Extracts from the Diary of the Late John Hunter of Craigcrook,"
        GOOD WORDS, XXIII (1882), 96-103.

1122   Stanley, Arthur P. SERMONS ON SPECIAL OCCASIONS. London:
        John Murray, 1882.

1123 U., C. B. "The Philosophy of Carlyle," INQUIRER, no. 2076 (April 8, 1882), 214-216.

1124 Wallace, William. "Thomas Carlyle: A History of the First Forty Years of His Life," ACADEMY, XXI (April 15, 1882), 259-261.

1125 Walsh, William S. PEN PICTURES OF MODERN AUTHORS. New York: G. P. Putnam, 1882.

1126 Watt, Francis. "Thomas Carlyle and Religious Thought," ST. JAMES MAGAZINE, XLII (May, 1882), 539-545.

1127 Welsh, Alfred H. DEVELOPMENT OF ENGLISH LITERATURE AND LANGUAGE. 2 vols. Chicago: S. C. Griggs, 1882.

1128 Whitman, Walt. SPECIMEN DAYS AND COLLECT. Philadelphia: Rees Welsh, 1882-1883.

1883

1129 Anon. "Anecdote of Carlyle," CHOICE LITERATURE, I (1883), 330.

1130 _____. "Mrs. Carlyle's Letters," GOOD WORDS, XXIV (1883), 334-340.

1131 _____. "Carlyle and Emerson," TIMES (January 15, 1883), 7.

1132 _____. "Emerson and Carlyle," NEW YORK TIMES (February 19, 1883), 3. See also NEW YORK TIMES (April 15, 1883), 6.

1133 _____. "Carlyle's Country," NEW YORK TIMES (February 23, 1883), 6.

1134 _____. "Carlyle and Emerson," LITERARY WORLD, XIV (March 10, 1883), 71-72.

1135 _____. "The Correspondence of Thomas Carlyle and Ralph Waldo Emerson," ATHENAEUM, no. 2890 (March 17, 1883), 335-336.

1136 _____. "Carlyle and Emerson," SATURDAY REVIEW, LV (March 24, 1883), 367-368.

1137   . "The Correspondence of Carlyle and Emerson," SPECTA-
TOR, LVI (March 24, 1883), 386-387.

1138   . "Mrs. Carlyle's Letters," TIMES (March 31, 1883), 4.

1139   . "Carlyle and Emerson," CONGREGATIONALIST, XII
(April, 1883), 325-334.

1140   . "Carlyle and Emerson," ATLANTIC MONTHLY, LI (April,
1883), 560-564.

1141   . "The Carlyle-Emerson Correspondence," WESTMINSTER
REVIEW, CXIX (April 1, 1883), 451-493.

1142   . "Carlyle and His Wife," NEW YORK TIMES (April 4,
1883), 2-3. See also NEW YORK TIMES (April 9, 1883), 5.

1143   . "Letters and Memorials of Jane Welsh Carlyle," ATHE-
NAEUM, no. 2893 (April 7, 1883), 435-437. Rpt. LITTELL'S
LIVING AGE, CLVII (May 5, 1883), 290-295.

1144   . "Mrs. Carlyle," SPECTATOR, LVI (April 7-14, 1883),
445-446, 483-485.

1145   . "Mrs. Carlyle's Letters," LITERARY WORLD, XIV (April
21, 1883), 121-122.

1146   . "Letters and Memorials of Jane Welsh Carlyle," SATUR-
DAY REVIEW, LV (April 21, 1883), 502-503.

1147   . "One of Carlyle's Letters," NEW YORK TIMES (April
22, 1883), 3.

1148   . "Carlyle and Two Queens," NEW YORK TIMES (April
22, 1883), 6.

1149   . "The Correspondence of Thomas Carlyle and Ralph Waldo
Emerson," MANHATTAN, I (May, 1883), 408-410.

1150   . "Jane Welsh Carlyle," ATLANTIC MONTHLY, LI (June,
1883), 837-840.

1151   . "Letters and Memorials of Jane Welsh Carlyle," HIBER-

NIA, II (June, 1883), 90-92.

1152 ____. "Thin Pessimism," SPECTATOR, LVI (June 2, 1883), 702-703.

1153 ____. "A Sister of Carlyle," NEW YORK TIMES (July 1, 1883), 8.

1154 ____. "Carlyle Worship," TIMES (August 8, 1883), 11.

1155 ____. "'In Suspense,'" CORNHILL MAGAZINE, XLVIII (September, 1883), 289-304.

1156 ____. "Some Reminiscences of Jane Welsh Carlyle," TEMPLE BAR, LXIX (October, 1883), 227-233. Rpt. LITTELL'S LIVING AGE, CLIX (November 3, 1883), 302-306.

1157 ____. "Vocabulary of Carlyle," NOTES AND QUERIES, sers. 6, VIII (October 6, 1883), 264-265.

1158 A Day Laborer [pseud.]. "Emerson and Carlyle as Related to the Common People," INTERNATIONAL REVIEW, XIV (May-June, 1883), 319-325.

1159 [Alden, Henry]. "[Carlyle-Emerson Correspondence]," HARPER'S MAGAZINE, LXVI (May, 1883), 956-957.

1160 Britton, Norman. "Carlyle and Emerson," PROGRESS, I (May, 1883), 277-287.

1161 [Browne, Francis F.]. "Letters and Memorials of Jane Welsh Carlyle," DIAL, IV (May, 1883), 17-18.

1162 Burroughs, John. "In Carlyle's Country," ATLANTIC MONTHLY, LI (March, 1883), 320-330. Rpt. FRESH FIELDS. Boston: Houghton Mifflin, 1885.

1163 ____. "Emerson and Carlyle Again," CRITIC (NY), III (July 14, 1883), 303-304.

1164 ____. "Carlyle," CENTURY MAGAZINE, XXVI (August, 1883), 530-543.

1165   Courthope, William J. "Johnson and Carlyle: Common Sense
        Versus Transcendentalism," NATIONAL REVIEW, II (November,
        1883), 317-332.

1166   Editor. "Carlyle and Emerson," MODERN REVIEW, IV (April,
        1883), 318-340.

1167   Foster, Fred W. "The Carlyle Statue at Chelsea," TIMES (Nov-
        ember 29, 1883), 7.

1168   Gould, Elizabeth P. "The Family Life of Carlyle and Emerson,"
        CRITIC (NY), III (June 30, 1883), 292-293.

1169   Hamilton, Gail. "The Day of Judgment," NORTH AMERICAN
        REVIEW, CXXXVII-CXXXVIII (December, 1883-January, 1884),
        563-583, 60-77.

1170   Harrison, Frederic. "Histories of the French Revolution," NORTH
        AMERICAN REVIEW, CXXXVII (October, 1883), 388-402. Rpt.
        THE CHOICE OF BOOKS. London: Macmillan, 1886.

1171   Hewlett, Henry G. "Two Letters from Thomas Carlyle to the
        Chorleys," ATHENAEUM, no. 2887 (February 24, 1883), 247.

1172   [Hubbard, Sara A.]. "Carlyle and Emerson," DIAL, III (April,
        1883), 265-270.

1173   Ireland, Alexander. "The Correspondence of Thomas Carlyle and
        Ralph Waldo Emerson," ACADEMY, XXIII (April 7, 1883), 231-
        233.

1174   James, Henry, Jr. "The Correspondence of Carlyle and Emerson,"
        CENTURY MAGAZINE, XXVI (June, 1883), 265-272.

1175   [Jenkins, M.]. "The Letters of Mrs. Carlyle," AMERICAN, VI
        (May 12, 1883), 73.

1176   Lane, William C. "The Carlyle Collection. Part I. Oliver Crom-
        well," HARVARD UNIVERSITY BULLETIN, III (January, 1883), 53-
        56.

1177   [Lyttleton, Arthur T.]. "Carlyle's Life and Works," CHURCH

QUARTERLY REVIEW, XV (January, 1883), 301-343. Rpt. MOD-
ERN POETS OF FAITH, DOUBT AND PAGANISM. London: John
Murray, 1904.

1178   McCosh, James. "Thomas Carlyle and His Influence on the English Language," MANHATTAN, II (November, 1883), 433-438.

1179   [Metcalfe, William M.]. "Mrs. Carlyle's Letters," SCOTTISH
REVIEW, II (May, 1883), 127-146.

1180   Morison, James C. "Thomas Carlyle," MACMILLAN'S MAGA-
ZINE, XLVII (January, 1883), 200-212. Rpt. LITTELL'S LIVING
AGE, CLVI (February 7, 1883), 438-448; and CHOICE LITERA-
TURE, I (1883), 142-148.

1181   Mounsey, A. C. "Madame Campan and Carlyle," NOTES AND
QUERIES, sers. 6, VIII (October 27, 1883), 338.

1182   Nicoll, Henry J. LANDMARKS OF ENGLISH LITERATURE. London: John Hogg, 1883.

1183   Oliphant, M. O. W. "Mrs. Carlyle," CONTEMPORARY REVIEW,
XLIII (May, 1883), 609-628. Rpt. LITTELL'S LIVING AGE, CLVII
(June 16, 1883), 673-684; and CHOICE LITERATURE, I (1883),
345-352.

1184   _____. "The Ethics of Biography," CONTEMPORARY REVIEW,
XLIV (July, 1883), 76-93. Rpt. LITTELL'S LIVING AGE,
CLVIII (August 11, 1883), 323-333.

1185   P., R. W. "Madame Campan and Carlyle," NOTES AND QUER-
IES, sers. 6, VIII (August 18, 1883), 126-127.

1186   Paterson, J. "Carlyle's Home at Craigenputtock," GOOD WORDS,
XXIV (1883), 128-131.

1187   [Perry, Thomas S.]. "The Carlyle and Emerson Correspondence,"
AMERICAN, V (March 10, 1883), 348-349.

1188   Robertson, A. J. "Carlyle Smirching the Idol," PROGRESS, I-
II (May-August, 1883), 370-374, 47-51.

1189   Schuyler, Montgomery. "'Carlyle and Emerson,'" ATLANTIC

MONTHLY, LI (June, 1883), 774.

1190   Shepherd, Richard H. "The Carlyle-Emerson Correspondence,"
        GENTLEMAN'S MAGAZINE, CCLIV (April, 1883), 415-427.

1191   [Skelton, John]. "Mrs. Carlyle's Letters," BLACKWOOD'S EDIN-
        BURGH MAGAZINE, CXXXIII (May, 1883), 614-627.

1192   Spence, R. M. "Thomas Carlyle on Wordsworth," NOTES AND
        QUERIES, sers. 6, VIII (August 4, 1883), 87.

1193   [Sullivan, Margaret F.]. "[Carlyle's Works]," DIAL, IV (Decem-
        ber, 1883), 201.

1194   Venables, G. S. "Carlyle in Society and at Home," FORTNIGHT-
        LY REVIEW, XXXIX (May, 1883), 622-642. Rpt. LITTELL'S LIV-
        ING AGE, CLVII (June 23, 1883), 725-738; and ECLECTIC MAG-
        AZINE, CI (July, 1883), 1-15.

1195   Wallace, William. "Letters and Memorials of Jane Welsh Carlyle,"
        ACADEMY, XXIII (April 21, 1883), 267-268.

1196   Whipple, Edwin P. "Emerson and Carlyle," NORTH AMERICAN
        REVIEW, CXXXVI (May, 1883), 431-445.

1197   Wise, Daniel. THOMAS CARLYLE. New York: Phillips and
        Hunt, 1883.

1884

1198   Anon. "Recreations of Men of Letters," ALL THE YEAR ROUND,
        n.s. XXXIII (February 2, 1884), 257-258.

1199   _____. "Proposed Memorial for Thomas Carlyle," TIMES (Febru-
        ary 16, 1884), 12.

1200   _____. "Carlyle's Birthplace," TIMES (May 26, 1884), 13.

1201   _____. "Carlyle on Libraries," LIBRARY JOURNAL, IX (June,
        1884), 103.

1202   _____. "Emerson and the Concord School," CRITIC (NY), V (August 2, 1884), 55-57.

1203   . "Carlyleana," BOOKBUYER, n.s. I (October, 1884), 199.

1204   . "Carlyle's Inner Life," NEW YORK TIMES (October 16, 1884), I. See also NEW YORK TIMES (October 19, November 2, 1884), 5, 6.

1205   . "Carlyle on the Politicians," SPECTATOR, LVII (October 18, 1884), 1367-1368.

1206   . "Carlyle's Life in London," CRITIC (NY), V (October 25, 1884), 193-194.

1207   . "Thomas Carlyle: A History of His Life in London," ATHE-NAEUM, no. 2974 (October 25, 1884), 524-526. Rpt. LITTELL'S LIVING AGE, CLXIII (November 22, 1884), 508-511.

1208   . "Carlyle on Religious Cant," SPECTATOR, LVII (October 25, 1884), 1401-1402.

1209   . "Thomas Carlyle," SPECTATOR, LVII (October 25-November I, 1884), 1406-1407, 1438-1439.

1210   . "The New Carlyle Memoirs," BOOKBUYER, n.s. I (November, 1884), 233-234.

1211   . "[Carlyle's Temperament]," CRITIC (NY), V (November I, 1884), 210.

1212   . "Carlyle's Great Services," NEW YORK TIMES (November 2, 1884), 14.

1213   . "Carlyle in London," LITERARY WORLD, XV (November 5, 1884), 383-384.

1214   . "Cant and Carlyle's Cant," NEW YORK TIMES (November 6, 1884), 2.

1215   . "[Froude's Defense]," CRITIC (NY), V (November 8, 1884), 225-226.

1216 _____ . "Almost a Tragedy," CRITIC (NY), V (December 20, 1884), 298-299.

1217 Adams, W. H. D. CELEBRATED ENGLISHWOMEN OF THE VIC-TORIAN ERA. 2 vols. London: F. V. White, 1884.

1218 Austin, Alfred. "Some Lessons from Carlyle's Life," NATIONAL REVIEW, IV (November, 1884), 330-341. Rpt. LITTELL'S LIVING AGE, CLXIII (December 6, 1884), 629-635.

1219 Beveridge, H. "Some Thoughts of Thomas Carlyle," CALCUTTA REVIEW, LXXIX (1884), 1-13.

1220 [Birrell, Augustine]. OBITER DICTA. London: Elliot Stock, 1884.

1221 Brewer, E. Cobham. "Carlyle's French Revolution," NOTES AND QUERIES, sers. 6, X (October 18, 1884), 307.

1222 Burroughs, John. "Arnold on Emerson and Carlyle," CENTURY MAGAZINE, XXVII (April, 1884), 925-932.

1223 _____ . "Another Word on Carlyle," CRITIC (NY), V (November 29, 1884), 253-254.

1224 Callaway, Morgan. "Letters and Memorials of Jane Welsh Carlyle," METHODIST QUARTERLY REVIEW, LXVI (January, 1884), 60-79.

1225 Congdon, Charles T. "Literary Resurrectionists," NORTH AMERI-CAN REVIEW, CXXXVIII (March, 1884), 274-283.

1226 Froude, James A. THOMAS CARLYLE: A HISTORY OF HIS LIFE IN LONDON, 1834-1881. 2 vols. London: Longmans, Green, 1884. See also ECLECTIC MAGAZINE, CIII (December, 1884), 791-800.

1227 Hannay, David. "Some Portraits of Carlyle," MAGAZINE OF ART, VII (1884), 76-83.

1228 Harris, James. "The Carlyle Correspondence," RED DRAGON MAGAZINE, VI (August, 1884), 164-167.

1229 _____ . "Wales as Carlyle Saw It Forty Years Ago," RED DRAGON MAGAZINE, VI (December, 1884), 519-527.

1230   Howells, John. "Carlyle's Holidays in Wales," RED DRAGON
        MAGAZINE, V (April–June, 1884), 333-341, 461-469, 553-563.

1231   Hubbard, Sara A. "More of Carlyle's Memoirs," DIAL, V (Nov-
        ember, 1884), 172-175.

1232   Ireland, Alexander. "The Carlyle-Emerson Correspondence,"
        CRITIC (NY), V (November 22, 1884), 251.

1233   [Morley, John]. "The Man of Letters as Hero," MACMILLAN'S
        MAGAZINE, LI (November, 1884), 62-70.

1234   Rhine, Alice H. "Neither Genius nor Martyr," NORTH AMERI-
        CAN REVIEW, CXXXVIII (March, 1884), 246-262.

1235   Robertson, A. J. "Carlyle on Diderot," PROGRESS, IV (Aug-
        ust, 1884), 65-71.

1236   [Sadler, Thomas]. "Carlyle and Neuberg," MACMILLAN'S MAG-
        AZINE, L (August, 1884), 280-297.

1237   Saladin [William S. Ross]. A VISIT TO CARLYLE'S GRAVE. Lon-
        don: W. Stewart, n.d. [1884].

1238   Seaton, R. C. "The Attitude of Carlyle and Emerson Towards
        Christianity," NATIONAL REVIEW, III (August, 1884), 775-788.
        Rpt. ECLECTIC MAGAZINE, CIII (October, 1884), 445-453.

1239   [Sedgwick, A. G.]. "Carlyle in London," NATION, XXXIX
        (November 20, 1884), 438-439.

1240   Tooley, G. W. LIVES: GREAT AND SIMPLE. London: Kent,
        1884.

1241   Toynbee, Arnold. LECTURES ON THE INDUSTRIAL REVOLUTION.
        London: Rivington, 1884.

1242   Venables, G. S. "Carlyle's Life in London," FORTNIGHTLY RE-
        VIEW, XLII (November, 1884), 594-608.

1243   Wallace, William. "Thomas Carlyle: A History of His Life in Lon-
        don," ACADEMY, XXVI (November 1, 1884), 281-282.

1244   West, Henry E. "JOHN INGLESANT" AND "SARTOR RESAR-
TUS." London: Modern Press, n.d. [1884].

1885

1245   Anon. "Thomas Carlyle: A History of His Life in London," BRIT-
ISH QUARTERLY REVIEW, LXXXI (January, 1885), 143-159.

1246   ____. "Froude's Thomas Carlyle," METHODIST QUARTERLY RE-
VIEW, LXVII (January, 1885), 160.

1247   ____. "[Cheyne Row]," CRITIC (NY), VI (January 17, 1885), 31.

1248   ____. "Carlyle in London," ATLANTIC MONTHLY, LV (March,
1885), 421-423.

1249   ____. "Thomas Carlyle," LONDON QUARTERLY REVIEW, LXIV
(April, 1885), 1-25.

1250   ____. "Dante's English Translators," BOOK-LORE, II (July,
1885), 42-46.

1251   ____. "A Pilgrimage to Carlyle's Country," PALL MALL GAZ-
ETTE (July 10, 1885), 10-11. Rpt. CRITIC (NY), VII (August 8,
1885), 67-69.

1252   ____. "A Letter by Carlyle," TIMES (August 13, 1885), 10.

1253   ____. "[Carlyle on Slavery]," NEW YORK TIMES (September
15, 1885), 4. See also NEW YORK TIMES (September 30, 1885),
6.

1254   ____. "[Carlyle Letters to Judge Beverly Tucker]," HARPER'S
MAGAZINE, LXXI (October, 1885), 797-800. See also CRITIC
(NY), VII (September 19, 1885), 142.

1255   ____. "Emerson's Letters Stolen," NEW YORK TIMES (October
13, 1885), 4. See also NEW YORK TIMES (October 14, 1885), 4.

1256   ____. "An Unpublished Letter of Carlyle's [to Gavan Duffy],"
IRISH MONTHLY, XIII (November, 1885), 597.

1257   . "Masson's Interpretation of Carlyle," POPULAR SCIENCE
MONTHLY, XXVIII (December, 1885), 224-236.

1258   Arnold, Matthew. DISCOURSES IN AMERICA. London: Macmillan,
1885.

1259   Barry, William F. "Carlyle," DUBLIN REVIEW, XCVI (January,
1885), 63-90. Rpt. HERALDS OF REVOLT. London: Hodder and
Stoughton, 1904.

1260   Burroughs, John. FRESH FIELDS. Boston: Houghton Mifflin, 1885.

1261   Chamberlain, D. H. "The Man, Thomas Carlyle, At Last," AND-
OVER REVIEW, III (March, 1885), 227-238.

1262   Coolidge, Susan. "A Gallery of Contemporary Portraits. By the
Late Thomas Carlyle," LITERARY WORLD, XVI (May 30, 1885),
185-187.

1263   Courthope, William J. THE LIBERAL MOVEMENT IN ENGLAND.
London: John Murray, 1885.

1264   Crozier, John B. CIVILIZATION AND PROGRESS. London:
Longmans, Green, 1885.

1265   Dowden, Edward. "George Eliot and Jane Carlyle," CRITIC (NY),
VI (February 28, 1885), 107.

1266   Emerson, George H. "The Incipiency of the French Revolution,"
UNIVERSALIST QUARTERLY REVIEW, XLII (January, 1885), 68-81.

1267   . "Thomas Carlyle," UNIVERSALIST QUARTERLY REVIEW,
XLII (October, 1885), 389-399.

1268   F., A. [A. F. Hewit]. "Carlyle as a Prophet," CATHOLIC WORLD,
XL-XLI (March-April, 1885), 724-734, 1-17.

1269   F., A. R. "Carlyle as a Philologist," NOTES AND QUERIES, sers.
6, XI (January 3, 1885), 9.

1270   Harris, William R. "Emerson's Relations to Goethe and Carlyle,"
THE GENIUS AND CHARACTER OF EMERSON. Ed. F. B. Sanborn

(Boston: J. Osgood, 1885), 386-419.

1271   Harrison, Frederic. "Froude's Life of Carlyle," NORTH AMERI-
        CAN REVIEW, CXL (January, 1885), 9-21. Rpt. THE CHOICE
        OF BOOKS. London: Macmillan, 1886. See also CRITIC (NY),
        VI (February 28, 1885), 107.

1272   Hedge, Frederick H. "Froude's Carlyle," UNITARIAN REVIEW,
        XXIII (February, 1885), 118-134.

1273   Hutton, Laurence. LITERARY LANDMARKS OF LONDON. Bos-
        ton: J. R. Osgood, 1885.

1274   Laing, Samuel. MODERN SCIENCE AND MODERN THOUGHT.
        London: Chapman and Hall, 1885.

1275   MacCall, William. "'Almost a Tragedy,' Again," CRITIC (NY),
        VI (February 14, 1885), 81-82.

1276   Mackintosh, Emily J. "Carlyle and Carlyle's Wife," PETERSON'S
        MAGAZINE, LXXXVII (May, 1885), 413-417.

1277   Masson, David. CARLYLE: PERSONALLY AND IN HIS WRITINGS.
        London: Macmillan, 1885.

1278   [Metcalfe, William M.]. "Froude's Carlyle's Life in London,"
        SCOTTISH REVIEW, V (January, 1885), 1-21.

1279   [Morris, Mowbray]. "Thomas Carlyle: A History of the First Forty
        Years of His Life," QUARTERLY REVIEW, CLIX (January, 1885),
        76-112.

1280   "Obiter Dicta" [Augustine Birrell]. "Views of Carlyle," BOOK-
        WORM, II (July, 1885), 20-21.

1281   O'Brady, F. S. "Carlyle as a Political Teacher," FORTNIGHTLY
        REVIEW, XLIV (October, 1885), 516-530. Rpt. ECLECTIC MAG-
        AZINE, CV (December, 1885), 794-804.

1282   Parton, James. SOME NOTED PRINCES, AUTHORS, AND STATES-
        MEN OF OUR TIME. New York: T. Y. Crowell, n.d. [1885].

1283   Petre, M. "Carlyle on Religious Ceremonies," MONTH, LV

(November, 1885), 314-321.

1284   Porter, John A. "Carlyle's Naseby Relics," NOTES AND QUER-
IES, sers. 6, XII (August 8, 1885), 107.

1285   Saintsbury, George. SPECIMENS OF ENGLISH PROSE STYLE.
London: Kagen Paul, 1885.

1286   Smith, John C. WRITINGS BY THE WAY. Edinburgh: William
Blackwood, 1885.

1287   Taylor, Henry. AUTOBIOGRAPHY. 2 vols. London: Longmans,
Green, 1885.

1288   Tulloch, John. MOVEMENTS OF RELIGIOUS THOUGHT IN
BRITAIN DURING THE NINETEENTH CENTURY. London: Longmans, Green, 1885.

1289   Wallace, William. "Carlyle, Personally and in His Writings,"
ACADEMY, XXVIII (July 11, 1885), 20.

1290   [Wells, N. W.]. "Carlyle and Lamb," NEW ENGLANDER,
XLIV (September, 1885), 605-619.

1886

1291   Anon. "Carlyle Tablet at Cheyne Row," PALL MALL GAZETTE
(February 6, 1886), 5. Rpt. CRITIC (NY), VIII (February 27,
1886), III.

1292   _____ . "[Froude on Carlyle]," CRITIC (NY), VIII (February 13,
1886), 86.

1293   _____ . "Carlyle on the Choice of Books," CRITIC (NY), VIII
(May 1, 1886), 221.

1294   _____ . "Carlyle's Writing Desk," NEW YORK TIMES (May 16,
1886), 3.

1295   _____ . "Chronicles of Scottish Counties," ALL THE YEAR ROUND,
n.s. XXXVIII (May 29, 1886), 340-346.

1296   _____ . "Five Letters of Carlyle's," ATHENAEUM, no. 3064 (July

17, 1886), 81-82.

1297 _____. "Goethe's Testimonial to Carlyle for the Chair of Moral Philosophy," ATHENAEUM, no. 3067 (August 7, 1886), 176.

1298 _____. "Carlyle to Coventry Patmore," CRITIC (NY), IX (August 14, 1886), 83.

1299 _____. "[Symington's Reminiscences]," LITERARY WORLD, XVII (September 4, 1886), 296.

1300 _____. "Carlyle Sneers at Lamb," CRITIC (NY), IX (September 25, 1886), 153-154.

1301 _____. "Early Letters of Thomas Carlyle," TIMES (November 6, 1886), 15.

1302 _____. "Early Letters of Thomas Carlyle," ATHENAEUM, no. 3080 (November 6, 1886), 593-595.

1303 _____. "Carlyle's Love Letters," NEW YORK TIMES (November 13, 1886), 2.

1304 _____. "Early Letters of Thomas Carlyle," SATURDAY REVIEW, LXII (November 13, 1886), 655-656.

1305 _____. "[Froude and the Reminiscences]," NEW YORK TIMES (November 15, 1886), 3.

1306 _____. "Prof. Norton's Portrait of Carlyle," CRITIC (NY), IX (December 11, 1886), 288-289.

1307 _____. "[Carlyle and Froude]," CRITIC (NY), IX (December 18, 1886), 307.

1308 Birch, W. J. "Carlyle and Greene on Shakespeare," NOTES AND QUERIES, sers. 7, II (July 31, 1886), 85.

1309 Browning, Oscar. "The Flight of Louis XVI. to Varennes. A Criticism of Carlyle," TRANSACTIONS OF THE ROYAL HISTORICAL SOCIETY, n.s. III (March, 1886), 319-341. Rpt. FLIGHT TO VARENNES AND OTHER ESSAYS. London: Swan, 1892.

1310   Burroughs, John. "Dr. Johnson and Carlyle," CRITIC (NY), VIII (June 2, 1886), 1-2.

1311   C., Th. "Carlyle and Whistler," AMERICAN, XIII (December 11, 1886), 121.

1312   Carlyle, Mary. "Carlyle Letters," TIMES (November 4, 1886), 10.

1313   Dawson, George. BIOGRAPHICAL LECTURES. Ed. George St. Clair. London: Kegan Paul, Trench, 1886.

1314   Edger, Samuel. AUTOBIOGRAPHICAL NOTES AND LECTURES. London: William Isbister, 1886.

1315   Francison, Alfred. NATIONAL LESSONS FROM THE LIFE AND WORKS OF CARLYLE. London: London Literary Society, n.d. [1886].

1316   Froude, James A. "Carlyle's Letters," TIMES (November 2, 1886), 8.

1317   Gridley, C. Oscar. "Thomas Carlyle's Tablet," TIMES (February 18, 1886), 4. See also (February 8, 1866), 6; and (February 15, 1886), 6.

1318   Haskins, D. G. "The Maternal Ancestors of Ralph Waldo Emerson," LITERARY WORLD, XVII (September 4, 1886), 297-299.

1319   Hooper, James. "'Cool as Dilworth's,'" NOTES AND QUERIES, sers. 7, II (September 18, 1886), 230.

1320   Larkin, Henry. CARLYLE AND THE OPEN SECRET OF HIS LIFE. London: Kegan Paul, Trench, 1886.

1321   Lewin, Walter. "Thomas Carlyle and the Open Secret of His Life," ACADEMY, XXIX (June 12, 1886), 407-408.

1322   Martin, Benjamin E. "Old Chelsea, II," CENTURY MAGAZINE, XXXIII (December, 1886), 225-236.

1323   Mounsey, A. C., and W. H. N. "'Cool as Dilworth's,'" NOTES

AND QUERIES, sers. 7, II (October 9, 1886), 297.

1324 Müller, Friedrich M. "Goethe and Carlyle," CONTEMPORARY
REVIEW, XLIX (June, 1886), 772-793. Rpt. LITTELL'S LIVING
AGE, CLXX (July 31, 1886), 259-272; and GOETHE AND
CARLYLE. London: D. Nutt, 1886. See also LITERARY WORLD,
XVII (June 26, 1886), 233.

1325 Norton, Charles E. "Recollections of Carlyle, with Notes Concerning His Reminiscences," NEW PRINCETON REVIEW, II (July-
November, 1886), 1-19, 283. See also CRITIC (NY), IX (July 3,
1886), II; and LITERARY WORLD, XVIII (July 10, 1886), 239.

1326 O'Donoghue, T. Griffin. "Carlyle's Irish Tours," IRISH MONTH-
LY, XIV (November, 1886), 613-625.

1327 Stephen, James F. THE LATE MR. CARLYLE'S PAPERS. London:
privately printed, 1886. Rpt. Froude, no. 1622.

1328 _____. "[Carlyle's Desk]," CRITIC (NY), VIII (May 15, 1886),
250.

1329 Wallace, William. "Early Letters of Thomas Carlyle," ACADEMY,
XXX (November 6, 1886), 301-302.

1330 Wasson, David A. "Carlyle on Happiness," UNITARIAN REVIEW,
XXV (May, 1886), 385-402.

1331 Wright, William A. "The Squire Papers," ENGLISH HISTORICAL
REVIEW, I (April, 1886), 311-348.

1887

1332 Anon. "[Facsimilie of Carlyle Letter]," COLLECTOR, I (January 15, 1887), 7.

1333 _____. "Carlyle's Early Letters," LITERARY WORLD, XVIII
(January 22, 1887), 21-22.

1334 _____. "Carlyle's Early Life," WESTMINSTER REVIEW, CXXVIII
(April, 1887), 211-224.

1335 ____ . "The Carlyle-Goethe Correspondence," CRITIC (NY), X (May 7, 1887), 226-227.

1336 ____ . "Correspondence Between Goethe and Carlyle," SATUR-DAY REVIEW, LXIII (May 14, 1887), 697-698.

1337 ____ . "More Carlyle Letters Coming," NEW YORK TIMES (May 29, 1887), 4.

1338 ____ . "The Goethe-Carlyle Correspondence," ATLANTIC MONTHLY, LIX (June, 1887), 849-852.

1339 ____ . "[Carlyle-Goethe Correspondence]," LITERARY WORLD, XVIII (June 11, 1887), 188.

1340 ____ . "Goethe and Carlyle," ALL THE YEAR ROUND, n.s. XL (June 18-25), 1887), 508-513, 533-539.

1341 ____ . "Carlyle Re-Edited," NEW YORK TIMES (June 19, 1887), 14.

1342 ____ . "Correspondence Between Goethe and Carlyle," BLACK-WOOD'S EDINBURGH MAGAZINE, CXLII (July, 1887), 120-123.

1343 ____ . "Correspondence Between Goethe and Carlyle," NEW PRINCETON REVIEW, IV (July, 1887), 134-137.

1344 ____ . "[Reminiscences]," LITERARY WORLD, XVIII (July 9, 1887), 220.

1345 ____ . "Carlyle and His Own Home," NEW YORK TIMES (July 18, 1887), 2.

1346 ____ . "Bismark and Carlyle," NEW YORK TIMES (July 25, 1887), 3.

1347 Anderson, John P. "Bibliography." See Garnett, no. 1354.

1348 Bayne, Thomas. "Carlyle's Definition of Genius," NOTES AND QUERIES, sers. 7, III (January 29, 1887), 84-85.

1349 Baynes, T. Spencer. "An Evening with Carlyle," ATHENAEUM, nos. 3101-3103 (April 2-16, 1887), 449-450, 511. Rpt. CRITIC (NY), X (April 27, 1887), 209-210.

1350　Bouchier, Jonathan. "Carlyle on Milton," NOTES AND QUER-IES, sers. 7, IV (November 26, 1887), 429.

1351　Cochrane, William. THE CHURCH AND THE COMMONWEALTH. Brantford, Ontario: Bradley, Garretson, 1887.

1352　Dawes, Anna L. "Some Sober After-Thoughts on Literature and Character," ANDOVER REVIEW, VIII (August, 1887), 161-168.

1353　F., A. J. "Carlyle Rehabilitated," AMERICAN, XIV (April 30, 1887), 24-25.

1354　Garnett, Richard. LIFE OF THOMAS CARLYLE. London: Walter Scott, 1887.

1355　Griswold, Hattie T. HOME LIFE OF GREAT AUTHORS. Chicago: A. C. McClurg, 1887.

1356　Holmes, Oliver W. OUR HUNDRED DAYS IN EUROPE. Boston: Houghton, Mifflin, 1887.

1357　Hubbard, Sara A. "Goethe and Carlyle," DIAL, VIII (May, 1887), 19-21.

1358　Hunt, Theodore W. REPRESENTATIVE ENGLISH PROSE AND PROSE WRITERS. New York: A. C. Armstrong, 1887.

1359　Hutton, Richard H. ESSAYS ON SOME OF THE MODERN GUIDES TO ENGLISH THOUGHT IN MATTERS OF FAITH. London: Macmillan, 1887.

1360　Jessop, A. "Books that Helped Me," FORUM, IV (September, 1887), 29-33.

1361　Kerr, James. CARLYLE AS SEEN IN HIS WORKS. London: W. H. Allen, 1887.

1362　Lane, William C. "The Carlyle Collection. Part II. Frederick the Great," HARVARD UNIVERSITY BULLETIN, V (October, 1887-January, 1888), 67-72, 107-116. See also THE CARLYLE

COLLECTION. Cambridge: Library of Harvard University, 1888.

1363   Lane-Poole, Stanley. CELEBRITIES OF THE CENTURY. London: Cassel, 1887.

1364   Mason, J. "Gallery of Illustrious Literary Characters," LEISURE HOUR, XXXVI (1887), 690-695.

1365   Palgrave, Reginald. "Carlyle, The 'Pious Editor' of Cromwell's Speeches," NATIONAL REVIEW, VIII (January, 1887), 588-604. See also LITERARY WORLD, XVIII (February 5, 1887), 47.

1366   Parkes, W. Kineton. THOMAS CARLYLE: AN ESSAY. London: Simpkin, Marshall, 1887.

1367   Pollock, William F. PERSONAL REMEMBRANCES. 2 vols. London: Macmillan, 1887.

1368   R., R. "Carlyle," NOTES AND QUERIES, sers. 7, IV (October 1, 1887), 276.

1369   Stephen, Leslie. DICTIONARY OF NATIONAL BIOGRAPHY. vol. IX. London: Smith, Elder, 1887.

1370   [Thomas, C.]. "Carlyle's Indebtedness to Goethe," NATION, XLIV (May 5, 1887), 391-392.

1371   Thorne, William H. MODERN IDOLS. Philadelphia: J. B. Lippincott, 1887.

1372   Whipple, Edwin P. AMERICAN LITERATURE AND OTHER PAPERS. Boston: Ticknor, 1887.

1373   [Woodberry, George E.]. "Carlyle's Early Letters," NATION, XLIV (January 13, 1887), 37-39.

1888

1374   Anon. "[J. H. Stirling's Pamphlet on Carlyle]," CRITIC (NY), XII (April 28, 1888), 205.

1375   _____. "Carlyle in an Anglican Church," FRANK LESLIE'S

POPULAR MAGAZINE, XXVI (August, 1888), 191.

1376   . "Carlyle and Mill," SPECTATOR, LXI (August 18, 1888), 1131-1132.

1377   . "[Jane Welsh Carlyle Letter to Mrs. Daubeny]," CRITIC (NY), XIII (September 8, 1888), 116.

1378   . "[Entrance to Carlyle's House]," CRITIC (NY), XIII (September 22, 1888), 132.

1379   Arnold, A. S. THE STORY OF THOMAS CARLYLE. London: Ward and Downey, 1888.

1380   Browning, Oscar. "Carlyle as an Historian," ATHENAEUM, no. 3185 (November 10, 1888), 625-626.

1381   Cochrane, Robert. GREAT THINKERS AND WORKERS. London: W. and R. Chambers, 1888.

1382   Evans, T. C. OF MANY MEN. New York: American News, 1888.

1383   Harris, W. M. "Carlyle on Milton," NOTES AND QUERIES, sers. 7, V (January 14, 1888), 33.

1384   Jenks, Edward. THOMAS CARLYLE AND JOHN STUART MILL. Orpington: George Allen, 1888.

1385   Kelly, J. J. "Points of View," IRISH ECCLESIASTICAL RE-CORD, IX (July, 1888), 589-599.

1386   Kennedy, W. S. "'Sartor,' 'Brahma,' and the 'Forest Hymn,'" CRITIC (NY), XII (February 4, 1888), 57-58.

1387   Laun, Henri Van. "Carlyle and the Prince Imperial," NOTES AND QUERIES, sers. 7, V (June 9, 1888), 447-448.

1388   P., E. "Charlemagne," NOTES AND QUERIES, sers. 7, VI (September 29, 1888), 247.

1389   Robinson, W. Clarke. "Epitaphs by Carlyle," NOTES AND QUER-

IES, sers. 7, V (June 23, 1888), 486.

1390   Smith, Lucy T. "Thomas Carlyle," ATALANTA, I (February, 1888), 287-291.

1391   Steggall, Julius., St. C. B., and C. C. B. "Charlemagne," NOTES AND QUERIES, sers. 7, VI (October 13, 1888), 297.

1392   Winsor, Justin. BIBLIOGRAPHICAL CONTRIBUTIONS. THE CARLYLE COLLECTION. Cambridge, Library of Harvard University, 1888.

1889

1393   Anon. "[Carlyle Letter to John L. Motley]," CRITIC (NY), XIV (March 23, 1889), 140.

1394   ____. "Letters of Thomas Carlyle," ATHENAEUM, no. 3204 (March 23, 1889), 367-368.

1395   ____. "Mrs. Carlyle Assailed," NEW YORK TIMES (March 24, 1889), 12.

1396   ____. "Further Letters from Carlyle," NEW YORK TIMES (March 31, 1889), 12.

1397   ____. "[Scribner's Edition of Sartor Resartus]," NEW YORK TIMES (April 7, 1889), 19.

1398   ____. "Carlyle's Early Letters," LITERARY WORLD, XX (May 11, 1889), 156.

1399   ____. "[Frederick Martin's MS, Ritchie's Early Letters, and Cromwell Letters]," NEW YORK TIMES (June 3, 1889), 3.

1400   ____. "Early Letters of Jane Welsh Carlyle," ATHENAEUM, no. 3218 (June 29, 1889), 815.

1401   ____. "Letters of Thomas Carlyle," ATLANTIC MONTHLY, LXIV (August, 1889), 279-281.

1402   ____. "Early Letters of Jane Welsh Carlyle," SATURDAY RE-

105

VIEW, LXVIII (August 3, 1889), 136-137.

1403   ____. "Early Letters of Jane Welsh Carlyle," NOTES AND QUERIES, sers. 7, VIII (August 24, 1889), 160.

1404   ____. "Carlyle's Tobacconist," NEW YORK TIMES (September 15, 1889), 3.

1405   ____. "Carlyle as a Schoolmaster," CRITIC (NY), XV (September 25, 1889), 155-156.

1406   ____. "[Carlyle Letter]," CRITIC (NY), XV (September 28, 1889), 148.

1407   ____. "[Leigh Hunt, Jane Welsh Carlyle, and 'Jenny Kissed Me']," DIAL, X (October, 1889), 140. Rpt. LITERARY WORLD, XX (October 25, 1889), 370-371.

1408   ____. "Mrs. Carlyle's Early Letters," SPECTATOR, LXIII (October 5, 1889), 442-443.

1409   Burroughs, John. INDOOR STUDIES. Boston: Houghton Mifflin, 1889.

1410   C., F. W. "Unpublished Lectures of Carlyle," NOTES AND QUERIES, sers. 7, VIII (October 12, 1889), 286.

1411   Conway, Moncure D. "Carlyle's Religion," OPEN COURT, III (July 11, 1889), 1719-1720.

1412   Dreer, Ferdinand J. A CATALOGUE OF THE COLLECTION OF AUTOGRAPHS FORMED BY FERDINAND JULIUS DREER. 2 vols. Philadelphia: privately printed, 1889-1893.

1413   E., M. B. "Carlyle and Goethe: A Comparison," TEMPLE BAR, LXXXVI (July, 1889), 399-403. Rpt. ECLECTIC MAGAZINE, CXII (September, 1889), 325-327.

1414   Gibbs, William E. "Thomas Carlyle," UNIVERSALIST QUARTERLY REVIEW, XLVI (April, 1889), 141-158.

1415   Hapgood, Norman. "Carlyle's Estimate of the Eighteenth Century," HARVARD MONTHLY, VIII (April, 1889), 53-59.

1416   Harrison, Frederic. "Letters of Thomas Carlyle," NINETEENTH
CENTURY, XXV (April, 1889), 625-628.

1417   James, Lewis G. "Carlyle's Philosophy of History," WESTMIN-
STER REVIEW, CXXXII (October, 1889), 414-423.

1418   Lee, Marian. "'Jenny Kissed Me,'" CRITIC (NY), XV (July
13, 1889), 20.   See also CRITIC, XV (October 26, 1889), 209.

1419   Marwick, William. "Jane Welsh and Thomas Carlyle," RUSKIN
READING GUILD JOURNAL, I (August, 1889), 235-241.

1420   Murroes, H. "The Religion of Carlyle," RUSKIN READING
GUILD JOURNAL, I (January-February, 1889), 7-12, 42-47.

1421   Robertson, J. M. ESSAYS TOWARDS A CRITICAL METHOD.
London: T. Fisher Unwin, 1889.

1422   Ross, William G. OLIVER CROMWELL AND HIS 'IRONSIDES.'
Chatham: W. and J. Mackay, 1889.

1423   West, Henry E. "The Carlyle Society of London," RUSKIN READ-
ING GUILD JOURNAL, I (January-November, 1889), 1-4, 21-
23, 57-58, 90, 125-126, 215-216, 345, 373-374.

1424   _____. "Carlyle as a Historian," RUSKIN READING GUILD
JOURNAL, I (February, 1889), 47-50.

1890

1425   Anon. "Carlyle and Augusta," NEW YORK TIMES (February 12,
1890), 2.

1426   _____. "More Carlyle Anecdotes," CRITIC (NY), XVI (May
17, 1890), 251-252.

1427   _____. "[Carlyle Letter to Jane Welsh Carlyle]," NEW YORK
TIMES (July 14, 1890), 3.

1428   _____. "Carlyle as an Aristocrat," NEW YORK TIMES (December 7, 1890), 2.

1429   Anderson, Jessie M. "Humor--Carlyle and Browning," POET-
LORE, II (August, 1890), 421-423.

1430   Bolton, Sarah K. FAMOUS ENGLISH AUTHORS OF THE NINE-
TEENTH CENTURY. New York: Crowell, n.d. [1890].

1431   Cocke, Zitella. "'At Carlyle's Grave,'" NEW ENGLAND MAG-
AZINE, VIII (March, 1890), 173. Rpt. REVIEW OF REVIEWS, I
(May, 1890), 147.

1432   Davidson, David. MEMORIES OF A LONG LIFE. Edinburgh:
David Douglass, 1890.

1433   Lewin, Walter. THOMAS CARLYLE. Liverpool: Cope, 1890.

1434   Lunan, George B. "Carlyle and Hero-Worship," IGDRASIL,
I (May, 1890), 195-202.

1435   Martin, William. THOMAS CARLYLE: HIS LIFE AND WORK.
Glasgow: Wilson and McCormick, n.d. [1890?].

1436   Matheson, A. "'Thomas Carlyle,'" SPECTATOR, LXV (December 6, 1890), 836.

1437   McPherson, J. G. "Carlyle and Kirkcaldy," IGDRASIL, I
(April, 1890), 155-157.

1438   Roose, Pauline W. "Carlyle and Old Women," NATIONAL
REVIEW, XVI (September, 1890), 77-83. Rpt. LITTELL'S
LIVING AGE, CLXXXVII (October 18, 1980), 185-189.

1439   Sime, David. "Carlyle as a Literary Man," HOME CHIMES,
LI (April, 1890), 212-222.

1440   _____. "Carlyle on Scott; or, Carlyle's Iconoclastic Criticism,"
IGDRASIL, I (August, 1890), 320-329, 365-374.

1441   Smalley, George W. LONDON LETTERS AND SOME OTHERS.
2 vols. London: Macmillan, 1890.

1442   Tyndall, John. "Personal Recollections of Carlyle," FORT-
NIGHTLY REVIEW, LIII (January, 1890), 5-32. Rpt. LIT-
TELL'S LIVING AGE, CLXXXIV (February 8, 1890), 323-
339; and NEW FRAGMENTS. London: Longmans, Green,
1892. See also REVIEW OF REVIEWS, I (January, 1890), 30-
31.

1443   Venturi, Emilie A. "A Memory of Thomas Carlyle," PATER-
NOSTER REVIEW (November, 1890), 122-129. See also RE-
VIEW OF REVIEWS, II (November, 1890), 451.

1444   West, Henry E. "The Carlyle Society of London," IGDRASIL,
I (August, 1890), 342-343.

1891

1445   Anon. "[Carlyle Letter to Emerson]," CRITIC (NY), XVIII
(June 13, 1891), 318.

1446   _____. "[Carlyle Letter to Dr. Hanna]," CRITIC (NY), XIX
(July 4, 1891), 12.

1447   _____. "Carlyle on Thiers," CRITIC (NY), XIX (July 18,
1891), 34.

1448   _____. "Self Tormentors," SPECTATOR, LXVII (July 25, 1891),
122-123.

1449   _____. "Ireland's Jane Welsh Carlyle," SATURDAY REVIEW,
LXXII (August 1, 1891), 140-141.

1450   _____. "[Ireland's Jane Welsh Carlyle]," CRITIC (NY), XIX
(August 15, 1891), 80. See also CRITIC, XIX (October 3, 1891),
167.

1451   _____. "James Russell Lowell," SPEAKER, IV (August 15, 1891),
191-192. Rpt. LITTELL'S LIVING AGE, CXC (September 19,
1891), 762-764.

1452   _____. "Professor Masson on Carlyle," IGDRASIL, III (September, 1891), 121-123.

1453   . "Carlyle and Ruskin (Two Letters)," ENGLISH ILLUS-
TRATED MAGAZINE, IX (October, 1891), 105-106.

1454   . "[Carlyle's Lectures]," CRITIC (NY), XIX (October
31, 1891), 241.

1455   . "[Martin of Kirkcaldy on Carlyle]," CRITIC (NY),
XIX (December 5, 1891), 326.

1456   . "[French Revolution]," NEW YORK TIMES (December
19, 1891), 3.

1457 Bayne, Thomas. "Carlyle and Lord Tennyson," NOTES AND
QUERIES, sers. 7, XI (March 14, 1891), 204.

1458   . "Date of Essay by Carlyle," NOTES AND QUERIES,
sers. 7, XI (April 18, 1891), 314.

1459 Bouchier, Jonathan. "Thomas Carlyle and 'N&Q,'" NOTES
AND QUERIES, sers. 7, XII (November 28, 1891), 428-429.

1460 Carryer, A. P. "Date of Essay by Carlyle," NOTES AND
QUERIES, sers. 7, XI (March 14, 1891), 208.

1461 C[ather], W[illa]. "Concerning Thomas Carlyle," NEBRASKA
STATE JOURNAL, XXI (March 1, 1891), 14. See also HESPER-
IAN, XX (March 1, 1891), 3-4.

1462 Davies, W. W. "Passage in Carlyle Wanted," NOTES AND
QUERIES, sers. 7, XI (April 25, 1891), 333.

1463 [Espinasse, Francis]. "The Carlyles and a Segment of Their
Circle: Recollections and Reflections," BOOKMAN (L), I-II
(October, 1891-September, 1892), 21-23, 57-59, 95-97, 133-
135, 167-168, 202-204, 11-12, 45-47, 75-76, 108-109, 144-
146, 170-171. Expanded in LITERARY RECOLLECTIONS AND
SKETCHES. London: Hodder and Stoughton, 1893.

1464 Ewing, Thomas J. "Carlyle's Essay 'The Opera,'" NOTES AND
QUERIES, sers. 7, XI (May 30, 1891), 425-426.

1465 Flügel, Ewald. THOMAS CARLYLE'S MORAL AND RELIGIOUS

DEVELOPMENT. Trans. J. G. Tyler. New York: M. L. Holbrook, 1891.

1466   Graham, P. Anderson. NATURE IN BOOKS: SOME STUDIES IN BIOGRAPHY. London: Methuen, 1891.

1467   Hitchcock, Thomas. UNHAPPY LOVES OF MEN OF GENIUS. New York: Harper, 1891.

1468   Ireland, Mrs. Alexander. LIFE OF JANE WELSH CARLYLE. London: Chatto and Windus, 1891.

1469   [Kingsland, W. G.]. "Letter of Advice to a Young Man, 1 April 1870," POET-LORE, III (January, 1891), 47-49. See also REVIEW OF REVIEWS, III (February, 1891), 133, 161; and CRITIC (NY), XIX (November 29, 1891), 310.

1470   Lecky, W[illiam] E. H. "Carlyle's Message to His Age," CONTEMPORARY REVIEW, LX (October, 1891), 520-528. Rpt. LITTELL'S LIVING AGE, CXCI (December 19, 1891), 758-762; and HISTORICAL AND POLITICAL ESSAYS. London: Longmans, Green, 1908.

1471   Martin, Edwin C. "Carlyle's Politics," SCRIBNER'S MONTHLY MAGAZINE, X (October, 1891), 506-512.

1472   Masson, David. CARLYLE. Glasgow: Carter and Pratt, 1891.

1473   Meldrum, David S. "Carlyle and Kirkcaldy," SCOTS MAGAZINE, n.s. VIII (November, 1891), 435-442.

1474   Murray, Patrick. "Dr. Murray as an Edinburgh Reviewer, with an Unpublished Letter of Thomas Carlyle," IRISH MONTHLY, XIX (November, 1891), 582-586.

1475   Robertson, J. M. MODERN HUMANISTS. London: Swan Sonnenschein, 1891.

1476   Rose, Henry. THE NEW POLITICAL ECONOMY. London: James Speirs, 1891.

1477   S., E. "Passage in Carlyle Wanted," NOTES AND QUERIES, sers. 7, XI (March 14, 1891), 208.

1478 Scherer, Edmond. ESSAYS ON ENGLISH LITERATURE. Trans. George Saintsbury. London: Sampson Low, 1891.

1892

1479 Anon. "[Mary Aitken Carlyle on Carlyle]," CRITIC (NY), XX (January 16, 1892), 39-40.

1480 _____. "Carlyle's Lectures of 1838," NEW YORK TIMES (January 31, 1892), 19.

1481 _____. "A New View of Carlyle," CRITIC (NY), XX (February 6, 1892), 92.

1482 _____. "Lectures on the History of Literature," SATURDAY REVIEW, LXXIII (February 6, 1892), 162-163.

1483 _____. "Carlyle's Lectures on Literature," BOOKMAN (L), I (March, 1892), 217.

1484 _____. "Lectures on the History of Literature," ATHENAEUM, no. 3358 (March 5, 1892), 301.

1485 _____. "Professor Blackie's Reminiscences," CRITIC (NY), XX (March 19, 1892), 177.

1486 _____. "Lectures on the History of Literature," NATION, LIV (March 24, 1892), 235.

1487 _____. "Letters of Jane Welsh Carlyle to Amely Bolte," NEW REVIEW, VI (April, 1892), 608-616.

1488 _____. "Carlyle's Posthumous Book," SPECTATOR, LXVII (April 9-16, 1892), 494-496, 531-533.

1489 _____. "Concerning Leigh Hunt," CORNHILL MAGAZINE, LV (May, 1892), 487-496.

1490 _____. "Carlyle's Lectures on Literature," CRITIC (NY), XX (May 28, 1892), 298.

1491 _____ . "[Lectures on the History of Literature]," WESTMIN-STER REVIEW, CXXXVII (June, 1892), 463.

1492 _____ . "Carlyle's Novel in Court," CRITIC (NY), XX (June 4, 1892), 318.

1493 _____ . "Another Book by Carlyle," NEW YORK TIMES (June 5, 1892), 19.

1494 _____ . "Two Carlyle Books," SATURDAY REVIEW, LXXIII (June 18, 1892), 722-723.

1495 _____ . "Last Words and Conversations with Carlyle," ATHE-NAEUM, no. 3374 (June 25, 1892), 815-816.

1496 _____ . "[Duffy's Conversations]," IRISH MONTHLY XX (July, 1892), 388.

1497 _____ . "Philosophy and Theology," WESTMINSTER REVIEW, CXXXVIII (July, 1892), 533-534.

1498 _____ . "[Duffy on Carlyle]," CRITIC (NY), XXI (July 2, 1892), 7.

1499 _____ . "Talks with Carlyle," NEW YORK TIMES (July 10, 1892), 19.

1500 _____ . "Carlyleana," BOOKMAN (L), II (August, 1892), 153-154.

1501 _____ . "Nichol's Life of Carlyle," LITERARY WORLD, XXIII (August, 1892), 287.

1502 _____ . "The Last Words of Thomas Carlyle," POPULAR SCIENCE MONTHLY, XLI (August, 1892), 555.

1503 _____ . "Nichol's Thomas Carlyle," SATURDAY REVIEW, LXXIV (August 6, 1892), 169-171.

1504 _____ . "Professor Nichol on Carlyle," NEW YORK TIMES (August 7, 1892), 19.

1505   ____. "Professor Nichol's Life of Carlyle," SPECTATOR, LXIX (August 13, 1892), 226-227.

1506   ____. "Carlyle's Last Words," CRITIC (NY), XXI (August 27, 1892), 104-105.

1507   ____. "[Carlyle and Thackeray]," CRITIC (NY), XXI (September 17, 1892), 150.

1508   ____. "A New Life of Carlyle," CRITIC (NY), XXI (September 24, 1892), 161.

1509   ____. "Carlyle and the 'Rose Goddess,'" NEW YORK TIMES (October 23, 1892), 4.

1510   ____. "Miss Jewsbury's Letters to Mrs. Carlyle," BOOKMAN (L), III (November, 1892), 55-56.

1511   ____. "Carlyle Once More," SPECTATOR, LXIX (November 5, 1892), 621-623.

1512   ____. "Miss Jewsbury's Letters," NEW YORK TIMES (November 28, 1892), 3.

1513   Atkinson, Blanche. "My Four Letters from Carlyle," GOOD WORDS, XXXIII (1892), 459-462. See also REVIEW OF REVIEWS, VI (August, 1892), 87-88.

1514   Bayne, Thomas. "Carlyle at Haddington," NOTES AND QUERIES, sers. 8, I (January 2, 1892), 6.

1515   Bouchier, Jonathan. "Sir Walter Scott and Carlyle," NOTES AND QUERIES, sers. 8, II (November 5, 1892), 366-367.

1516   Boyesen, H. H. ESSAYS ON GERMAN LITERATURE. London: T. Fisher Unwin, 1892.

1517   Cade, R. "Carlyle's Lectures on Literature; A Note Respecting the Various Manuscripts," LIBRARY, IV (1892), 225-227.

1518   Caird, Edward. ESSAYS ON LITERATURE AND PHILOSOPHY. 2 vols. Glasgow: James Maclehose, 1892.

1519   Dalgleish, W. S. GREAT AUTHORS. London: Thomas Nelson, 1892.

1520   Duffy, Charles G. "Conversations and Correspondence with Thomas Carlyle," CONTEMPORARY REVIEW, LXI (January-April, 1892), 120-152, 279-304, 430-456, 576-608. Rpt. LITTELL'S LIVING AGE, CXCII-CXCIII (February 27-June 4, 1892), 531-550, 795-810, 234-250, 596-615; ECLECTIC MAGAZINE, CXXIII (March-May, 1892), 326-333, 503-515, 598-704; and CONVERSATIONS WITH CARLYLE. London: Sampson Low, 1892. See also REVIEW OF REVIEWS, V (February-April, 1892), 92, 231, 342.

1521   Gibbins, H. de B. ENGLISH SOCIAL REFORMERS. London: Methuen, 1892.

1522   Hill, George B. WRITERS AND READERS. New York: G. P. Putnam, 1892.

1523   Holyoake, George J. SIXTY YEARS OF AN AGITATOR'S LIFE. 2 vols. London: T. Fisher Unwin, 1892.

1524   How, Harry. "Professor Blackie," STRAND MAGAZINE, III (March, 1892), 225-236.

1525   Hudson, Robert, and L. L. K. "Sir Walter Scott and Carlyle," NOTES AND QUERIES, sers. 8, II (December 3, 1892), 455.

1526   Johnson, Lionel. "Nichol's Thomas Carlyle," ACADEMY, XLII (September 10, 1892), 205-206.

1527   Kennedy, W. S. "Varnhagen Von Ense and Carlyle," CRITIC (NY), XXI (July 9, 1892), 21-22.

1528   [Morris, Mowbray]. "Leaves from a Note-Book of Some Books," MACMILLAN'S MAGAZINE, LXV (March, 1892), 386-393.

1529   Nichol, John. THOMAS CARLYLE. London: Macmillan, 1892.

1530   Oliphant, M. O. W., and E. R. Oliphant. THE VICTORIAN

AGE OF ENGLISH LITERATURE. London: Percival, 1892.

1531   Pelly, Lewis. "Glimpses of Carlyle," FORTNIGHTLY RE-
VIEW, LVII (May, 1892), 723-728. Rpt. LITTELL'S LIVING
AGE, CXCIV (July 16, 1892), 187-190.

1532   [Preuss, Richard]. "Letters of Carlyle to Varnhagen von Ense,"
NEW REVIEW, VI (April-May, 1892), 408-429, 593-608.
Rpt. LITTELL'S LIVING AGE, CXCIII-CXCIV (June 18-Aug-
ust 20, 1892), 744-756, 480-488; and LAST WORDS OF THO-
MAS CARLYLE. London: Longmans, Green, 1892.

1533   Smith, Mary. SCHOOLMISTRESS AND NONCONFORMIST.
London: Bemrose, 1892.

1534   Smith, William. "Ruskin and Carlyle on 'Sir Walter Scott,'"
IGDRASIL, III (March, 1892), 304-323.

1535   Strachey, G. "Carlyle and the 'Rose-Goddess,'" NINETEEN-
TH CENTURY, XXXII (September, 1892), 470-486. Rpt.
LITTELL'S LIVING AGE, CXCV (November 5, 1892), 360-372.

1536   Tyndall, John. NEW FRAGMENTS. London: Longmans, Green,
1892.

1537   Young, J. "Sir Walter Scott and Carlyle," NOTES AND
QUERIES, sers. 8, II (December 31, 1892), 537-538.

1893

1538   Anon. "John Nichol's Thomas Carlyle," CALCUTTA REVIEW,
XCVI (January, 1893), xli-xliii.

1539   _____. "Thomas Carlyle to Thomas Aird, October, 1840,"
BOOKMAN (L), III (January, 1893), 120-121.

1540   _____. "Memorial To Carlyle," TIMES (January 19, 1893), 6.

1541   _____. "Ecclefechan," ATLANTIC MONTHLY, LXXI (February, 1893), 287-288.

1542   _____. "The Literary Lounger," SKETCH, I (February 22, 1893),
223.

1543   ____ . "[The Diamond Necklace]," CRITIC (NY), XXII (March 11, 1893), 143.

1544   ____ . "[Carlyle and Sarah Austin]," CRITIC (NY), XXII (March 18, 1893), 165-166.

1545   ____ . "Unpublished Letters of Carlyle," SCRIBNER'S MAGAZINE, XIII (April, 1893), 416-425.

1546   ____ . "[Carlyle's Essays on the Greater German Poets and Writers]," WESTMINSTER REVIEW, CXXXIX (June, 1893), 698.

1547   ____ . "[French Revolution]," NEW YORK TIMES (December 10, 1893), 23.

1548   ____ . "Another Carlyle Book," NEW YORK TIMES (December 11, 1893), 3.

1549   Clarke, William. "Carlyle and Ruskin and Their Influence on English Social Thought," NEW ENGLAND MAGAZINE, XV (December, 1893), 473-488.

1550   Leland, Charles G. MEMOIRS. New York: D. Appleton, 1893.

1551   M. "Tennyson and Carlyle," NOTES AND QUERIES, sers. 8, III (May 13, 1893), 367.

1552   Markscheffel, Louise. "The Last of the Carlyles," LADIES' HOME JOURNAL, X (May, 1893), 5.

1553   Minnow in a Creek [pseud.]. "Sartor Resartus," NOTES AND QUERIES, sers. 8, IV (August 26, 1893), 168.

1554   Muir, John. THOMAS CARLYLE'S APPRENTICESHIP. Glasgow: R. M'Clure, 1893.

1555   ____ . "Addition to the Carlyle Bibliography," NOTES AND QUERIES, sers. 8, IV (September 23, 1893), 246.

1556   Oswald, O. S. B. "Sartor Resartus," NOTES AND QUERIES, sers. 8, IV (October 14, 1893), 319.

1557 Sinclair, C. M. "Glimmerings of Sartor Resartus," CANADI-
AN MAGAZINE, I (June, 1893), 273-276.

1558 Strachey, G. "Reminiscences of Carlyle, with Some Unpublished Letters," NEW REVIEW, IX (July, 1893), 17-33.

1559 Wilson, H. Schurz. "Goethe and Carlyle," GENTLEMAN's
MAGAZINE, CCLXXV (November, 1893), 509-516. Rpt.
ECLECTIC MAGAZINE, CXXI (December, 1893), 775-779;
and HISTORY AND CRITICISM. London: T. Fisher Unwin,
1896.

1894

1560 Anon. "[Westminster Gazette's Carlyle]," CRITIC (NY), XXIV
(June 23, 1894), 425.

1561 ____. "Carlyle's Cromwell," CRITIC (NY), XXV (July 7,
1894), 8.

1562 ____. "Carlyle's House in Chelsea," TIMES (September 21,
1894), 7.

1563 ____. "[Andrew Carnegie and Carlyle's House]," CRITIC
(NY), XXV (October 7, 1894), 279.

1564 ____. "Carlyle Memorial Fund," TIMES (November 22, 1894),
9. This begins the appeal for funds to preserve Carlyle's house
at Chelsea. Hereafter, until the take over of the residence by
the National Trust in 1936, reports of the activities of the Memorial Trust Fund Committee--headed by luminaries such as Leslie Stephen, John Morley, David Masson, James Crichton-
Browne, and Reginald Blunt--appeared in the TIMES under various
titles. The following is the chronological history that is not
without biographical importance: (November 22, 1894), 9;
(December 20, 1894), 6; (December 29, 1894), 11; (December 31,
1894), 6; (January 2, 1895), 5; (February 2, 1895), 10; (February 23, 1896), 11; (July 23, 1895), 6; (July 26, 1895), 8; (October 21, 1895), 13; (November 15, 1895), 12; (November 18,
1895), 9; (December 5, 1895), 6; (February 18, 1986), 5; (February 19, 1906), 10; (February 16, 1909), 11; (February 21, 1910),
10; (March 3, 1910), 12; (February 18, 1916), 9; (February 21,

1916), 9; (July 14, 1925), 10; (January 14, 1926), 8; (January 15, 1926), 8; (June 19, 1926), 17; (March 16, 1929), 15; (April 3, 1933), 10; (September 22, 1933), 8; (February 3, 1934), 15-16; (March 28, 1934), 17; (April 27, 1934), 10; (June 9, 1934), 10, 15; (June 12, 1934), 11; and (March 23, 1936), 9. The NEW YORK TIMES also supported appeals for funds to help preserve Carlyle's house and attendant memorabilia. See NEW YORK TIMES (January 31, 1895), 16; (February 23, 1895), 5; (March 8, 1895), 7; (March 13, 1895), 4; (June 1, 1895), 4; (July 28, 1895), 1; (August 8, 1895), 4; (September 13, 1895), 15; (December 16, 1895), 2; (August 17, 1926), 20; (May 7, 1933), 2, Section IV; (April 15, 1934), 3, Section IV; and (May 29, 1936), 20.

1565   _____. "Carlyle's London Home," CRITIC (NY), XXV (December 15, 1894), 415.

1566   _____. "The Carlyle Museum," CRITIC (NY), XXV (December 29, 1894), 453.

1567   Besant, Walter. "[The Purchasing of the Chelsea Home]," QUEEN, XCVI (September 29, 1894), 508.

1568   Dawson, William J. "Carlyle: The Man and His Message," YOUNG MAN, VIII (October-December, 1894), 343-346, 384-386, 410-412.

1569   Harrison, Frederic. "Carlyle's Place in Literature," FORUM, XVII (July, 1894), 537-550. Rpt. CARLYLE'S PLACE IN LITERATURE. London: Arnold, n.d. [1894]; and STUDIES IN EARLY VICTORIAN LITERATURE. London: Arnold, 1895.

1570   Hutton, Richard H. CRITICISMS ON CONTEMPORARY THOUGHT AND THINKERS. 2 vols. London: Macmillan, 1894.

1571   Huxley, Thomas H. "Professor Tyndall," NINETEENTH CENTURY, XXXV (January, 1894), 1-11.

1572   McMahon, Morgan. "Carlyle and Tennyson," NOTES AND QUERIES, sers. 8, V (February 3, 1894), 81-82.

1573   Mercer, Elizabeth A. "Carlyle and the 'Blumine' of Sartor
       Resartus," WESTMINSTER REVIEW, CXLII (July, 1894), 164-
       165. See also REVIEW OF REVIEWS, X (September, 1894),
       318.

1574   Murray, John. "Carlyle and Tennyson," NOTES AND QUER-
       IES, sers. 8, V (February 24, 1894), 152.

1575   Robertson, J. Logie. A HISTORY OF ENGLISH LITERATURE.
       Edinburgh: William Blackwood, 1894.

1576   Schooling, J. H. "The Handwriting of Thomas Carlyle from
       1809 to 1875," STRAND MAGAZINE, VIII (October, 1894),
       360-368.

1577   Shelley, Henry C. "Gleanings in Carlyle's Country," NEW
       ENGLAND MAGAZINE, XVII (October, 1894), 194-205.

1578   Skelton, John. "Reminiscences of James Anthony Froude,"
       BLACKWOOD'S EDINBURGH MAGAZINE, CLVI-CLVII
       (December, 1894-January, 1895), 756-776, 40-63.

1579   Strachey, Edward. "Some Letters and Conversations of
       Thomas Carlyle," ATLANTIC MONTHLY, LXXIII (June, 1894),
       821-834.

1580   Wallace, William. GREAT MEN AND FAMOUS WOMEN.
       New York: Selmar Hess, n.d. [1894].

                              1895

1581   Anon. "Carlyle's Talk with the Queen," NEW YORK TIMES
       (February 13, 1895), 13.

1582   _____. "[Carlyle and America]," CRITIC (NY), XXVI (March
       2, 1895), 159.

1583   _____. "[S. R. Crockett and Carlyle's House]," CRITIC (NY),
       XXVI (March 16, 1895), 207.

1584   _____. "[Carlyle's House and Study]," BOOKMAN (NY),
       II (October, 1895), 84-85.

1585   . "Wordsworth and Carlyle--A Literary Parallel," TEM-
PLE BAR, XVI (October, 1895), 261-267. Rpt. LITTELL'S LIV-
ING AGE, CCVII (November 9, 1895), 356-359.

1586   . "Thomas Carlyle Centenary," NEW YORK TIMES (December 5, 1895), 5.

1587   . "The Carlyle Centenary," SPECTATOR, LXXV (December 7, 1895), 810-811.

1588   . "Blunt's The Carlyle's Chelsea Home," CRITIC (NY),
XXVII (December 14, 1895), 410-411.

1589   . "Carlyle Criticized by a Cook," NEW YORK TIMES
(December 15, 1895), 3.

1590   Anderson, F. "The Mask of Cromwell," ENGLISH ILLUSTRA-
TED MAGAZINE, XIV (November, 1895), 117-118.

1591   Blunt, Reginald. THE CARLYES' CHELSEA HOME. London:
George Bell, 1895.

1592   Bouchier, Jonathan. "Thomas Carlyle," NOTES AND QUERIES,
sers. 8, VIII (December 28, 1895), 508.

1593   Chancellor, E. Beresford. LITERARY TYPES. London: Swan
Sonnenschein, 1895.

1594   [Cochrane, Robert, and Mary Cochrane]. THOMAS CARLYLE:
THE STORY OF HIS LIFE AND WRITINGS. London: W. and
R. Chambers, n.d. [1895].

1595   C[ollins], J[ohn] C. "A Reminiscence of Carlyle," SATURDAY
REVIEW, LXXX (November 30, 1895), 722-724. See LIFE AND
MEMORIALS. London: John Lane, 1912.

1596   Common, Thomas. "Carlyle and Nietzsche," TIMES (December
9, 1895), 10.

1597   Fleming, George. "Thomas Carlyle and the Winter-Shoeing of
Horses," TIMES (December 11, 1895), 6.

1598   Garnett, Richard. "The Preservation of Carlyle's House,"
        NATION, LX (February 7, 1895), 105.

1599   Hale, C. P. "'Carrion Heath,'" NOTES AND QUERIES, sers.
        8, VIII (August 31, 1895), 168.

1600   [Hoarr, John N.]. "Carlyle's Interview with the Queen,"
        ATHENAEUM, no. 3510 (February 2, 1895), 149-151. Rpt.
        LITTELL'S LIVING AGE, CCIV (March 9, 1895), 636-637.

1601   _____. "Carlyle," ATHENAEUM, no. 3513 (February 23,
        1895), 251.

1602   Horsley, R. THOMAS CARLYLE. Edinburgh: W. and R. Cham-
        bers, 1895.

1603   Hubbard, Elbert. LITTLE J OURNEYS TO THE HOMES OF
        GOOD MEN AND GREAT. New York: G. P. Putnam, n.d.
        [1895].

1604   Lee, Gerald S. "Thomas Carlyle," CRITIC (NY), XXVII
        (November 30, 1895), 359-360.

1605   Lilly, William S. FOUR ENGLISH HUMORISTS OF THE NINE-
        TEENTH CENTURY. London: John Murray, 1895.

1606   Marshall, Edward H. "Carlyle Relic," NOTES AND QUERIES,
        sers. 8, VIII (October 19, 1895), 311.

1607   Newland, H. W., Edward Peacock, and Edward H. Marshall.
        "'Carrion Heath,'" NOTES AND QUERIES, sers. 8, VIII
        (September 14, 1895), 215.

1608   Nicoll, W. Robertson, and Thomas J. Wise. LITERARY ANEC-
        DOTES OF THE NINETEENTH CENTURY. 2 vols. London:
        Hodder and Stoughton, 1895-1896.

1609   O'Connor, T. P. SOME OLD LOVE STORIES. London: Chap-
        man and Hall, 1895.

1610   Peet, William H. "Tyndall and Carlyle," NOTES AND QUER-
        IES, sers. 8, VII (February 2, 1895), 98.

1611   Saintsbury, George. ESSAYS IN ENGLISH LITERATURE. New
        York: Charles Scribner, 1895.

1612   _____. CORRECTED IMPRESSIONS. London: William Heine-
        mann, 1895.

1613   [Shelley, Henry C.]. THE HOMES AND HAUNTS OF THOMAS
        CARLYLE. London: Westminster Gazette Library, 1895.

1614   Smalley, George W. STUDIES OF MEN. London: Macmillan,
        1895.

1615   Smalley, Phillips. "Thomas Carlyle's House (Chelsea, London)
        Purchase Fund," CRITIC (NY), XXVII (August 31, 1895), 141.

1616   Spencer, F. M. "Tyndall on Carlyle," NOTES AND QUER-
        IES, sers. 8, VII (January 26, 1895), 68.

1617   Stearns, Frank P. SKETCHES FROM CONCORD AND APPLE-
        DORE. New York: G. P. Putnam, 1895.

1618   Stephen, Leslie. "Carlyle's House at Chelsea," ACADEMY,
        XLVII (January 5, 1895), 120.

1619   T., J. E. "Carlyle Relic," NOTES AND QUERIES, sers. 8,
        VIII (September 21, 1895), 229.

1620   Thayer, William R. "Thomas Carlyle: His Work and Influence,"
        FORUM, XX (December, 1895), 465–479. Rpt. THRONE-
        MAKERS. Boston: Houghton Mifflin, n.d. [1895].

1621   Thorne, William H. "'Carlyle,'" GLOBE QUARTERLY RE-
        VIEW, V (October, 1895), 469.

1622   Waugh, Arthur. "[Carlyle's Chelsea Home]," CRITIC (NY),
        XXVI (February 9, 1895), 111.

1623   _____. "[Extract of John Morley's Centenary Speech]," CRITIC
        (NY), XXVII (December 21, 1895), 431–432.

1624   Wolfe, Theodore F. A LITERARY PILGRIMAGE AMONG THE
        HAUNTS OF FAMOUS BRITISH AUTHORS. Philadelphia: J.

B. Lippincott, 1895.

1896

1625   Anon. ILLUSTRATED MEMORIAL VOLUME OF THE CARLYLE'S
HOUSE PURCHASE FUND COMMITTEE WITH CATALOGUE OF
CARLYLE'S BOOKS, MANUSCRIPTS, PICTURES, AND FURNI-
TURE EXHIBITED THEREIN. London: Carlyle Memorial Trust,
1896.

1626   ____. "The Centenary of Thomas Carlyle," POET-LORE, VIII
(January, 1896), 54-56.

1627   ____. "Mr. Zangwill on the Carlyles," LITTELL'S LIVING
AGE, CCVIII (January 18, 1896), 191-192.

1628   ____. "The Carlyle Centenary," AMERICAN ARCHITECT,
LI (February 8, 1896), 64-65.

1629   ____. "Carlyle's Chelsea Home," NEW YORK TIMES
(March 8, 1896), 26.

1630   ____. "Errors in Carlyle's French Revolution," CATHOLIC
WORLD, LXIII (June, 1896), 421-422.

1631   ____. "[Carlyle's Windowpane Verse]," CRITIC (NY),
XXVIII (June 27, 1896), 470.

1632   ____. "On Heroes and Hero-Worship," CRITIC (NY), XXIX
(November 28, 1896), 341.

1633   Alger, J. G. "Corrigenda in Carlyle's French Revolution,"
WESTMINSTER REVIEW, CXLV (January, 1896), 14-22.

1634   [Henshaw, Mary]. "Recollections of Thomas Carlyle," BLACK-
WOOD'S EDINBURGH MAGAZINE, CLIX (January, 1896), 31-
37. Rpt. LITTELL'S LIVING AGE, CCVIII (January 25, 1896),
248-254; and ECLECTIC MAGAZINE, CXXVI (February,
1896), 213-218.

1635   Hershey, O. F. "Thomas Carlyle on Our Present Political
Situation," HARPER'S WEEKLY, XL (August 29, 1896), 850.

1636   Hope, Andrew. "Carlyle and Burns," NOTES AND QUER-
        IES, sers. 8, X (December 19, 1896), 498.

1637   Macpherson, Hector C. THOMAS CARLYLE. Edinburgh:
        Oliphant, Anderson and Ferrier, n.d. [1896].

1638   Mayo, I. F. "Thomas Carlyle," LEISURE HOUR, XLV (1896),
        15-21, 93-97.

1639   Muir, John. "Carlyle and Burns," NOTES AND QUERIES,
        sers. 8, X (December 5, 1896), 456.

1640   N. N. [E. R. Pennell]. "The Carlyle House in Chelsea,"
        NATION, LXII (April 9, 1896), 286-287.

1641   Prideaux, W. F. "Carlyle's Window-pane Verse," NOTES
        AND QUERIES, sers. 8, X (September 19, 1896), 237.

1642   Ritchie, Annie T. "The First Number of 'The Cornhill,'"
        CORNHILL MAGAZINE, LXXIV (July, 1896), 4-5.

1643   Saintsbury, George. A HISTORY OF THE NINETEENTH-CEN-
        TURY LITERATURE. New York: Macmillan, 1896.

1644   Smithers, Charles G., Francis W. Jackson, and Edward P.
        Belben. "Carlyle's Window-pane Verse," NOTES AND QUER-
        IES, sers. 8, X (October 10, 1896), 301.

1645   Wilson, H. Schurz. HISTORY AND CRITICISM. London: T.
        Fisher Unwin, 1896.

                                1897

1646   Anon. "[Centenary Edition of Sartor Resartus]," NEW YORK
        TIMES (January 23, 1897), 3, Saturday Supplement.

1647   _____. "Thomas Carlyle's Abhandlung uber Goethe's Faust aus
        dem Jahre 1821," NOTES AND QUERIES, sers. 8, XI (February
        6, 1897), 120.

1648   _____. "A Page of Carlyle," NEW YORK TIMES (April 17,
        1897), 4, Book Review Section.

                                125

1649 _____ . "[Carlyle and Emerson]," CRITIC (NY), XXX (May 1, 1897), 305.

1650 _____ . "Letters from Carlyle," NEW YORK TIMES (May 8, 1897), 3, Book Review Section.

1651 _____ . "The Centenary Carlyle," CRITIC (NY), XXX (May 22, 1897), 352.

1652 _____ . "[Sale of Carlyle Letters at Sotheby's]," CRITIC (NY), XXX (May 29, 1897), 372.

1653 _____ . "Sartor Resartus," NOTES AND QUERIES, sers. 8, XII (July 17, 1897), 60.

1654 _____ . "[Craigenputtock]," BOOKMAN (NY), VI (October, 1897), 97-98.

1655 _____ . "Carlyle's Essay on Goethe's Faust," NEW YORK TIMES (October 9, 1897), 4, Book Review Section.

1656 _____ . "Carlyle's Encyclopaedia Essays," CRITIC (NY), XXXI (October 23, 1897), 230.

1657 _____ . "Carlyle and Delia Bacon," NEW YORK TIMES (November 6, 1897), 5-6, Book Review Section.

1658 _____ . "[Carlyle and His Canadian Sister]," CRITIC (NY), XXXI (November 13-December 18, 1897), 284, 389.

1659 _____ . "[Carlyleana]," BOOKMAN (NY), VI (December, 1897), 279-281.

1660 _____ . "Thomas Carlyle's Sister Dead," NEW YORK TIMES (December 14, 1897), 3.

1661 A., J. L. "Quotation on the Title-Page of Carlyle's Latter-Day Pamphlets," NOTES AND QUERIES, sers. 8, XII (November 6, 1897), 377.

1662 B., C. C. "Quotation on the Title-Page of Carlyle's Latter-Day Pamphlets," NOTES AND QUERIES, sers. 8, XII (September 18, 1897), 227.

1663   Black, William. "Some Recollections of Carlyle's Talk,"
GOOD WORDS, XXXVIII (1897), 20-23. Rpt. LITTELL'S
LIVING AGE, CCXII (January 23, 1897), 248-251.

1664   Burroughs, John. "On the Re-Reading of Books," CENTURY
MAGAZINE, LV (November, 1897), 146-150.

1665   Crichton-Browne, James. "Young Dumfries and Old Carlyle,"
DUMFRIES AND GALLOWAY STANDARD AND ADVERTISER,
LIV (November 10, 1897), 3. See also editorial comment, pp.
3, 6.

1666   Farrar, Frederick W. MEN I HAVE KNOWN. New York:
T. Y. Crowell, n.d. [1897].

1667   Forster, Joseph. FOUR GREAT TEACHERS. London: George
Allen, 1890. Rpt. GREAT TEACHERS. London: George Red-
wey, 1898 [1897].

1668   Graham, P. Anderson. "Thomas Carlyle," ACADEMY, LI
(May 15, 1897), 524.

1669   [Hardy, E. J.]. LOVE AFFAIRS OF SOME FAMOUS MEN.
London: T. Fisher Unwin, 1897.

1670   Herford, C. H. THE AGE OF WORDSWORTH. London: George
Bell, 1897.

1671   Jenkins, Owen B. "A Carlyle Will in An American Court,"
GREEN BAG, IX (October, 1897), 452-453.

1672   Mackinnon, James. LEISURE HOURS IN THE STUDY   London:
T. Fisher Unwin, 1897.

1673   MacMechan, Archibald. "Carlyle's Prentice Hand," CITIZEN,
III (November, 1897), 200-201.

1674   Shorter, Clement K. VICTORIAN LITERATURE. London: James
Bowden, 1897.

1675 _____. "Victorian Literature," BOOKMAN (NY), V (August, 1897), 480-483.

1676 Smith, Elizabeth L. "Carlyle upon His Contemporaries," BOOKBUYER, n.s. XIV (June, 1897), 469-473.

1677 Stearns, Frank P. MODERN ENGLISH PROSE WRITERS. New York: G. P. Putnam, 1897.

1678 Walker, Hugh. THE AGE OF TENNYSON. London: George Bell, 1897.

1898

1679 Anon. "A Reminiscence of Carlyle," ATLANTIC MONTHLY, LXXXI (February, 1898), 284-286.

1680 _____. "Carlyle's Benefactor," NEW YORK TIMES (March 28, 1898), 2.

1681 _____. "The Centenary Carlyle," CRITIC (NY), XXXII (June 4, 1898), 372.

1682 _____. "[Centenary Edition of Works]," NEW YORK TIMES (August 6, 1898), 513-514, Book Review Section.

1683 _____. "Carlyle," NEW YORK TIMES (September 3, 1898), 587, Book Review Section.

1684 _____. "Letters from Carlyle," NEW YORK TIMES (October 1, 1898), 643, Book Review Section.

1685 _____. "[Carlylean Biography]," BOOKMAN (NY), VIII (November, 1898), 189-192.

1686 _____. "[Historical Sketches]," NEW YORK TIMES (December 17, 1898), 849-850, Book Review Section.

1687 A Scotchwoman. "A Week with Mrs. Carlyle," INDEPENDENT (NY), L (January 27, 1898), 105.

1688 Arthur, William. PROPHETS OF THE CENTURY. London:

Ward, Lock, n.d. [1898].

1689 [Browning, Elizabeth B.]. "Mrs. Browning's Opinion of Carlyle," POET-LORE, X (December, 1898), 612-617.

1690 Clark, J. Scott. A STUDY OF ENGLISH PROSE WRITERS. New York: Charles Scribner, 1898.

1691 Copeland, Charles T. "Unpublished Letters of Carlyle," ATLANTIC MONTHLY, LXXXII (September-December, 1898), 289-307, 445-461, 673-686, 785-792.

1692 _____. "Carlyle as a Letter Writer," ATLANTIC MONTHLY, LXXXII (November, 1898), 687-697.

1693 Crozier, John B. MY INNER LIFE. London: Longmans, Green, 1898.

1694 [Franklin, G. M.]. "Carlyle's Letters to His Sister," CRITIC (NY), XXXII (May 15-June 14, 1898), 335, 387-388.

1695 [Gosse, Edmund]. "Carlyle and Macaulay," LITTELL'S LIV-ING AGE, CCXVII (May 14, 1898), 491-494. From A SHORT HISTORY OF MODERN ENGLISH LITERATURE. London: William Heinemann, 1898 [1897].

1696 H., S. "Essay by Carlyle," NOTES AND QUERIES, sers. 9, I (May 7, 1898), 368.

1697 Harland, Marion. WHERE GHOSTS WALK: THE HAUNTS OF FAMILIAR CHARACTERS IN HISTORY AND LITERATURE. New York: G. P. Putnam, 1898.

1698 Hodgkins, Louise M. A GUIDE TO THE STUDY OF NINE-TEENTH-CENTURY AUTHORS. Boston: D. C. Heath, 1898.

1699 Muir, John. CARLYLE ON BURNS. Glasgow: William Hodge, 1898.

1700 Patrick, David. "Essay by Carlyle," NOTES AND QUERIES, sers. 9, II (July 2, 1898), 10.

1701   Saintsbury, George. A SHORT HISTORY OF ENGLISH LIT-
        ERATURE. New York: Macmillan, 1898.

1702   Scudder, Vida D. SOCIAL IDEALS IN ENGLISH LETTERS.
        Boston: Houghton Mifflin, 1898.

1703   Wilson, David A. MR. FROUDE AND CARLYLE. London:
        William Heinemann, 1898.

1704   Wilson, Peter. LEADERS IN LITERATURE. Edinburgh: Oli-
        phant, Anderson, and Ferrier, 1898.

                            1899

1705   Anon. "Historical Sketches," LITERARY WORLD, XXX (April
        15, 1899), 118.

1706   _____. "Historical Sketches," ATHENAEUM, no. 3731 (April
        29, 1899), 525-527.

1707   _____. "[Copeland's Letters of Carlyle to His Youngest Sister],"
        CRITIC (NY), XXXV (July, 1899), 654-655.

1708   _____. "[Letters of Thomas Carlyle to His Youngest Sister],"
        BOOKMAN (NY), X (September, 1899), 86.

1709   _____. "[Carlyle and Burns]," BOOKMAN (NY), X (October,
        1899), 116.

1710   Aylesworth, B. O. "'Carlyle,'" ARENA, XXI (April, 1899),
        508.

1711   Dawson, William J. THE MAKERS OF MODERN PROSE. Lon-
        don: Hodder and Stoughton, 1899.

1712   Garnett, Richard. "Eight Unpublished Letters of Thomas
        Carlyle," ARCHIV FÜR DAS STUDIUM DER NEUEREN SPRA-
        CHEN UND LITERATUREN, CII (1899), 317-330.

1713   Hotchkiss, Florence. "Carlyle's Dramatic Portrayal of Charac-
        ter," CENTURY MAGAZINE, LVII (January, 1899), 415-422.

1714   Malsby, David L. THE GROWTH OF SARTOR RESARTUS. Malden, Mass.: H. W. Whittemore, 1899.

1715   Morris, Martin. "The Philosophy of Poetry," NINETEENTH
        CENTURY, XLVI (September, 1899), 504-513.

1716   Painter, Franklin V. A HISTORY OF ENGLISH LITERATURE.
        Boston: Sibley and Ducker, n.d. [1899].

1717   Patrick, John. "The Carlyles in Scotland," CENTURY MAG-
        AZINE, LVII (January, 1899), 321-330.

1718   Trevelyan, George M. "Carlyle as an Historian," NINE-
        TEENTH CENTURY, XLVI (September, 1899), 493-503. Rpt.
        LITTELL'S LIVING AGE, CCXXIII (November 11, 1899), 366-
        375; ECLECTIC MAGAZINE, CXXXIV (January, 1900), 75-
        84; and LIFE AND LETTERS, V (December, 1930), 391-410.
        See also LISTENER, XXXVIII (October 2, 1947), 567-568.

1719   Wells, John T. THOMAS CARLYLE: HIS RELIGIOUS EXPER-
        IENCE AS REFLECTED IN SARTOR RESARTUS. Edinburgh:
        J. R. Fairgrieve, 1899.

1720   Wilson, S. Law. THE THEOLOGY OF MODERN LITERATURE.
        Edinburgh: T. and T. Clark, 1899.

THE TWENTIETH CENTURY

1900

1721 Anon. "Carlyle's Translation of Goethe's Wilhelm Meister,"
GOETHE JAHRBUCH, band 21, (1900), 306.

1722 _____. "Burns's Sister," NEW YORK TIMES (April 14, 1900),
252, Book Review Section.

1723 _____. "The Greatest Books of the Century," OUTLOOK,
LXVI (December 1, 1900), 789-804.

1724 Bayne, Thomas, and V. R. "Quotation from Carlyle," NOTES
AND QUERIES, sers. 9, VI (July-December, 1900), 338-454.

1725 Bouchier, Jonathan. "Scott and Carlyle on Laughter,"
NOTES AND QUERIES, sers. 9, VI (July-December, 1900),
226.

1726 C., E. S. C. "Carlyle and Robert Chambers: Unpublished
Letters," CHAMBERS'S JOURNAL, LXXVII (March 24, 1900),
257-261. Rpt. LITTELL'S LIVING AGE, CCXXV (April 28,
1900), 211-216; and ECLECTIC MAGAZINE, CXXXIV (June,
1900), 787-792.

1727 Curwen, Alfred F. "Quotation from Carlyle," NOTES AND
QUERIES, sers. 9, VI (July-December, 1900), 376.

1728 du Bois, Henri P. LOVE AFFAIRS OF FAMOUS MEN AND
WOMEN. London: Gibbings, 1900.

1729 Gates, Lewis E. "English Literature of the Nineteenth Century:
A Retrospect; The Return to Conventional Life," CRITIC (NY),
XXXVI (March, 1900), 268-275. Rpt. STUDIES AND APPRE-
CIATIONS. New York: Macmillan, 1900.

1730 Larminie, W. "Carlyle and Shelley: A Parallel and a Con-
trast," CONTEMPORARY REVIEW, LXXVII (May, 1900), 728-
741.

1731 Monkhouse, Cosmo. "George Frederick Watts," OUTLOOK,
LXVI (October 6, 1900), 321-328.

1732   Morris, Edward E. "'Rotatory Calabash,'" NOTES AND QUER-
IES, sers. 9, V (January–June, 1900), 186–187.

1733   Nadal, E. S. "The Blumine of Sartor Resartus," BOOKMAN
(NY), XII (October, 1900), 126–129.

1734   Pickford, John. "'Rotatory Calabash,'" NOTES AND QUER-
IES, sers. 9, V (January–June, 1900), 381.

1735   Sharp, R. F. ARCHITECTS OF ENGLISH LITERATURE. London:
Swan, Sonnenschein, 1900.

1736   Ward, May A. PROPHETS OF THE NINETEENTH CENTURY.
London: Gay and Bird, 1900.

1901

1737   Anon. "Literature Portraits, XIV. Thomas Carlyle; also
'Bibliography of Thomas Carlyle,' 'An Unpublished Letter from
Carlyle,' and 'Carlyle as Schoolmaster,'" LITERATURE,
Supplement to TIMES, no. 199 (August 10, 1901), 123–132.

1738   Blunt, Reginald. "Mrs. Carlyle and Her Housemaid," CORN-
HILL MAGAZINE, LXXXIV (September, 1901), 456–467. Rpt.
CRITIC (NY), XXXIX (October, 1901), 346–353; and IN
CHEYNE WALK AND THEREABOUT. London: Mills and Boon,
1914.

1739   Brownell, William C. "Thomas Carlyle," SCRIBNER'S MAG-
AZINE, XXX (October, 1901), 401–416.

1740   _____. VICTORIAN PROSE MASTERS. New York: Charles
Scribners, 1901.

1741   Buckley, George W. THE WIT AND WISDOM OF JESUS.
Boston: James H. West, n.d. [1901].

1742   Dakers, R. A. "The Jane Welsh Carlyle Centenary, Interesting
Carlyle Letters," GLASGOW HERALD (July 13, 1901), 7.

1743   MacNeil, Jane. "The Homes of Thomas Carlyle," MUNSEY'S
MAGAZINE, XXV (August, 1901), 633–639.

1744 Murray, Henry. ROBERT BUCHANAN: A CRITICAL APPRE-
      CIATION AND OTHER ESSAYS. London: Philip Welby, 1901.

1745 Prentiss, George L. THE BRIGHT SIDE OF LIFE. 2 vols. Ash-
      bury Park, New Jersey: privately printed, 1901.

1746 Taylor, E. R. "'Carlyle,'" BOOK-LOVER'S MAGAZINE, II
      (May, 1901), 300.

1747 Tebbutt, C. P. "Carlyle and Cromwell's Statue," TIMES
      (October 22, 1901), 5.

1748 Thompson, Francis. "Sartor Re-read," ACADEMY, LXI (July
      6, 1901), 17-18.

                              1902

1749 Anon. "[Carlyle and Heraldry]," ANCESTOR, no. 2 (July,
      1902), 190.

1750 Chesterton, Gilbert K. TWELVE TYPES. London: A. L.
      Humphreys, 1902.

1751 [____, and J. E. Hodder Williams]. "Carlyle Number,"
      BOOKMAN (L), XXII (May, 1902), 39-67. Rpt. THOMAS
      CARLYLE. London: Hodder and Stoughton, 1902.

1752 Cuyler, Theodore L. "Memories of Famous Literary Men" CUR-
      RENT LITERATURE, XXXIII (October, 1902), 420-423.

1753 ____. RECOLLECTIONS OF A LONG LIFE. New York: Baker
      and Taylor, 1902.

1754 Fischer, Thomas A. "Allusions in Sartor Resartus," NOTES
      AND QUERIES, sers. 9, X (December 27, 1902), 507-508.

1755 Hague, J. D. "A Personal Recollection of Carlyle By a 'Cap-
      tain of Industry,'" CENTURY MAGAZINE, LXIV (July, 1902),
      430-432.

1756 Heggie, D. HOW I READ CARLYLE'S FRENCH REVOLUTION.
      Toronto: William Briggs, 1902.

1757 Matz, Bertram W. THOMAS CARLYLE: A BRIEF ACCOUNT
OF HIS LIFE AND WRITINGS. London: Chapman and Hall,
1902.

1758 Moody, William V., and Robert M. Lovett. A FIRST VIEW
OF ENGLISH LITERATURE. New York: Charles Scribner,
1902.

1759 Sheenan, Patrick A. "Books that Influenced 'Luke Delmege,'"
IRISH MONTHLY, XXX (February, 1902), 109-114.

1760 Stephen, Leslie. STUDIES OF A BIOGRAPHER. 4 vols. New
York: G. P. Putnam, 1902.

1761 Wallace, E. Williamson. "Some Domestic Reminiscences of
Thomas Carlyle and His Wife," GENTLEMAN'S MAGAZINE,
CCXCII (May, 1902), 448-455. Rpt. LITTELL'S LIVING AGE,
CCXXXIII (June 21, 1902), 757-762.

1903

1762 Anon. "A Re-estimate of Carlyle's French Revolution,"
NATION, LXXVI (February 12, 1903), 133-134.

1763 _____. "Living History," ACADEMY, LXIV (April 18, 1903),
391-392.

1764 _____. "The Carlyles," INDEPENDENT, LV (April 23, 1903),
975-976.

1765 _____. "Jane Welsh Carlyle," TIMES LITERARY SUPPLEMENT
(May 1, 1903), 133-134.

1766 _____. "The Carlyle Love Letters," OUTLOOK, LXXIV
(May 16, 1903), 157-161.

1767 _____. "The Carlyles," NATION, LXXVI (May 28, 1903),
439-440.

1768 _____. "New Letters and Memorials of Jane Welsh Carlyle,"
ATLANTIC MONTHLY, XCI (June, 1903), 503-508.

1769   ____. "A Carlyle Sensation," NEW YORK TIMES (June 9, 1903), 5.

1770   ____. "Chatter About Jane," DIAL, XXXV (July 16, 1903), 29-31.

1771   ____. "The Famous Froude-Carlyle Controversy Reviewed," BOOK-LOVER'S MAGAZINE, II (August, 1903), 221-224.

1772   ____. "The French Revolution," ATHENAEUM, II (August 29, 1903), 276-278.

1773   ____. "Thomas Carlyle on Free Trade," BRITISH WEEKLY, no. 892 (December 3, 1903), 213.

1774   Bensly, E. "Carlyle's Past and Present," NOTES AND QUER-IES, sers. 9, XI (May 23, 1903), 418.

1775   Bicknell, Percy F. "The Queen of Letter Writers," DIAL, XXXIV (April 16, 1903), 264-266.

1776   Birrell, Augustine. "Some More Letters of Mrs. Carlyle," NINETEENTH CENTURY, LIII (May, 1903), 813-820. Rpt. LITTELL'S LIVING AGE, CCXXXVII (June 13, 1903), 657-663; and ECLECTIC MAGAZINE, CXLI (August, 1903), 231-237.

1777   [Browne, J. C.]. "A Revived Scandal," BLACKWOOD'S EDINBURGH JOURNAL, CLXXIV (July, 1903), 110-114. Rpt. LITTELL'S LIVING AGE, CCXXXVIII (August 22, 1903), 506-509.

1778   Burns, J. "An Ancient Scots Burgh and the Carlyles," ENG-LISH ILLUSTRATED MAGAZINE, XXX (October, 1903), 20-27.

1779   Carlyle, Alexander, and James Crichton-Browne. THE NEME-SIS OF FROUDE. London: John Lane, 1903.

1780   Chesterton, Gilbert K. VARIED TYPES. New York: Dodd, Mead, 1903.

1781   Cook, Emily. "A Chelsea Menage," NATIONAL REVIEW,

XLI (June, 1903), 609-615. Rpt. LITTELL'S LIVING AGE, CCXXXVIII (July 25, 1903), 237-242.

1782 Crichton-Browne, James. "Froude and Carlyle: The Imputation Medically Considered," BRITISH MEDICAL JOURNAL, I (June 27, 1903), 1498-1502.

1783 Duffy, Charles G. "The Real Carlyle," CONTEMPORARY REVIEW, LXXXIV (September, 1903), 337-348.

1784 Fischer, Thomas A. "Carlyle's Past and Present," NOTES AND QUERIES, sers. 9, XI (February 7, 1903), 108.

1785 Froude, James A. MY RELATIONS WITH CARLYLE. London: Longmans, Green, 1903.

1786 Garnett, Richard, and Edmund Gosse. ENGLISH LITERATURE. New York: Macmillan, 1903.

1787 Gilder, Jeannette L. "The Rehabilitation of the Carlyles," CRITIC (NY), XLII (June, 1903), 503-508.

1788 Gould, George M. BIOGRAPHIC CLINICS. Vols. I-II. Philadelphia: P. Blakiston's, 1903-1904.

1789 Harvey, George. "New Letters and Memorials of Jane Welsh Carlyle," HARPER'S MAGAZINE, XVII (July, 1903), 311-312.

1790 [Horwill, H. W.]. "New Letters and Memorials of Jane Welsh Carlyle," FORUM, XXXV (July, 1903), 70-75.

1791 Jones, Samuel A. "Carlyle's Apprenticeship," COLLECTANEA THOMAS CARLYLE (Canton, Penna.: Kirgate Press, 1903), 127-143.

1792 [Lang, Andrew]. "The Carlyle Scandal," INDEPENDENT, LV (July 2, 1903), 1565-1567, 1582-1583. Rpt. LONGMAN'S MAGAZINE, XLIII (November, 1903), 18-29.

1793 Lee, Sydney. DICTIONARY OF NATIONAL BIOGRAPHY. London: Smith, Elder, 1903.

1794   Lilly, William S. "New Light on the Carlyle Controversy,"
FORTNIGHTLY REVIEW, LXXIX (June, 1903), 1000-1009.

1795   Mallock, William H. "The Secret of Carlyle's Life," FORT-
NIGHTLY REVIEW, LXXX (July, 1903), 180-192.

1796   Matthew, G. A. "Allusions in Sartor Resartus," NOTES AND
QUERIES, sers. 9, XI (April 4, 1903), 273.

1797   McCarthy, Justin. PORTRAITS OF THE SIXTIES. London: T.
Fisher Unwin, 1903.

1798   McNeill, R. "The Real Froude," CONTEMPORARY REVIEW,
LXXXIV (August, 1903), 224-232.

1799   Mead, Edwin D. THE INFLUENCE OF EMERSON. Boston:
American Unitarian Association, 1903.

1800   Scott, Fred N. "Carlyle's Dante," NATION, LXXVII (December 24, 1903), 502-503.

1801   Shipman, C. "New Letters and Memorials of Jane Welsh
Carlyle," LAMP, XXVI (June, 1903), 386-391.

1802   Skeat, W. W. "Carlyle's Past and Present," NOTES AND
QUERIES, sers. 9, XI (February 21, 1903), 158.

1803   Smith, Goldwin. "The Froude and Carlyle Controversy,"
NATION, LXXVII (July 9, 1903), 29-30.

1804   Sykes, W. "Allusions in Sartor Resartus," NOTES AND QUER-
IES, sers. 9, XI (February 3, 1903), 117.

1805   Thompkins, Elizabeth A. "[New Letters and Memorials of Jane
Welsh Carlyle]," BOOKMAN (NY), XVII (June, 1903), 400-
402.

1904

1806   Anon. "Carlyle in Old Age," SUNDAY MAGAZINE, XXXIV
(1904), 306-307.

1807   . "Herbert Spencer: A Portrait," BLACKWOOD'S MAG-
AZINE, CLXXV (January, 1904), 100-116.

1808   . "The Nemesis of Froude," NATION, LXXVIII (January 28, 1904), 76.

1809   . "Mrs. George Bancroft's Letters from England in 1840-
1849," SCRIBNER'S MAGAZINE, XXXV (February-April,
1904), 163-180, 286-304, 424-447.

1810   . "New Letters of Thomas Carlyle," ATLANTIC MONTH-
LY, XCIII (May, 1904), 709-710.

1811   . "New Letters of Thomas Carlyle," ARENA, XXXII
(June, 1904), 95-103.

1812   . "A Portrait of Carlyle by Himself," OUTLOOK,
LXXVII (August, 1904), 950-954.

1813 B., W. C. "P. P., Clerk of the Parish," NOTES AND QUER-
IES, sers. 10, I (January 13, 1904), 137.

1814 Batt, Max. "Carlyle's Life of Schiller," MODERN PHILO-
LOGY, I (January, 1904), 391-392.

1815 Bicknell, Percy F. "New Letters of the Chelsea Sage,"
DIAL, XXXVI (April I, 1904), 231-232.

1816 Conway, Moncure D. AUTOBIOGRAPHY. 2 vols. Boston:
Houghton, Mifflin, 1904.

1817 Dickberry, F. [F. Blaze de Bury]. THE STORM OF LONDON:
A SOCIAL RHAPSODY. London: John Lane, 1904.

1818 Knight, William. RETROSPECTS. London: Smith, Elder, 1904.

1819 "Lee, Vernon" [Violet Paget]. "Studies in Literary Psycho-
logy: Carlyle and the Present Tense," CONTEMPORARY RE-
VIEW, LXXXV (March, 1904), 386-392. Rpt. LITTELL'S LIV-
ING AGE, CCXLI (April 23, 1904), 213-217; and THE HAN-
DLING OF WORDS. New York: Dodd, Mead, 1923.

1820 Marston, E. AFTER WORK: FRAGMENTS FROM THE WORK-
SHOP OF AN OLD PUBLISHER. London: William Heinemann,
1904.

1821 Meiklejohn, J. M. D. ENGLISH LITERATURE. London: Meiklejohn and Holden, 1904.

1822 Newman, C. A. "P. P., Clerk of the Parish," NOTES AND
QUERIES, sers. 10, I (January 30, 1904), 88.

1823 P., H. T. [New Letters of Thomas Carlyle]," BOOKMAN
(NY), XIX (June, 1904), 502-503.

1824 Saintsbury, George. A HISTORY OF CRITICISM AND LITER-
ARY TASTE. 3 vols. London: William Blackwood, 1904.

1825 Salmon, David. "P. P., Clerk of the Parish," NOTES AND
QUERIES, sers. 10, I (January 13, 1904), 137.

1826 Sharp, William. LITERARY GEOGRAPHY. New York:
Charles Scribner, 1904.

1827 Sloan, John M. THE CARLYLE COUNTRY WITH A STUDY OF
CARLYLE'S LIFE. London: Chapman and Hall, 1904.

1828 Vandyopādyāya, H. NOTES ON THOMAS CARLYLE'S HEROES
AND HERO-WORSHIP. Lahore: Students' Own Agency, 1904.

1829 Warner, Percy. THOMAS CARLYLE: THE MAN AND HIS IN-
FLUENCE. London: Chapman and Hall, 1904.

1905

1830 Bevan, Henry E. J. "The Religion and Philosophy of Thomas
Carlyle," TRANSACTIONS OF THE ROYAL SOCIETY OF
LITERATURE, sers. 2, XXVI (1905), 211-230.

1831 Brookfield, Charles, and Frances Brookfield. MRS. BROOK-
FIELD AND HER CIRCLE. London: Isaac Pitman, 1905.

1832 Brown, John M. THE "SARTOR RESARTUS" OF CARLYLE.
Christchurch: Whitcombe and Tombs, n.d. [1905?].

1833   Cosh, T. R. THE ETHICAL TEACHING OF CARLYLE IN
        "SARTOR RESARTUS." Greenock: Blair, 1905.

1834   Fletcher, J. B. "Newman and Carlyle: An Unrecognized
        Affinity," ATLANTIC MONTHLY, XCV (May, 1905), 669-
        679.

1835   Goodwin, Charles J. "Carlyle's Ethics," INTERNATIONAL
        JOURNAL OF ETHICS, XV (January, 1905), 198-210.

1836   Griggs, Edward H. MORAL LEADERS. New York: B. W.
        Huebsch, n.d. [1905].

1837   Hix, Melvin. FIFTY ENGLISH CLASSICS BRIEFLY OUTLINED.
        New York: Hinds, Noble, and Eldredge, n.d. [1905].

1838   Hunt, W. Holman. PRE-RAPHAELISM AND THE PRE-RAPH-
        AELITE BROTHERHOOD. 2 vols. New York: Macmillan,
        1905.

1839   Laughlin, Clara E. STORIES OF AUTHORS' LOVES. London:
        Isbistes, 1905.

1840   Macmillan. D. "The Carlyles and Crawfords," GLASGOW
        HERALD (July 29, 1905), 9.

1841   Masterman, C. F. G. IN PERIL OF CHANGE. London: T.
        Fisher Unwin, 1905.

1842   More, Paul E. "The Spirit of Carlyle," SHELBURNE ESSAYS
        (London: G. P. Putnam, 1905), 85-102.

1843   Nevinson, Henry W. BOOKS AND PERSONALITIES. London:
        John Lane, 1905.

1844   Paul, Herbert. THE LIFE OF FROUDE. London: Isaac Pitman,
        1905.

1906

1845   Anon. "Classics from Carlyle," SCRAP BOOK, I (April, 1906),
        220-221.

1846   Bayne, Thomas. "'Mother of Dead Dogs,'" NOTES AND
        QUERIES, sers. 10, VI (July 14, 1906), 32.

1847   Brookfield, Francis M. THE CAMBRIDGE "APOSTLES. " New
        York: Charles Scribner, 1906.

1848   Crozier, John B. THE WHEEL OF WEALTH. London: Longmans,
        Green, 1906.

1849   Dawson, William J. LITERARY LEADERS OF MODERN ENG-
        LAND. Chautauque, N. Y.: Chautauqua Press, 1906.

1850   Duncan, Robert. "'Mother of Dead Dogs,'" NOTES AND QUER-
        IES, sers. 10, VI (July 14, 1906), 32.

1851   F., C. L. "'Mother of Dead Dogs,'" NOTES AND QUERIES,
        sers. 10, V (June 30, 1906), 509.

1852   Hadden, J. Cuthbert. "Carlyle's First Love," GLASGOW
        HERALD (February 10, 1906), 9.

1853   Harrison, Frederic. CARLYLE AND THE LONDON LIBRARY.
        London: Chapman and Hall, 1906.

1854   _____. MEMORIES AND THOUGHTS. London: Macmillan,
        1906.

1855   MacMichael, J. Holden. "'Mother of Dead Dogs,'" NOTES
        AND QUERIES, sers. 10, VI (July 14, 1906), 32-33.

1856   Nicoll, W. Robertson, and Thomas Seccombe. THE BOOKMAN
        ILLUSTRATED HISTORY OF ENGLISH LITERATURE. 2 vols.
        London: Hodder and Stoughton, 1906.

1857   Shelley, Henry C. LITERARY BY-PATHS IN OLD ENGLAND.
        Boston: Little, Brown, 1906.

1858   Simpson, H. M. "The Mother of Carlyle," METHODIST RE-
        VIEW, LXXXVIII (May, 1906), 415-421.

1859   Smith, Goldwin. "Froude," ATLANTIC MONTHLY, XCVII
        (May, 1906), 680-687.

1907

1860   Anon. "A Forgotten Essay of Carlyle," SCOTTISH REVIEW,
        IV (February 28, 1907), 236-237.

1861   _____. "Cheyne Row--How Do Londoners Pronounce It?"
        ATLANTIC MONTHLY, C (August, 1907), 285-286.

1862   _____. "Reminiscences of Scott and Carlyle," SCOTTISH RE-
        VIEW, V (October 3, 1907), 289.

1863   _____. "An Unpublished Carlyle Letter," SCOTTISH REVIEW,
        V (October 17, 1907), 356.

1864   Allingham, William. A DIARY. Ed. H. Allingham and D.
        Radford. London: Macmillan, 1907.

1865   Bradbrook, W. "Carlyle on Painting Foam," NOTES AND
        QUERIES, sers. 10, VII (May 11, 1907), 373.

1866   Bullock, J. M. "Carlyle and Lady Bannerman," NOTES AND
        QUERIES, sers. 10, VII (March 16, 1907), 210.

1867   Durand, Walter Y. "De Quincey and Carlyle in Their Relation
        to the Germans," PUBLICATIONS OF THE MODERN LANGUAGE
        ASSOCIATION, XXII (1907), 521-530.

1868   Flint, Thomas. "Carlyle on the Painting Foam," NOTES AND
        QUERIES, sers. 10, VII (April 20, 1907), 310.

1869   _____. "Carlyle on Painting Foam," NOTES AND QUERIES,
        sers. 10, VI (June 8, 1907), 456-457.

1870   _____. "'Mother of Dead Dogs,'" NOTES AND QUERIES,
        sers. 10, VII (June 8, 1907), 457.

1871   _____. "Carlyle's French Revolution," NOTES AND QUERIES,
        sers. 10, VIII (November 30, 1907), 428.

1872   Giles, E. "Carlyle's Heroes and Hero Worship," JOURNAL
        OF EDUCATION, LXVI (December 26, 1907), 691-692; LXVII
        (January 2-May 7, 1908), 21, 47-48, 124-125, 153-155, 318-

319, 355, 377-378, 411-412, 432-433, 459-460, 489, 494, 517-518; LXVIII (October 15-October 29, 1908), 401-402, 427-428, 455-456.

1873　McGovern, J. B. "Cromwell and Milton: A Famous Picture," NOTES AND QUERIES, sers. 10, VIII (July 13, 1907), 22-24.

1874　Nicoll, W. Robertson, and Thomas Seccombe. A HISTORY OF ENGLISH LITERATURE. 3 vols. New York: Dodd, Mead, 1907.

1875　Reed, Marcus. "The Value of Humor in History," GENTLE-MAN'S MAGAZINE, CCCIII (September, 1907), 262-275. Rpt. LITTELL'S LIVING AGE, CCLV (November 2, 1907), 287-295.

1876　Reed, Myrtle. LOVE AFFAIRS OF LITERARY MEN. New York: G. P. Putnam, 1907.

1877　Strachan, L. R. M. "Carlyle on Painting Foam," NOTES AND QUERIES, sers. 10, VII (June 8, 1907), 456.

1878　Traubel, Horace. "Whitman in Old Age," CENTURY MAGA-ZINE, LXXIV (September-October, 1907), 740-755, 911-922.

1879　Yardley, E. "Carlyle on Painting Foam," NOTES AND QUER-IES, sers. 10, VII (May 11, 1907), 373.

1908

1880　B., C. C. "Carlyle's French Revolution," NOTES AND QUER-IES, sers. 10, IX (February 22, 1908), 157.

1881　B., R. "Carlyle's French Revolution," NOTES AND QUERIES, sers. 10, IX (February 22, 1908), 158.

1882　C., C. B. "Carlyle's French Revolution," NOTES AND QUER-IES, sers. 10, IX (February, 1908), 157.

1883　Craig, Robert S. THE MAKING OF CARLYLE. London: George Bell, 1908.

1884　Hinckman, Walter S., and Francis B. Gummere. LIVES OF

GREAT ENGLISH WRITERS FROM CHAUCER TO BROWNING.
Boston: Houghton Mifflin, 1908.

1885 Jennings, P. "Carlyle's French Revolution," NOTES AND
QUERIES, sers. 10, IX (February 22, 1908), 157-158.

1886 Lucis [pseud.]. "Carlyle on the Griffin: Hippogriff," NOTES
AND QUERIES, sers. 10, X (December 26, 1908), 509-510.

1887 Magnus, Laurie. "Byron and Carlyle," TRANSACTIONS OF
THE ROYAL SOCIETY OF LITERATURE, sers. 2, XXVIII
(1908), 235-252.

1888 Masson, David. "Memories of London in the 'Forties," BLACK-
WOOD'S MAGAZINE, CLXXXIII (February-May, 1908), 260-
269, 336-349, 542-556, 660-671. Rpt. LITTELL'S LIVING
AGE, CCLVII-CCLVIII (April 11-July 4, 1908), 95-102, 220-
230, 528-539, 24-34; and MEMORIES OF LONDON IN THE
'FORTIES. Edinburgh: William Blackwood, 1908.

1889 Politician [pseud.]. "Parliamentary Applause: Its Early Use,"
NOTES AND QUERIES, sers. 10, X (November 7, 1908), 376.

1890 Swithin, St. "Carlyle's French Revolution," NOTES AND
QUERIES, sers. 10, IX (February 22, 1908), 157.

1909

1891 Anon. "The Love Affairs of the Carlyles," PALL MALL GAZ-
ETTE (March 25, 1909), 4.

1892 _____. "Love and Letters," BOOK MONTHLY, VI (May,
1909), 563-566.

1893 _____. "Proposed Carlyle Memorial," TIMES (May 7, 1909),
12.

1894 _____. "New Light on the Stormy Courtship of Thomas Carlyle,"
CURRENT LITERATURE, XLVI (June, 1909), 624-627.

1895 _____. "Carlyle's First Love," SPECTATOR, CIII (October 9,
1909), 559-560.

1896 _____ . "[Margaret Gordon, Granddaughter of Walter Patterson of Ramelton, Donegal]," IRISH BOOK LOVER, I (November, 1909), 44.

1897 Abbott, Lyman. "Carlyle's Love Letters," OUTLOOK, XCII (June 12, 1909), 368-370.

1898 Archibald, Raymond C. CARLYLE'S FIRST LOVE: MARGARET GORDON, LADY BANNERMAN. London: John Lane, 1909.

1899 Bicknell, Percy F. "The Carlyle-Welsh Love Letters," DIAL, XLVI (May 1, 1909), 290-292.

1900 Clarke, C. "Carlyle on Freemasonry," NOTES AND QUERIES, sers. 10, XI (May 29, 1909), 437.

1901 Douglas, A. Johnstone. "Thomas Carlyle: Proposed National Memorial," TIMES (June 9, 1909), 12.

1902 Flint, Thomas. "Carlyle on the Griffin: Hippogriff," NOTES AND QUERIES, sers. 10, XI (June 5, 1909), 456-457.

1903 _____ . "Carlyle on the Peneus," NOTES AND QUERIES, sers. 10, XII (July 31, 1909), 87.

1904 Geddes, Patrick. "The Early Homes and Haunts of Carlyle," OXFORD AND CAMBRIDGE REVIEW, no. 8 (Michaelmas Term, 1909), 11-17. Rpt. LITTELL'S LIVING AGE, CCLXIV (March 19, 1910), 724-727; and HOMES AND HAUNTS OF FAMOUS AUTHORS. London: Wells, Gardner, and Dorton, n.d.

1905 Gerish, W. B. "Carlyle on the Griffin: Hippogriff," NOTES AND QUERIES, sers. 10, XI (February 6, 1909), 114.

1906 Lewis, Arthur M. TEN BLIND LEADERS OF THE BLIND. Chicago: H. Kerr, 1909.

1907 Lilly, William S. "The End of a Legend," NINETEENTH CENTURY AND AFTER, LXV (May, 1909), 826-837. Rpt. LITTELL'S LIVING AGE, CCLXI (May 29, 1909), 594-603.

1908 Long, William J. ENGLISH LITERATURE. Boston: Ginn, 1909.

1909 Magnus, Laurie. ENGLISH LITERATURE IN THE NINETEENTH CENTURY. London: Andrew Melrose, 1909.

1910 [McCarthy, D.?]. "Carlyle's Letters to the Socialists of 1830," NEW QUARTERLY, II (April, 1909), 277-288.

1911 McCarthy, Justin. "London: Its Politics and Literature," IN-DEPENDENT, LXVI (April 8, 1909), 758-759.

1912 McMahon, Morgan. "Voltaire and Carlyle," NOTES AND QUERIES, sers. 10, XII (December 18, 1909), 486.

1913 Mellish, J. T. "Carlyle and Lady Bannerman," NOTES AND QUERIES, sers. 10, XII (October 23, 1909), 331-332.

1914 Nicklin, T. "Cromwell and the 117th Psalm," NOTES AND QUERIES, sers. 10, XII (November 20, 1909), 417-418.

1915 Noyes, Alfred. "'Thomas Carlyle,'" BLACKWOOD'S MAG-AZINE, CLXXXVI (July, 1909), 137-142.

1916 Peet, William H. "Carlyle on Fanny Elssler," NOTES AND QUERIES, sers. 10, XII (October 30, 1909), 349.

1917 Phelps, William L. "New Light on Carlyle," FORUM, XLI (June, 1909), 594-599. Rpt. ESSAYS ON BOOKS. New York: Macmillan, 1914.

1918 Price, Warwick J. "Old Chelsea and Its Famous People," MUNSEY'S MAGAZINE, XL (March, 1909), 795-805.

1919 Seed, T. Alexander. "The Carlyle Love-Letters," LONDON QUARTERLY REVIEW, CXII (July, 1909), 40-51.

1920 Shore, W. Teignmouth. CHARLES DICKENS AND HIS FRIENDS. London: Cassell, 1909.

1921 Strachey, Lytton. "Some New Carlyle Letters," SPECTATOR, CII (April 10, 1909), 577-578. Rpt. LITTELL'S LIVING AGE, CCLXI (May 22, 1909), 495-498.

1922   Synge, M. B. THE GREAT VICTORIAN AGE. London: Hodder and Stoughton, 1909.

1923   Walker, A. S. "Some New Pen-Portraits of Carlyle," CHAMBERS'S JOURNAL, LXXXV (December 18, 1909), 33-35. Rpt. LITTELL'S LIVING AGE, CCLXIV (February 19, 1910), 488-492.

1924   [Wilberforce, Wilfrid]. "More Carlyle Letters," NATION, LXXXVIII (April 22, 1909), 416-418.

1925   _____ . "Froude and Carlyle," CATHOLIC WORLD, XC (October, 1909), 37-49.

1910

1926   Anon. "A Hitherto Unpublished Letter by Carlyle," SPECTATOR, XIV (March 19, 1910), 466.

1927   _____ . "Ecclefechan and Carlyle," TIMES (November 15, 1910), 12.

1928   Benton, Jay. "'You Have Forced Me to Do This Unwillingly,'" NOTES AND QUERIES, sers. 11, 11 (December 17, 1910), 493-494.

1929   _____ . "Carlyle on Singing at Work," NOTES AND QUERIES, sers. 11, 11 (December 17, 1910), 494.

1930   Brown, Frances. "Miss Martineau and the Carlyles," ATLANTIC MONTHLY, CVI (September, 1910), 381-387.

1931   Brown, H. "Goethe on English Literature," TRANSACTIONS OF THE ROYAL SOCIETY OF LITERATURE, sers. 2, XXX (1910), 59-86.

1932   Brownell, A. "Thomas Carlyle," LANTERN, I (1910), 20-24.

1933   Burns, J. "Mr. Burns and Carlyle," TIMES (January 13, 1910), 10.

1934   Chapman, Edward M. ENGLISH LITERATURE IN ACCOUNT

WITH RELIGION. Boston: Houghton Mifflin, 1910.

1935   Earland, Ada. RUSKIN AND HIS CIRCLE. New York: G. P. Putnam, 1910.

1936   Flint, Helen C. "Indications in Carlyle's French Revolution of the Influence of Homer and the Greek Tragedians," CLASSICAL JOURNAL, V (January, 1910), 118-126.

1937   Flint, Thomas. "Carlyle's French Revolution in a French Version," NOTES AND QUERIES, sers. II, II (September 10, 1910), 206.

1938   Matthews. Brander. "The Devil's Advocate," CENTURY MAGAZINE, LXXX (July, 1910), 335-340. Rpt. GATEWAYS TO LITERATURE. New York: Charles Scribner, 1912.

1939   Miller, Frank. THE POETS OF DUMFRIESSHIRE. Glasgow: Maclehose, 1910.

1940   Roe, Frederick W. THOMAS CARLYLE AS A CRITIC OF LITERATURE. New York: Columbia University Press, 1910.

1941   Russell, Constance. THE ROSE GODDESS. London: Longmans, Green, 1910.

1942   St. Helier, Mary J. MEMORIES OF FIFTY YEARS. London: Edward Arnold, 1910.

1943   Stephen, Leslie. "Thomas Carlyle," ENCYCLOPEDIA BRITANNICA. 11th ed. Vol. V. Cambridge: University Press, 1910-1911.

1944   Vaughan, C. E. "Carlyle and His German Masters," ESSAYS AND STUDIES, I (1910), 168-196.

1945   Walker, Hugh. THE LITERATURE OF THE VICTORIAN ERA. Cambridge: University Press, 1910.

1911

1946   Anon. CARLYLE'S BIRTHPLACE: THE ARCHED HOUSE, ECCLEFECHAN. London: Carlyle Memorial Trust, 1911.

CARLYLE BIBLIOGRAPHY

1947 ____. "Carlyle's Birthplace," TIMES (February 27, 1911), 6.

1948 ____. "Carlyle's Birthplace," OUTLOOK, XCVIII (July 8, 1911), 519.

1949 Bacon, L. "Illegitimate Lectures in Literature: IV. Thomas Carlyle," HARPER'S WEEKLY, LV (May 20, 1911), 16.

1950 Barbour, J. "The Carlyle Farm and Dwelling-Place at Birrens," PUBLICATIONS OF THE DUMFRESSHIRE AND GALLOWAY NATURAL HISTORY AND ANTIQUARIAN SOCIETY. n.s. XXIV (1911-1912), 163-165.

1951 Bensly, E. "Carlyle and Charles I," NOTES AND QUERIES, sers. II, III (May 13, 1911), 371.

1952 Carlyle, Alexander. "Eleventh Edition of the Encyclopedia Britannica," TIMES (June 9, 1911), 13.

1953 ____. "Frank Harris and His (Imaginary) 'Talks with Carlyle'; a Reply by Frank Harris," ENGLISH REVIEW, IX (November, 1911), 599-608.

1954 Courtney, William P. "Carlyle and Charles I," NOTES AND QUERIES, sers. II, III (May 13, 1911), 371.

1955 F., A. L. "Carlyle on Cromwell's Head," NOTES AND QUERIES, sers. II, III (June 10, 1911), 445.

1956 Flint, Thomas. "'Schicksal und Eigene Schuld,'" NOTES AND QUERIES, sers. II, III (May 27, 1911), 407.

1957 Harris, Frank. "Talks with Carlyle," ENGLISH REVIEW, VII (February, 1911), 419-434.

1958 Haskell, J. J. "Study Plan for Carlyle's Essay on Burns," JOURNAL OF EDUCATION, LXXIV (October 26, 1911), 432-433.

1959 Hogben, J. "Jane Welsh Carlyle," SCOTIA, V (1911), 26-33.

1960 Johnson, William S. THOMAS CARLYLE: A STUDY OF HIS

LITERARY APPRENTICESHIP, 1814-1831. New Haven: Yale University Press, 1911.

1961   Kingsley, M. E. "Examination Questions on Carlyle's Essay on Burns," EDUCATION, XXXII (December, 1911), 237-238.

1962   Macdonald, Frederic W. RECREATIONS OF A BOOK-LOVER. London: Hodder and Stoughton, 1911.

1963   Murray, Thomas. AUTOBIOGRAPHICAL NOTES. Dumfries: Standard Office, 1911.

1964   Orr, Lyndon. "Famous Affinities of History: the Story of the Carlyles," MUNSEY'S MAGAZINE, XLV (May, 1911), 209-219.

1965   Prideaux, W. F. "Sir Charles Hanbury Williams, Sir Woodbine Parish, and Thomas Carlyle," NOTES AND QUERIES, sers. II, III (May 4, 1911), 163.

1966   R., G. M. [G. McRobert]. "Three Days' Tramp in Dumfriesshire," BORDER MAGAZINE, XVI (June-October, 1911), 140-142, 159-160, 182-184, 200-201, 236-237.

1967   Saintsbury, George. A HISTORY OF ENGLISH CRITICISM. Edinburgh: William Blackwood, 1911.

1968   Stawell, F. Melian. "Goethe's Influence on Carlyle," INTERNATIONAL JOURNAL OF ETHICS, XXI (January-April, 1911), 178-189, 269-282.

1969   Tennyson, Hallam. TENNYSON AND HIS FRIENDS. London: Macmillan, 1911.

1970   Williams, J. B. "Carlyle and Some Historians," IRISH ECCLESIASTICAL RECORD, XXX (November, 1911), 479-500.

1971   Wilson, David A. EAST AND WEST. London: Methuen, n.d. [1911].

1912

1972   Anon. "Past and Present," TIMES (April 8, 1912), 7.

CARLYLE BIBLIOGRAPHY

1973 ____. "Carlyle and Doctors," BRITISH MEDICAL JOURNAL, II (November, 1912), 1569-1570.

1974 Bayne, Thomas. "Casanova and Carlyle," NOTES AND QUERIES, sers. II, V (June 1, 1912), 428; VI (August 31, 1912), 172; VI (September 21, 1912), 235.

1975 Callicot, T. C. "The Philosophy of Clothes," FORTNIGHTLY REVIEW, XCVII (March, 1912), 521-528.

1976 Cazamian, Louis. MODERN ENGLAND. London: J. M. Dent, 1912.

1977 Chesterton, Gilbert K. SIMPLICITY AND TOLSTOY. London: A. L. Humphreys, 1912.

1978 Duncan, Robert. "Casanova and Carlyle," NOTES AND QUERIES, sers. II, VI (August 3, 1912), 94.

1979 Elton, Oliver. A SURVEY OF ENGLISH LITERATURE, 1780-1830. London: Edward Arnold, 1912.

1980 Fitch, George H. MODERN ENGLISH BOOKS OF POWER. San Francisco: Paul Elder, n.d. [1912].

1981 Flint, Thomas. "Carlyle's French Revolution in a French Version," NOTES AND QUERIES, sers. II, V (April 20, 1912), 306.

1982 Hunter, R. W. G. "A Tale of Two Cities and the French Revolution," DICKENSIAN, VIII (August, 1912), 210-212.

1983 Kelman, John. AMONG FAMOUS BOOKS. 2nd ed. London: Hodder and Stoughton, n.d. [1912].

1984 Kerlin, Robert T. "Contemporary Criticism of Carlyle's French Revolution," SEWANEE REVIEW, XX (July, 1912), 282-296.

1985 Mackall, L. L. "Goethe and the Carlyles: Some Notes and Corrections," ATHENAEUM, II (August 10, 1912), 142.

1986 Saintsbury, George. A HISTORY OF ENGLISH PROSE RHYTHM.

London: Macmillan, 1912.

1987 Sparke, Archibald. "Carlyle's 'Carcassonne,'" NOTES AND QUERIES, sers. II, VI (December 21, 1912), 489.

1988 Strachan, L. R. M. "Carlyle," NOTES AND QUERIES, sers. II, V (June 1, 1912), 435.

1989 _____. "Casanova and Carlyle," NOTES AND QUERIES, sers. II, VI (July 6, 1912), 16.

1990 _____. "A Goethe Quotation in Carlyle and Ruskin," NOTES AND QUERIES, sers. II, VI (August 10, 1912), 106-107.

1991 Trevelyan, George M. "Carlyle's Sartor Resartus," NOTES AND QUERIES, sers. II, V (April 20, 1912), 315.

1992 Watt, Lauchlan M. THOMAS CARLYLE. London: T. C. Jack, n.d. [1912].

1913

1993 Anon. "Carlyle Letters in New York," TIMES (February 4, 1913), 2.

1994 _____. "Glasgow and Carlyle," TIMES (May 21, 1913), 4.

1995 _____. "Carlyle's Tip," LITERARY DIGEST, XLVII (October 4, 1913), 596-597.

1996 _____. "[Duffy's Conversations with Carlyle]," IRISH BOOK LOVER, V (November, 1913), 63.

1997 Chesterton, Gilbert K. THE VICTORIAN AGE IN LITERATURE. New York: Henry Holt, n.d. [1913].

1998 Clare, Maurice [May C. Byron]. A DAY WITH THOMAS CARLYLE. London: Hodder and Stoughton, n.d. [1913].

1999 FitzGerald, Percy. "Glimpses of Thomas Carlyle," CONTEMPORARY REVIEW, CIII (June, 1913), 787-796. Rpt. LITTELL'S LIVING AGE, CCLXXVIII (July 26, 1913), 216-223.

2000   Flint, Thomas. "Carlyle Quotation," NOTES AND QUER-
        IES, sers. II, VIII (December 27, 1913), 472.

2001   Gooch, George P. HISTORY AND HISTORIANS IN THE
        NINETEENTH CENTURY. London: Longmans, Green, 1913.

2002   Goudie, Gilbert. DAVID LAING. Edinburgh: T. and A.
        Constable, 1913.

2003   Hall, Sophy. "The Two Thomas Carlyles," NINETEENTH
        CENTURY AND AFTER, LXXIII (April, 1913), 829-833.

2004   Hayward, F. "Carlyle Quotation," NOTES AND QUERIES,
        sers. II, VIII (December 13, 1913), 472.

2005   Lucis [pseud.]. "Carlyle Quotation," NOTES AND QUER-
        IES, sers. II, VIII (November 22, 1913), 406.

2006   Norton, Sara, and M. A. De Howe. "English Friends: From
        the Letters and Journals of Charles Eliot Norton," SCRIB-
        NER'S MAGAZINE, LIII (April-June, 1913), 577-578, 775-
        786.

2007   Scrutator [pseud.]. "Carlyle on the Repeal of the Union,"
        TIMES (November 1, 1913), 8.

2008   Tassin, Algernon. "The Grub Street Problem," BOOKMAN
        (NY), XXXVII (July, 1913), 524-534.

2009   Vaughan, John S. "Thomas Carlyle: His Language, Style and
        Manner," IRISH ECCLESIASTICAL RECORD, II (November,
        1913), 449-458.

2010   Wilson, David A. THE TRUTH ABOUT CARLYLE. London:
        Alston Rivers, 1913.

                            1914

2011   Anon. "Carlyle's Birthplace--Purchase of the Ecclefechan
        House," TIMES (February 5, 1914), 5.

2012   _____. "New Carlyle Letters," NEW YORK TIMES (June

29, 1914), 4.

2013 _____. "New Letters of Carlyle--Criticism and Advice as to Literature," TIMES (June 29, 1914), 6.

2014 _____. "[Suffragette] Chops a Millais Picture [of Carlyle]," NEW YORK TIMES (July 18, 1914), 3.

2015 _____. "Thomas Carlyle and the Thirty Soldiers of Dumdrudge," CRAFTSMAN, XXVII (November, 1914), 197.

2016 Bensly, E. "Carlyle's Past and Present," NOTES AND QUERIES, sers. II, X (September 26, 1914), 255.

2017 Benson, Arthur C. WHERE NO FEAR WAS: A BOOK ABOUT FEAR. London: Smith, Elder, 1914.

2018 Carlyle, Alexander. "Eight New Love Letters of Jane Welsh," NINETEENTH CENTURY AND AFTER, LXXV (January, 1914), 86-113.

2019 _____. "More New Letters of Jane Welsh Carlyle," NINETEENTH CENTURY AND AFTER, LXXVI (August, 1914), 317-349.

2020 Cramb, John A. GERMANY AND ENGLAND. London: John Murray, 1914.

2021 Crichton-Browne, James. "Thomas Carlyle," FAMOUS EDINBURGH STUDENTS (Edinburgh: T. H. Foulis, 1914), 99-114.

2022 Flint, Thomas. "Higginbotham in Carlyle's Cromwell," NOTES AND QUERIES, sers. II, IX (May 9, 1914), 365.

2023 Gorrie, Daniel. "Letters by Carlyle to a Fellow Student," FORTNIGHTLY REVIEW, CI (April, 1914), 628-639.

2024 Gunn, Sidney. "Carlyle and Germany of the Present Day," NATION, XCIX (November 19, 1914), 605.

2025 Mair, G. H. MODERN ENGLISH LITERATURE FROM CHAUCER TO THE PRESENT DAY. London: Williams and Norgate,

1914.

2026   McMahon, James. "Carlyle's Translation of Legendre's Geometry," NATION, XCIX (August 20, 1914), 222.

2027   Weaver, F. "Dickens and Carlyle," DICKENSIAN, X (December, 1914), 329-330.

1915

2028   Anon. "Lamb and Carlyle Manuscripts--Important Sale in America," TIMES (March 23, 1915), 6.

2029   _____. "Carlyle's Apology for His Letter in 'The Times' in 1870," SATURDAY REVIEW, CXIX (April 24, 1915), 421-422.

2030   _____. "[Carlyle's Irascibility]," NEW YORK TIMES (April 25, 1915), 164, Section IV.

2031   _____. "The Late Miss Stanley--A Friend of Carlyle," TIMES (July 19, 1915), 9.

2032   Blunt, Reginald. "Mrs. Carlyle and Her Little Charlotte," STRAND MAGAZINE, XLIX (March-April, 1915), 280-291, 413-420.

2033   Carlyle, Alexander. "Correspondence between Carlyle and Browning," CORNHILL MAGAZINE, CXI (May, 1915), 642-669.

2034   Glover, Terrot R. POETS AND PURITANS. London: Methuen, n.d. [1915].

2035   Harris, Frank. CONTEMPORARY PORTRAITS. New York: Mitchell Kennerley, 1915.

2036   Hearn, Lafcadio. "On the Philosophy of Sartor Resartus," INTERPRETATIONS OF LITERATURE. Ed. J. Erskine (New York: Dodd, Mead, 1915), I, 208-232.

2037   Kelly, Marshall. "Carlyle and the War," OPEN COURT, XXIX (September, 1915), 527-556. See also CARLYLE AND

THE WAR. New York: Jean Wick, 1915.

2038   Perry, Bliss. THOMAS CARLYLE: HOW TO KNOW HIM.
       Indianapolis: Bobbs-Merrill, n.d. [1915].

2039   Sloan, John M. "Carlyle's Germans," HIBBERT JOURNAL,
       XIII (April, 1915), 592-603.

2040   Sparrow, W. S. "A Message from Carlyle," SATURDAY RE-
       VIEW, CXX (August 28, 1915), 201-202.

2041   Thwing, Charles F. "Education According to Carlyle,"
       SCHOOL AND SOCIETY, II (November 6, 1915), 649-661.

2042   Walker, Hugh. THE ENGLISH ESSAY AND ESSAYISTS. Lon-
       don: Dent, n.d. [1915].

                              1916

2043   Anon. "Dickens Letter to Carlyle," DICKENSIAN, XII
       (January, 1916), 21-22.

2044   _____ . "Carlyle's Advice on the Choosing of Books," LI-
       BRARY JOURNAL, XLI (July, 1916), 478.

2045   _____ . "Carlyle as a Music Critic," LITERARY DIGEST,
       LIII (September 30, 1916), 832-833.

2046   _____ . "Carlyle on the French-German War, 1870-1871,"
       OPEN COURT, XXX (December, 1916), 724-732.

2047   Dunn, Waldo H. ENGLISH BIOGRAPHY. London: J. M.
       Dent, 1916.

2048   Guthrie, Lord. THOMAS CARLYLE: AN APPRECIATION.
       Glasgow: Aird and Coghill, 1916.

2049   Lew, J. W. T. "Dickens and Carlyle," DICKENSIAN, XII
       (December, 1916), 313-316. Rpt. LITTELL'S LIVING AGE,
       CCXCIII (May 5, 1917), 308-311.

2050   Medico [pseud.]. "Carlyle and Germany," OPEN COURT,

XXX (December, 1916), 719-723.

2051 Morgan, W. "Carlyle and German Thought," QUEEN'S QUARTERLY, XXIII (April, 1916), 438-452.

2052 Robertson, J. G. "Carlyle," CAMBRIDGE HISTORY OF ENGLISH LITERATURE. Vol. XIII. Ed. A. W. Ward and A. R. Waller (Cambridge: University Press, 1916), 1-24.

2053 Scobie [pseud.]. "The 'As-You-Were' Result," TIMES (March 28, 1916), 9.

2054 Wilson, David A. "Carlyle and the German Empire," FORT-NIGHTLY REVIEW, CV (February, 1916), 326-333.

1917

2055 Anon. "Poland's Willful Men," NEW YORK TIMES (March 12, 1917), 10.

2056 Rose, John H. "Motive in the French Revolution," TRANS-ACTIONS OF THE ROYAL SOCIETY FOR LITERATURE, sers. 2, XXXV (1917), 23-38.

2057 Stewart, Herbert L. "Carlyle's Conception of Religion," AMERICAN JOURNAL OF THEOLOGY, XXI (January, 1917), 43-57.

2058 ____. "Carlyle's Conception of History," POLITICAL SCI-ENCE QUARTERLY, XXXII (December, 1917), 570-589.

2059 V. H.I.L.I.C.I.V. [pseud.]. "Carlyle and Newman," NOTES AND QUERIES, sers. 12, III (April 14, 1917), 277-278.

2060 Wilson, David A. "Carlyle on the German Style of Lying," TIMES LITERARY SUPPLEMENT (May 17, 1917), 237.

1918

2061 Anon. "Thomas Carlyle's Bookplate," PUBLISHER'S CIR-CULAR, XVIII (March 23, 1918), 267.

2062 _____ . "[Carlyle's Dual Personality]," NEW YORK TIMES (July 7, 1918), 308, Section V.

2063 _____ . "A Great Dramatist," NEW YORK TIMES (September 15, 1918), 1, Section III.

2064 _____ . "Carlyle's Lapse into Germanism," CURRENT OPIN- ION, LXV (October, 1918), 251-252.

2065 [Gunn, Sidney]. "Carlyle and Kultur," UNPOPULAR RE- VIEW, X (July, 1918), 66-78.

2066 Millar, Moorhouse I. S. "Carlyle and the Nineteenth Cen- tury," CATHOLIC WORLD, XVI (March, 1918), 772-781.

2067 Porritt, Norman. "Carlyle and the Germans," NATIONAL REVIEW, LXX (February, 1918), 748-754.

2068 Sherman, Stuart P. "Carlyle and Kaiser-Worship," NATION, CVII (September 14, 1918), 286-289.

2069 Smith, N. "Thomas Carlyle," MODERN CHURCHMAN, VIII (August-October, 1918), 338-343.

2070 Stewart, Herbert L. "The Alleged Prussianism of Thomas Carlyle," INTERNATIONAL JOURNAL OF ETHICS, XXVIII (January, 1918), 159-178.

2071 Trevelyan, George M. "The Two Carlyles," CORNHILL MAGAZINE, XLIV (June, 1918), 561-573. Rpt. LITTELL'S LIVING AGE, CCXCVIII (July 27, 1918), 220-229.

2072 Upham, A. H. "Rabelaisianism in Carlyle," MODERN LANG- UAGE NOTES, XXXIII (November, 1918), 408-414.

2073 Wright, Hagberg. "The Sources of Carlyle's Lecture on 'The Hero As Divinity,'" MODERN LANGUAGE REVIEW, XIII (January, 1918), 87-90.

1919

2074 Anon. "The Uses of Advertisement," SPECTATOR, CXXIII

(August 9, 1919), 168-170.

2075 Cook, Davidson. "A Strange Old Brown MS. The Story of an Anglo-American Franklin Relic, with Some Hitherto Unpublished Carlyle Letters," BOOKMAN (L), LVI (July, 1919), 128-130.

2076 Dunn, T. O. D. "An Anglo-Indian Romance Involving Thomas Carlyle, a Scottish Philosopher; James Achilles Kirkpatrick, Resident at the Court of the Nizam of Hyderabad; and the Marquis of Wellesley, Governor-General of India," CALCUTTA REVIEW, n.s. VII (January, 1919), 56-71.

2077 Elliott, J. J. "Carlyle as a Poet," SPECTATOR, CXXIII (August 16, 1919), 212.

2078 Flint, Thomas. "Carlyle on Constellations," NOTES AND QUERIES, sers. 12, V (June, 1919), 150.

2079 Hunter, J. "Thomas Carlyle," MODERN CHURCHMAN, IX (November, 1919), 349-359.

2080 Jones, Samuel A. A CATALOGUE OF THE DR. SAMUEL A. JONES CARLYLE COLLECTION. Ed. Mary E. Wead. Ann Arbor: University of Michigan Library, 1919.

2081 Macleod, Euphemia. SEANCES WITH CARLYLE. Boston: Four Seas, 1919.

2082 Miller, Frank. "Carlyle as a Poet," SPECTATOR, CXXIII (August 23, 1919), 244.

2083 Stewart, Herbert L. "Carlyle and His Critics," NINETEENTH CENTURY AND AFTER, LXXXVI (September, 1919), 505-514.

2084 _____. "Carlyle's Place in Philosophy," MONIST, XXIX (April, 1919), 161-189.

2085 Willcocks, M. P. "Thomas Carlyle," NATION (L), XXVI (December 27, 1919), 453-456.

1920

2086 Anon. "[William H. Mallock on Carlyle]," BOOKMAN (NY), LI (June, 1920), 510-511.

2087 Brand, C. Neville. "A Letter of Carlyle's," TIMES LITER-ARY SUPPLEMENT (June 10, 1920), 368.

2088 Bryan, William J. WHAT SPIRITUALISM REALLY IS. New York: Alberta Publishing, n.d. [1920].

2089 Carlyle, Alexander. "'Christopher North,'" NINETEENTH CENTURY AND AFTER, LXXXVII (January, 1920), 103-117.

2090 _____. "A Story from Real Life. By Jane Welsh Carlyle," CORNHILL MAGAZINE, CXXI (March, 1920), 296-304.

2091 de Castro, J. Paul. "Carlyle's Inaccuracy," NOTES AND QUERIES, sers. 12, VII (August 14, 1920), 128.

2092 Elton, Oliver. A SURVEY OF ENGLISH LITERATURE: 1830-1880. 2 vols. London: Edward Arnold, 1920.

2093 Grierson, Philip H. J. "Mrs. Carlyle's Claim to Descent from John Knox," TRANSACTIONS OF THE DUMFRIES-SHIRE AND GALLOWAY NATURAL HISTORY AND ANTI-QUARIAN SOCIETY, sers. 3, VIII (November 12, 1920), 61-68.

2094 Hoggan, J. C. "Miss Willcocks on Thomas Carlyle," NATION (L), XXVI (January 17, 1920), 537-538.

2095 Johnson, J. Ruddiman. "A Memorandum of Carlyle's," NOTES AND QUERIES, sers. 12, VII (September 18, 1920), 230.

2096 Lyster, T. W. "Carlyle in Dublin," TIMES LITERARY SUPPLE-MENT (September 16, 1920), 600. Rpt. IRISH BOOK LOVER, XII (December, 1920), 55-56.

2097 Ralli, Augustus. GUIDE TO CARLYLE. 2 vols. London: Allen and Unwin, n.d. [1920].

2098 Saintsbury, George. "Carlyle," ATHENAEUM, II (October 29, 1920), 577-579.

2099   Stewart, Herbert L. "The Declining Fame of Thomas Carlyle," TRANSACTIONS OF THE ROYAL SOCIETY OF CANADA, sers. 3, XIV (May, 1920), 11-29.

2100   Thorndike, Ashley H. LITERATURE IN A CHANGING AGE. New York: Macmillan, 1920.

2101   Williams, Stanley T. "Carlyle's Life of John Sterling," SOUTH ATLANTIC QUARTERLY, XIX (October, 1920), 341-349. Rpt. STUDIES IN VICTORIAN LITERATURE. New York: E. P. Dutton, 1923.

1921

2102   Anon. "Tammas and Amos," NEW YORK TIMES (May 22, 1921), 2, Section II.

2103   _____. "[Restoration of Jane Welsh Carlyle's Grave]," TIMES (December 14, 1921), 7.

2104   Armstrong, T. Percy. "Carlyle's French Revolution," NOTES AND QUERIES, sers. 12, VIII (January 22, 1921), 78.

2105   Bathurst, Katharine. "Carlyle's Unpublished Letters to Miss Wilson," NINETEENTH CENTURY AND AFTER, LXXXIX (May-June, 1921), 802-811, 1017-1023.

2106   Bensly, E. "Errors in Carlyle's French Revolution," NOTES AND QUERIES, sers. 12, VIII (February 5, 1921), 105-106.

2107   Blunt, Reginald. "Mrs. Carlyle and Her 'Carina,'" LONDON MERCURY, V (November, 1921), 41-53.

2108   _____. "Jane Carlyle's Unpublished Letters," FORUM, LXVI (November-December, 1921), 394-400, 538-543; LXVII (January, 1922), 46-53.

2109   Carlyle, Alexander. "Thomas Carlyle and Thomas Spedding: Their Friendship and Correspondence," CORNHILL MAGAZINE, CXXIII (May-June, 1921), 513-537, 742-768.

2110   Falconer, J. A. "The Source of A Tale of Two Cities," MOD-

ERN LANGUAGE NOTES, XXXVI (January, 1921), 1-10.

2111   Gorrie, Daniel. "More Letters by Carlyle to a Fellow Student," FORTNIGHTLY REVIEW, XCVI (October, 1921), 677-684.

2112   Hodgins, James. "Some Reminiscences of the Carlyle Family," CANADIAN MAGAZINE, LVI (February, 1921), 317-319.

2113   Hohlfeld, A. R. "The Poems in Carlyle's Translation of Wilhelm Meister," MODERN LANGUAGE NOTES, XXXVI (April, 1921), 205-211.

2114   Jalbert, Arthur. THE ACTIVISM OF THOMAS CARLYLE. Torino: G. Bonis and Rossi, 1921.

2115   Johnson, J. Ruddiman. "Carlyle and a Bookseller," NOTES AND QUERIES, sers. 12, IX (July 30, 1921), 88.

2116   MacDonald, P. M. "Carlyle as a Prophet," CANADIAN MAGAZINE, LVI (February, 1921), 314-316.

2117   Masson, Rosaline. "Silhouettes: Thomas Carlyle," CORNHILL MAGAZINE, CXXIII (April, 1921), 421-425.

2118   Roe, Frederick W. THE SOCIAL PHILOSOPHY OF CARLYLE AND RUSKIN. New York: Harcourt, Brace, 1921.

2119   Sloan, John M. "Carlyle and Emerson," LANDMARK, III (April, 1921), 265-268. Rpt. LITTELL'S LIVING AGE, CCCIX (May 21, 1921), 486-489.

2120   Starnes, De Witt T. "The Influence of Carlyle upon Tennyson," TEXAS REVIEW, VI (July, 1921), 316-336.

2121   Stewart, Herbert L. "Carlyle and Canada," CANADIAN MAGAZINE, LVI (February, 1921), 320-323.

1922

2122   Anon. "Thomas Carlyle in the Movies," NEW YORK TIMES (January 1, 1922), 14, Section III.

2123   . "Emerson and Carlyle," NEW YORK TIMES (June 4, 1922), 4, Section III.

2124   . "The Wives of the Hag-Ridden--A Tragic Marriage," TIMES (August 3, 1922), 10.

2125   Allen, Anna O. JOHN ALLEN AND HIS FRIENDS. London: Hodder and Stoughton, n.d. [1922].

2126   Bradley, Herbert D. THE ETERNAL MASQUERADE. London: T. Werner Laurie, 1922.

2127   Bruce, Harold L. "Blake, Carlyle, and the French Revolution," CHARLES MILLS GAYLEY ANNIVERSARY PAPERS (Berkeley: University of California Press, 1922), 165-176.

2128   Carlyle, Alexander. "Notes on a Three Days' Tour to the Netherlands: August, 1842.--T. Carlyle," CORNHILL MAGAZINE, CXXVI (October-November, 1922), 493-512, 626-640.

2129   Chapman, J. A. "The Carlyle Legend," CALCUTTA REVIEW, sers. 3, II (February, 1922), 204-221.

2130   Crichton-Browne, James. 'The Wives of the Hag-Ridden,'" TIMES (August II, 1922), 13.

2131   Masson, Rosaline. "Two Edinburgh Literary Homes,'" CHAMBERS'S JOURNAL, sers. 7, XII (August 5, 1922), 564-569, 584-587.

2132   Morley, Edith J. "Carlyle in the Diary, Reminiscences and Correspondence of Henry Crabb Robinson," LONDON MERCURY, VI (October, 1922), 607-618.

2133   Scott, J. W. "Carlyle's Sartor Resartus," UNIVERSITY OF CALIFORNIA CHRONICLE, XXIV (April-October, 1922), 153-161, 337-346, 427-439.

2134   Spence, Lewis. "Two Carlyle Letters," TIMES (May 1, 1922), 18.

2135   Williams, Stanley T. "Carlyle's Past and Present: A Prophecy,"

SOUTH ATLANTIC QUARTERLY, XXI (January, 1922), 30-40. Rpt. STUDIES IN VICTORIAN LITERATURE. New York: E. P. Dutton, 1923.

1923

2136   Anon. "Carlyle and Burns," SATURDAY REVIEW, CXXXV (January 27, 1923), 108-109.

2137   _____. "[Carlyle's Will]," HARVARD LIBRARY NOTES, no. 10 (February, 1923), 222-225.

2138   _____. "On Two Lord Rectors," NATION (L), XXXII (March 10, 1923), 854-855.

2139   _____. "Thomas Carlyle," VILLAGER, no. 263 (October 21, 1923). [Listed in Dyer, untraced]

2140   Arnold, William H. VENTURES IN BOOK COLLECTING. New York: Charles Scribner, 1923.

2141   Chesterton, Gilbert K. "William Cobbett," TRANSACTIONS OF THE ROYAL SOCIETY OF LITERATURE, sers. 3, III (1923), 89-97.

2142   Clark, J. B. M. "An Hour with Thomas Carlyle," AMERICAN FEDERATIONIST, XXX (August, 1923), 668-669.

2143   Davidson, Mabel. "A Lady Who Deserves to be Remembered," SEWANEE REVIEW, XXXI (July, 1923), 287-295.

2144   Harwood, H. C. "Victorian Glimpses," LONDON MERCURY, VIII (June, 1923), 167-174.

2145   Helm, W. H. "The Young Carlyle," BOOKMAN (L), LXV (November, 1923), 116-118.

2146   Housman, Laurence. ECHO DE PARIS. London: Jonathan Cape, n.d. [1923].

2147   "Sartor Resartus" [pseud.]. "Thomas Carlyle as the Catspaw of the Hohenzollerns," NATIONAL REVIEW, LXXX (February,

1923), 901-913.

2148   Wilson, David A. CARLYLE TILL MARRIAGE (1795-1826).
London: Kegan Paul, 1923.

1924

2149   Anon. "Lord Jeffrey's Loving Salute to Jane Carlyle,"
NEW YORK TIMES (January 27, 1924), 10, Section VIII.

2150   _____ . "Carlyle's Monk Who Kept the Faith," NEW YORK
TIMES (February 24, 1924), 5, Section III.

2151   _____ . "New Letters of Mrs. Carlyle: What It Means to be
the Wife of a Genius," CURRENT OPINION, LXXVII
(August, 1924), 167-168.

2152   _____ . "Carlyle, Cinematographer," ATLANTIC MONTH-
LY, CXXXIV (August, 1924), 282-283.

2153   Abbott, Wilbur C. CONFLICTS WITH OBLIVION. New
Haven: Yale University Press, 1924.

2154   Addison, James T. "Carlyle Transposed," FORUM, LXXII
(December, 1924), 760-762.

2155   Bell, Elizabeth G. "A 'Not Unblessed Pilgrimage': The
Carlyles' Married Life," CORNHILL MAGAZINE, CXXX
(July, 1924), 51-78.

2156   Brownell, William C. THE GENIUS OF STYLE. New York:
Charle s Scribner, 1924.

2157   Carson, Gerald H. "[Carlyle Redivivus]," BOOKMAN (NY),
LXX (August, 1924), 736-737.

2158   Ernle, Lord. "Mrs. Carlyle and English Letter Writing,"
QUARTERLY REVIEW, CCXLII (July, 1924), 193-210.

2159   Flint, Thomas. "Carlyle on Constellations," NOTES AND
QUERIES, sers. 13, II (March 29, 1924), 240.

2160   Holland, Bernard. "On a Re-reading of Carlyle's Cromwell,"
        DUBLIN REVIEW, CLXXIV (April, 1924), 260-278.

2161   Huxley, Leonard. "Family Letters of Jane Welsh Carlyle,"
        CENTURY MAGAZINE, XVII (January-February, 1924), 348-
        358, 510-519. Rpt. CORNHILL MAGAZINE, CXXIX (Janu-
        ary-February, 1924), 1-21, 129-150.

2162   Kelman, John. PROPHETS OF YESTERDAY AND THEIR
        MESSAGE FOR TO-DAY. Cambridge: Harvard University
        Press, 1924.

2163   Matz, Bertram W. "Dickens, Carlyle, and Hard Times,"
        DICKENSIAN, XX (January, 1924), 32-33.

2164   Neff, Emery. CARLYLE AND MILL: MYSTIC AND UTILI-
        TARIAN. New York: Columbia University Press, 1924.

2165   Roe, Frederick W. "New Lights on Carlyle," SEWANEE RE-
        VIEW, XXXII (July, 1924), 357-361.

2166   Ryan, W. P. "Jane Welsh Carlyle," BOOKMAN (L), LXVI
        (June, 1924), 149-151.

2167   Stephen, Leslie. SOME EARLY IMPRESSIONS. London:
        Hogarth Press, 1924.

2168   Thrall, Miriam M. "A Phase of Carlyle's Relationship to
        Fraser's Magazine," PUBLICATIONS OF THE MODERN LANG-
        UAGE ASSOCIATION, XXXIX (December, 1924), 919-931.

2169   Wainewright, J. B. "Carlyle and Montesquieu," NOTES
        AND QUERIES, sers. 13, II (June 7, 1924), 415.

2170   Wilson, David A. CARLYLE TO "THE FRENCH REVOLUTION"
        (1826-1827). London: Kegan Paul, 1924.

                              1925

2171   Anon. CARLYLE'S HOUSE, 24 CHEYNE ROW, CHELSEA.
        London: Carlyle Memorial Trust, 1925.

2172   _____. "The Best Years of Thomas Carlyle," CURRENT OPIN-

ION, LXXVIII (March, 1925), 295-296.

2173 Addy, S. P. "'Infants in the Porch,'" NOTES AND QUER-
IES, CXLIX (November 7, 1925), 330.

2174 Bodelsen, Carl A. STUDIES IN MID-VICTORIAN IMPERI-
ALISM. New York: A. A. Knopf, 1925.

2175 Chrisman, Lewis H. "Sartor Resartus," METHODIST REVIEW,
CVIII (March-April, 1925), 193-208.

2176 Davidson, Mabel. "The Record of a Broken Friendship,"
SOUTH ATLANTIC QUARTERLY, XXIV (July, 1925), 278-
292.

2177 Harris, Frank. MY LIFE AND LOVES. 3 vols. New York
and Nice: privately printed, 1925-1927.

2178 Liljegren, S. B. "The Origin of Sartor Resartus," PALAES-
TRIA, no. 148 (1925), 400-433.

2179 Marx, Olga. CARLYLE'S TRANSLATION OF WILHELM
MEISTER. Baltimore: Johns Hopkins Press, 1925.

2180 Mott, Frank L. "Carlyle's American Public," PHILOLO-
GICAL QUARTERLY, IV (July, 1925), 245-264.

2181 Roe, Frederick W. "More About the Carlyles," SEWANEE
REVIEW, XXXIII (April, 1925), 233-236.

2182 Rye, W. TWO CROMWELLIAN MYTHS. Norwick: H. W.
Hunt, 1925.

2183 Thackeray, C. B. "The Melancholy Humourist and His
Friends. A Victorian Scrap Book," LONDON MERCURY,
XII (May, 1925), 54-68.

2184 Wilson, David A. CARLYLE ON CROMWELL AND OTHERS
(1837-1848). London: Kegan Paul, 1925.

1926

2185 Anon. "[Letters of Jane Welsh Carlyle]," NOTES AND

QUERIES, CLI (October 2–November 6, 1926), 235, 326.

2186 _____. "Gifted Couples Run Risk of Rival Glory," NEW YORK
TIMES (November 21, 1926), 18, Section V.

2187 Creek, H. L. "The Opinions of Jane Welsh Carlyle," SE-
WANEE REVIEW, XXXIV (April, 1926), 156-168.

2188 Gessendoerfer, Theodore. "Carlyle and Jean Paul Friedrich
Richter," JOURNAL OF ENGLISH AND GERMANIC PHIL-
OLOGY, XXV (October, 1926), 540-553.

2189 George. W. L. "Great Love Stories of the World: The
Carlyles," McCALL'S MAGAZINE, LIII (April, 1926), 13,
40, 44, 57, 63.

2190 Hamilton, Mary A. THOMAS CARLYLE. London: Leonard
Parsons, n.d. [1926].

2191 Huxley, Leonard. "A Sheaf of Letters from Jane Welsh
Carlyle," CORNHILL MAGAZINE, CXXIV (October-November, 1926), 493-510, 622-638.

2192 Knight, George. "Carlyle Recalled," TIMES (March 9, 1926),
12.

2193 Phelps, Sydney K. "Two More of Our Invisible Hosts," NINE-
TEENTH CENTURY AND AFTER, XCIX (May, 1926), 759-768.

2194 Phelps, William L. "[Carlyle and His Works]," SCRIBNER'S
MAGAZINE, LXXIX (February, 1926), 209-216.

2195 Simon Pure [pseud.]. "[Satirization of Carlyle]," BOOKMAN
(NY), LXXIII (May, 1926), 330-331.

2196 Speck, William A. "New Letters of Carlyle to Eckermann,"
YALE REVIEW, n.s. XV (July, 1926), 736-757. Rpt. NEW
LETTERS OF CARLYLE. New Haven: Yale University Press,
1926.

2197 Willcocks, M. P. BETWEEN THE OLD WORLD AND THE
NEW. New York: Frederick A. Stokes, 1926.

1927

2198   Barrett, James A. S. "Carlyle on Novels," TIMES LITER-
ARY SUPPLEMENT (January 20, 1927), 44.

2199   Blankenagel, John C. "Carlyle as a Critic of Grillparzer,"
PUBLICATIONS OF THE MODERN LANGUAGE ASSOCIA-
TION, XLII (December, 1927), 1027-1035.

2200   Broadbent, Henry. "Carlyle's French Revolution--A Sug-
gestion," TIMES LITERARY SUPPLEMENT (July 21, 1927),
504.

2201   Burdett, Osbert. "Thomas Carlyle," OUTLOOK, LX
(September 10, 1927), 342.

2202   Carson, Gerald H. "A Live Prophet," SATURDAY REVIEW
OF LITERATURE, IV (September 24, 1927), 232.

2203   Chrisman, Lewis H. "Past and Present," METHODIST RE-
VIEW, CX (September, 1927), 713-727.

2204   Crichton-Browne, James. STRAY LEAVES FROM A PHYSI-
CIAN'S PORTFOLIO. London: Hodder and Stoughton,
n.d. [1927].

2205   Davidson, Mabel. "The Religion of Mrs. Carlyle," SEWANEE
REVIEW, XXXV (October, 1927), 448-459.

2206   Fisher, W. J. "The Influence of Carlyle," DICKENSIAN,
XXIII (Summer, 1927), 197-199.

2207   Francke, Kuno. "Carlyle, and Goethe's Symbolum," PHILO-
LOGICAL QUARTERLY, VI (April, 1927), 97-101.

2208   Heseltine, Olive. CONVERSATION. London: Methuen,
n.d. [1927].

2209   Hilles, Frederick W. "'Mother of Dead Dogs,'" MODERN
LANGUAGE NOTES, XLII (December, 1927), 506-508.

2210   Hutchinson, Keith. "The Victorian Isaiah," BOOKMAN (NY),

LXVI (September, 1927), 101-102.

2211   McGovern, J. B. "Carlyle and Dickens, " NOTES AND QUERIES, CLIII (July 16, 1927), 45.

2212   Moody, John. A COMMENTARY AND QUESTIONNAIRE ON PAST AND PRESENT. London: Isaac Pitman, 1927.

2213   Peel, Albert. "A New Carlyle Letter, " YALE REVIEW, XVI (July, 1927), 830-832.

2214   Robertson, J. M. MODERN HUMANISTS RECONSIDERED. London: Watts, 1927.

2215   Thompson, Frank T. "Emerson and Carlyle, " STUDIES IN PHILOLOGY, XXIV (July, 1927), 438-453.

2216   Tyrrell, T. W. "Carlyle and Dickens, " NOTES AND QUER-IES, CLIII (July 30, 1927), 87.

2217   Wilson, David A. CARLYLE AT HIS ZENITH (1848-1853). London: Kegan Paul, 1927.

2218   Young, Norwood. CARLYLE: HIS RISE AND FALL. London: Duckworth, n.d. [1927].

1928

2219   Anon. "[Gabriel Wells] Gives Carlyle Draft to British Museum, " NEW YORK TIMES (July 20, 1928), 6.

2220   _____. "Autograph Letters of Carlyle, " TIMES (December 15, 1928), 15.

2221   _____. "Macaulay and Carlyle, " TIMES (December 15, 1928), 15.

2222   Baker, C. F. "Carlyle and Goethe, " TIMES LITERARY SUP-PLEMENT (May 10, 1928), 358.

2223   Barrett, James A. S. "Carlyle on Blake and Vitalis, " TIMES LITERARY SUPPLEMENT (April 26, 1928), 313.

2224   . THE PRINCIPLE PORTRAITS AND STATUES OF THOMAS CARLYLE. London: Spurr and Swift, n.d. [1928]. See also Dyer, no. 2231.

2225   Carlyle, Alexander. "Carlyle on Horse-Shoes." See Dyer, no. 2231.

2226   Caw, James L. "A Commentary on Carlyle's Portraits." See Dyer, no. 2231.

2227   Chamberlin, Benjamin B. "Carlyle as a Portrait Painter," SEWANEE REVIEW, XXXVI (July, 1928), 328-341.

2228   Davidson, Mabel. "Time and Little Charlotte," SEWANEE REVIEW, XXXVI (January, 1928), 30-34.

2229   Davies, Blodwen. "The Love Story of Carlyle and His Canadian Sweetheart," CANADIAN MAGAZINE, LXIX (June, 1928), 10-11, 42.

2230   Drew, Elizabeth A. JANE WELSH AND JANE CARLYLE. London: Jonathan Cape, n.d. [1928].

2231   Dyer, Isaac W. A BIBLIOGRAPHY OF THOMAS CARLYLE'S WRITINGS AND ANA. Portland, Maine: Southworth Press, 1928.

2232   Firkins, O. W. TWO PASSENGERS FOR CHELSEA AND OTHER PLAYS. London: Longmans, Green, 1928. Rpt. "Two Passengers for Chelsea," GOLDEN BOOK MAGAZINE, XI (January, 1930), 95-103.

2233   Forbes, H. M. "The Belle of Haddington," SCOTS MAGAZINE, n.s. IX (September, 1928), 420-425.

2234   G[ibson], J. P. "Carlyle's Past and Present," BRITISH MUSEUM QUARTERLY, III (1928), 75-76.

2235   Grierson, Herbert J. C. "Scott and Carlyle," ESSAYS AND STUDIES, XIII (1928), 88-111. Rpt. ESSAYS AND ADDRESSES. London: Chatto and Windus, 1940.

2236 Guedalla, Philip. "Jane Welsh Carlyle," GOOD HOUSE-
KEEPING, LXXXVI (June, 1928), 34-35, 182, 184, 187-
188, 191-192.

2237 _____. BONNET AND SHAWL: AN ALBUM. London: Hodder and Stoughton, 1928.

2238 Harrold, Charles F. "The Translated Passages in Carlyle's
French Revolution," JOURNAL OF ENGLISH AND GERMAN-
IC PHILOLOGY, XXVII (January, 1928), 51-66.

2239 _____. "Two Critics of Democracy," SOUTH ATLANTIC
QUARTERLY, XXVII (April, 1928), 130-141.

2240 _____. "Carlyle's Interpretation of Kant," PHILOLOGICAL
QUARTERLY, VII (October, 1928), 345-357.

2241 _____. "Carlyle's General Method in The French Revolution," PUBLICATIONS OF THE MODERN LANGUAGE
ASSOCIATION, XLIII (December, 1928), 1150-1169.

2242 Lehman, Benjamin H. CARLYLE'S THEORY OF THE HERO.
Durham: Duke University Press, 1928.

2243 Morris, Rose. "Thomas Carlyle: An Unpublished Letter,"
SPECTATOR, CXL (January 7, 1928), 8.

2244 Orrick, James B. "Matthew Arnold and Goethe," PUBLI-
CATIONS OF THE ENGLISH GOETHE SOCIETY, IV (1928),
1-54.

2245 Platt, Charles. "The Development of an Attitude: The
Carlyles and Their Good Friend Froude," CENTURY MAGA-
ZINE, CXVI (July, 1928), 318-325.

2246 Reilly, Joseph J. "Jane Carlyle Looks at Thomas," CATH-
OLIC WORLD, CXXVIII (November, 1928), 156-163. Rpt.
OF BOOKS AND MEN. New York: J. Messner, 1942.

2247 Stawell, F. Melian. "The Case Against Carlyle," TIMES
LITERARY SUPPLEMENT (March 1, 1928), 150.

2248 _____ . "Carlyle and Goethe, " TIMES LITERARY SUPPLE-
MENT (May 3, 1928), 334.

2249 Strachan, L. R. M. "The Case Against Carlyle, " TIMES
LITERARY SUPPLEMENT (February 23, 1928), 130.

2250 Strachey, Lytton. "Four English Historians: IV.--Carlyle, "
NATION (L), XLII (January 28, 1928), 646-648.

2251 _____ . "Carlyle, " A CHATTO & WINDUS MISCELLANY
(London: Chatto and Windus, 1928), 3-12. See also POR-
TRAITS IN MINIATURE. London: Chatto and Windus,
1931.

2252 Tristram, Henry. "Two Leaders--Newman and Carlyle, "
CORNHILL MAGAZINE, CXXXVIII (September, 1928),
367-382.

2253 Young, Norwood. "Carlyle and Goethe, " TIMES LITER-
ARY SUPPLEMENT (May 10, 1928), 358.

1929

2254 Anon. "Geraldine and Jane, " TIMES LITERARY SUPPLE-
MENT (February 28, 1929), 149-150.

2255 _____ . "[Carlyle's Concept of 'Gigmanity'], " NEW YORK
TIMES (April 15, 1929), 24.

2256 _____ . "Gift to Carlyle's House, " TIMES (May 2, 1929),
13.

2257 _____ . "National Library of Scotland--Gift of Carlyle
Papers, " TIMES (July 13, 1929), 9.

2258 _____ . "A Carlyle Memorial, " TIMES (August 9, 1929), 8.

2259 _____ . "Thomas Carlyle Statue To Be Unveiled To-Day at
Ecclefechan, " TIMES (September 3, 1929), 9.

2260 _____ . "The Ecclefechan Statue, " TIMES (September 3,
1929), 13.

2261 _____. "Carlyle's Statue Unveiled," NEW YORK TIMES (September 4, 1929), 30.

2262 _____. "Did Bust of Shelley Portray His Disgust?" NEW YORK TIMES (December 8, 1929), 5, Section III.

2263 _____. "Rare Manuscripts of Carlyle Arrive," NEW YORK TIMES (December 22, 1929), 20, Section II.

2264 Bickley, F. "Poets and the Others," BOOKMAN (L), LXXVII (December, 1929), 199-200.

2265 Bonnard, G. A. "A Letter of Carlyle to A. Vinet," REVIEW OF ENGLISH STUDIES, V (January, 1929), 70-72.

2266 Dixon, E. H. "Geraldine and Jane," TIMES LITERARY SUPPLEMENT (March 7, 1929), 185.

2267 Dudley, O. H. T. "Geraldine and Jane," TIMES LITERARY SUPPLEMENT (March 7, 1929), 185.

2268 Guedalla, Philip. "Bonnet and Shawl," MENTOR, XVII (June, 1929), 53-55.

2269 Housman, Laurence. "The Fire-Lighters: A Dialogue on a Burning Topic," LONDON MERCURY, XIX (January, 1929), 263-277.

2270 Hutton, W. H. "Geraldine and Jane," TIMES LITERARY SUPPLEMENT (March 7, 1929), 185.

2271 Leopold, Werner. "Thomas Carlyle and Franz Horn," JOURNAL OF ENGLISH AND GERMANIC PHILOLOGY, XXVIII (April, 1929), 215-219.

2272 Macy, John. "Carlyle: From Ecclefechan to the World," BOOKMAN (NY), LXIX (August, 1929), 609-615.

2273 Maurois, Andrè. "[Carlylean Biography]," BOOKMAN (NY), LXIX (June, 1929), 343.

2274 Morley, Edith J. "Geraldine and Jane," TIMES LITERARY

SUPPLEMENT (March 7, 1929), 185.

2275 Murray, Robert H. STUDIES IN ENGLISH SOCIAL AND
POLITICAL THINKERS OF THE NINETEENTH CENTURY.
2 vols. Cambridge: W. Heffer, 1929.

2276 Patterson, W. P. "Books that Have Influenced Our Epoch:
Carlyle's Sartor Resartus," EXPOSITORY TIMES, XLI
(October, 1929), 32-38.

2277 Stockley, V. A. GERMAN LITERATURE AS KNOWN IN
ENGLAND: 1750-1830. London: G. Routledge, 1929.

2278 Storrs, Margaret. THE RELATION OF CARLYLE TO KANT
AND FICHTE. Bryn Mawr: Bryn Mawr College: 1929.

2279 Wellek, René. "Carlyle and German Romanticism,"
XENIA PRAGENSIA (Prague, 1929), 375-403. Rpt. CON-
FRONTATIONS. Princeton: Princeton University Press,
1965.

2280 Wilson, David A. CARLYLE TO THREESCORE-AND-TEN
(1853-1865). London: Kegan Paul, 1929.

2281 Woodruff, E. H. "Geraldine and Jane," TIMES LITERARY
SUPPLEMENT (April 4, 1929), 276.

2282 Woolf, Virginia. "Geraldine and Jane," BOOKMAN (NY),
LXVIII (February, 1929), 612-620.

1930

2283 Anon. "An Original Letter of Thomas Carlyle," JOURNAL
OF THE FRIENDS HISTORICAL SOCIETY, XXVII (1930),
25-26.

2284 ____. "Carlyle's Letters to Neuberg," TIMES (March 22,
1930), 9.

2285 ____. "Carlyle and Froude," TIMES (December 11, 1930),
10.

2286 Bernbaum, Ernest. GUIDE THROUGH THE ROMANTIC

MOVEMENT. New York: Ronald Press, 1930.

2287 Burdett, Osbert. THE TWO CARLYLES. London: Faber and Faber, 1930.

2288 Carlyle, Alexander. "Carlyle and His Biographers," TIMES (April 1, 1930), 12.

2289 _____. THE CARLYLE MYTH REFUTED. Edinburgh: Constable, 1930.

2290 Crichton-Browne, James. "Carlyle and His Biographers," TIMES (March 7, 1930), 17.

2291 Cushendun, Lord. "Carlyle and His Biographer--The 'Inaccuracy' of Froude--A Vindication," TIMES (March 6, 1930), 15-16.

2292 _____. "Carlyle's Biographers," TIMES (April 2, 1930), 10.

2293 Dunn, Waldo H. FROUDE AND CARLYLE. London: Longmans, Green, 1930.

2294 Harrold, Charles F. "Carlyle and Novalis," STUDIES IN PHILOLOGY, XXVII (January, 1930), 47-63.

2295 _____. "A Defense of Froude," SATURDAY REVIEW OF LITERATURE, VI (July 19, 1930), 1205.

2296 Holmes, T. Rich. "Carlyle and His Biographers--The 'Inaccuracy' of Froude," TIMES (March 11, 1930), 12.

2297 Howe, Susanne. WILHELM MEISTER AND HIS ENGLISH KINSMEN. New York: Columbia University Press, 1930.

2298 James, Stanley B. "A Mediaeval Carlyle," MONTH, CLVI (August, 1930), 116-122.

2299 Joynt, J. W. "Carlyle and His Biographers," TIMES (March 10, 1930), 10.

2300 Norman, F. "Henry Crabb Robinson and Goethe," PUBLI-

CATIONS OF THE ENGLISH GOETHE SOCIETY, VI &
VIII (1930-1931), 1-102, 1-123.

2301 Quennell, Peter. "A Literary Enigma, " NEW STATESMAN
AND NATION, XXXIV (March 22, 1930), 772-773.

2302 Reuter, Gabrielle. "Jane Welsh Carlyle, " DIE LITERATUR,
XXXIII (December, 1930), 237-238.

2303 Sagar, S. ROUND BY REPENTANCE TOWER: A STUDY
OF CARLYLE. London: Burns, Oates, and Wasborne, 1930.

2304 Saintsbury, George. "Froude and Carlyle, " BOOKMAN
(L), LXXVIII (April, 1930), 7-8.

2305 Yeigh, Frank. "Scott, Carlyle, Dickens, and Canada, "
QUEEN'S QUARTERLY, XXXVII (April, 1930), 335-347.

1931

2306 Anon. "Carlyle's House Visited, " NEW YORK TIMES
(February 8, 1931), 4, Section III.

2307 ____. "Tammas of Ecclefechan, " NEW YORK TIMES
(March 8, 1931), 1, Section III.

2308 ____. "Mr. Alexander Carlyle, " TIMES (December 2,
1931), 14.

2309 ____. "Yale Gets Manuscript of a Carlyle Work, " NEW
YORK TIMES (December 20, 1931), 5, Section II.

2310 ____. "Finds Hero Worship Our National Trait, " NEW
YORK TIMES (December 29, 1931), 5.

2311 Barrett, James A. S. "Carlyle's Debt to Goethe, " HIB-
BERT JOURNAL, XXX (October, 1931), 61-75.

2312 Calder, Grace J. "Carlyle's Past and Present, " YALE UNI-
VERSITY LIBRARY GAZETTE, VI (October, 1931), 33-35.

2313 Clark, Henry W. "Carlyle: Fifty Years After, " CONTEM-

PORARY REVIEW, CXXXIX (February, 1931), 219-225.

2314   Cofer, David B. SAINT-SIMONISM IN THE RADICALISM OF THOMAS CARLYLE. Austin, Texas: Von Boeckermann-Jones, 1931.

2315   Dunn, Waldo H. "The Centennial of Sartor Resartus," LON-DON QUARTERLY REVIEW, CLV (January, 1931), 39-51.

2316   Friedell, Egon. "Carlyle Fifty Years On," LITTELL'S LIV-ING AGE, CCCXL (April, 1931), 188-192.

2317   Mabbott, Thomas O. "Carlyle: A Bibliographical Item," NOTES AND QUERIES, CLX (February 14, 1931), 114.

2318   MacKinnon, Murdock. "Carlyle's 'Imperious Queen of Hearts,' A Canadian," QUEEN'S QUARTERLY, XXXVIII (Winter, 1931), 52-62.

2319   Masson, Flora. VICTORIANS ALL. Edinburgh: W. and R. Chambers, 1931.

2320   Muirhead, J. H. THE PLATONIC TRADITION IN ANGLO-SAXON PHILOSOPHY. London: Allen and Unwin, 1931.

2321   Nichols, Elizabeth. THE CONSISTENCY OF CARLYLE'S LITERARY CRITICISM. Cambridge: Cambridge University Press, 1931.

2322   O'Brien, Mrs. William. "A Tragic Pair," CATHOLIC BUL-LETIN, XXI (August, 1931), 818-823.

2323   Olivero, Frederico. "The Campaign of 1792 in Carlyle and Goethe," STUDI DI BRITANNICI (Torino: Bocca, 1931), 165-186.

2324   Sarolea, Charles. "The Tragedy of Thomas Carlyle: A New Interpretation," ENGLISH REVIEW, LII (April, 1931), 465-477.

2325   Strachan, L. R. M. "Carlyle Query," NOTES AND QUER-IES, CLX (March 14, 1931), 193.

2326   Thrall, Miriam M. "Two Articles Attributed to Carlyle," MODERN LANGUAGE NOTES, XLVI (May, 1931), 316-321.

2327   Wellek, René. IMMANUEL KANT IN ENGLAND: 1793-1838. Princeton: Princeton University Press, 1931.

2328   Wilson, Grove. TEMPERAMENTAL JANE: THE STRANGE STORY OF CARLYLE'S WIFE. New York: Ives Washburn, 1931.

1932

2329   Anon. "[Sotheby Sale of Carlyleana]," TIMES (May 17, 18 -June 14, 15, 1932), 7, 14, 11, 9.

2330   _____. "Carlyle's Books Sold," NEW YORK TIMES (June 14, 1932), 19.

2331   _____. "[Ralli on Carlyle and Shakespeare]," TIMES (November 18, 1932), 12.

2332   Blunt, Reginald. "Carlyle's Chelsea Home," TIMES (June 8, 1932), 10.

2333   Burdett, Osbert. "[Jane Welsh Carlyle]," BOOKMAN (NY), LXXV (April, 1932), 54.

2334   Cazamian, Louis. CARLYLE. Trans. E. K. Brown. New York: Macmillan, 1932.

2335   Clapton, George T. "Carlyle and Some Early English Critics of Baudelaire," A MISCELLANY OF STUDIES IN ROMANCE LANGUAGES AND LITERATURES PRESENTED TO LEON E. KASTNER. Ed. Mary Williams and James A. Rothschild (Cambridge, England: W. Heffer, 1932), 128-146.

2336   Dunn, Waldo H. "Wilson's Carlyle," SEWANEE REVIEW, XL (November, 1932), 460-475.

2337   Edmunds, A. J. "Carlyle Query," NOTES AND QUERIES, CLXII (February 20, 1932), 142.

2338   Harrold, Charles F. "The Mystical Element in Carlyle
        (1827-1834)," MODERN PHILOLOGY, XXIX (May, 1932),
        459-475.

2339   Huxley, Leonard. "Carlyle and Huxley: Early Influences,"
        CORNHILL MAGAZINE, CXLV (March, 1932), 290-302.

2340   Irvine, Lyn L. [Lyn L. Newman]. TEN LETTER-WRITERS.
        London: Hogarth Press, 1932.

2341   Keys, D. R. "Bengough and Carlyle," UNIVERSITY OF
        TORONTO QUARTERLY, II (October, 1932), 49-73.

2342   "Kingsmill, Hugh" [H. K. Lunn]. "Some Modern Light-
        Bringers, As They Might Have Been Extinguished by
        Thomas Carlyle," BOOKMAN (NY), LXXV (December,
        1932), 766-768.

2343   Lovett, Robert M. "Goethe in English Literature," OPEN
        COURT, XLVI (April, 1932), 217-233.

2344   Morse, B. J. "Crabb Robinson and Goethe in England,"
        ENGLISCHE STUDIEN, LXVII (1932), 199-227.

2345   Neff, Emery. CARLYLE. London: George Allen, 1932.

2346   Paston, George [Emily M. Symonds]. AT JOHN MURRAY'S;
        RECORDS OF A LITERARY CIRCLE: 1843-1892. London:
        John Murray, 1932.

2347   Sotheby. CATALOGUE OF PRINTED BOOKS, AUTOGRAPH
        LETTERS, LITERARY MANUSCRIPTS. . .FORMERLY THE
        PROPERTY OF THOMAS CARLYLE. London: J. Davy, 1932.

2348   Tilby, A. Wyatt. "Thomas Carlyle," THE GREAT VICTORI-
        ANS. Ed. H. J. Massingham and Hugh Massingham (London:
        Ivor Nicholson and Watson, 1932), 121-133.

1933

2349   Anon. "[Carlyle Cambridge Scholarship]," TIMES (March
        1, 1933), 16.

2350   Baker, Joseph E. "Carlyle Rules the Reich," SATURDAY RE-
VIEW OF LITERATURE, X (November 25, 1933), 291.

2351   Brinton, C. Crane. ENGLISH POLITICAL THOUGHT IN
THE NINETEENTH CENTURY. London: E. Benn, 1933.

2352   Coffin, Edward F. "American First Editions of Carlyle,"
AMERICAN BOOK COLLECTOR, IV (November, 1933), 236-
238.

2353   Crone, J. C. "Sgéala ó Chathair na gCeó (Carlyle's Influence Over the Young Irelanders)," IRISH BOOK LOVER,
XXI (May–June, 1933), 51.

2354   Dunn, Waldo H. "Carlyle and the Eternal Verities," LEC-
TURES ON THREE EMINENT VICTORIANS (Claremont:
Scripps College Papers, 1933), 5-30.

2355   Dyer, Isaac W. "Carlyle Reconsidered," SEWANEE REVIEW,
XLI (January–June, 1933), 104-108, 141-151.

2356   Grierson, Herbert J. C. CARLYLE AND HITLER. Cambridge,
England: The University Press, 1933. Rpt. ESSAYS AND
ADDRESSES. London: Chatto and Windus, 1940.

2357   Ishida, Kenji. "Arnold or Carlyle?" STUDIES IN ENGLISH
LITERATURE (Tokyo), XIII (1933), 507-512.

2358   "Kingsmill, Hugh" [H. K. Lunn]. "Some Modern Light-
Bringers Extinguished by Thomas Carlyle," ENGLISH REVIEW,
LVI (January, 1933), 23-27.

2359   _____. "The Table of Truth," BOOKMAN (NY), LXXVI
(January, 1933), 29-35.

2360   Knickerbocker, Kenneth L. "The Source of Swinburne's Les
Noyades," PHILOLOGICAL QUARTERLY, XII (January,
1933), 82-83.

2361   Olivier, Sydney H. THE MYTH OF GOVERNOR EYRE. London: L. and V. Woolf, 1933.

2362   Parsons, Coleman O. "A Goethe Poem and Carlyle's Trans-

lation," ARCHIV FÜR DAS STUDIUM DER NEUEREN
SPRACHEN UND LITERATUREN, CLXIV (1933), 252-253.

2363   Phelps, William L. "[Froude's Carlyle]," SCRIBNER'S MAG-
AZINE, XCIII (January, 1933), 60-64.

2364   Ralli, Augustus. LATER CRITIQUES. London: Longmans,
Green, 1933.

2365   Robinson, William H. A MISCELLANY OF RARE BOOKS.
London: William H. Robinson, 1933.

2366   Smith, Mae T. NO. 5 CHEYNE ROW: A DRAMA IN FIVE
ACTS. Herrin, Ill.: Egyptian Publications, 1933.

2367   Turner, G. M. S. "Carlyle and Kirkcaldy," CHAMBERS'S
JOURNAL, 8 sers., II (September, 1933), 687-688.

1934

2368   Anon. "The Rembrandt of English Prose," TIMES LITERARY
SUPPLEMENT (June 7, 1934), 397-398.

2369   ____. "[Letter Praising Carlyle]," NEW YORK TIMES
(June 17, 1934), 5, Section IV.

2370   Barrett, James A. S. "Two Note Books of Thomas Carlyle,"
NOTES AND QUERIES, CLXVI (March 10, 1934), 164-165.

2371   Brooks, Richard. "Manuscripts Pertaining to Carlyle's Frederick the Great," YALE UNIVERSITY LIBRARY GAZETTE, IX
(October, 1934), 38-41.

2372   Haldane, Elizabeth S. "Edward Irving," QUARTERLY REVIEW,
CCLXIII (July, 1934), 111-126.

2373   Harrold, Charles F. CARLYLE AND GERMAN THOUGHT:
1819-1834. New Haven: Yale University Press, 1934.

2374   Holmberg, A. O. DAVID HUME IN CARLYLE'S "SARTOR
RESARTUS." Lund: C. W. K. Gleerups, 1934.

2375   Leopold, Werner. "Carlyle's Handbooks on the History of

German Literature." See Harrold, no. 2373.

2376   Milner, Gamaliel. THE THRESHOLD OF THE VICTORIAN
        AGE. London: Williams and Norgate, 1934.

2377   Parsons, Coleman O. "Carlyle on Ramsay and Ferguson,"
        MODERN LANGUAGE REVIEW, XXIX (July, 1934), 324-
        325.

2378   Simpson, James S. "The House at Craigenputtock,"
        SCOTTISH COUNTRY LIFE, XXIII (February, 1934), 50-51.

2379   Stevenson, G. H. "The Little House," FORTNIGHTLY RE-
        VIEW, CXLI (March, 1934), 349-356.

2380   Thrall, Miriam M. REBELLIOUS FRASER'S. New York:
        Columbia University Press, 1934.

2381   Watt, M. H. "Carlyle and Irving: The Story of a Friendship,"
        SCOTS MAGAZINE, n.s. XXII (December, 1934), 202-208.

2382   Wilson, David A., and David W. MacArthur. CARLYLE IN
        OLD AGE (1865-1881). London: Kegan Paul, 1934.

2383   Wilson, T. C. "'And to Carlyle,'" NEW REPUBLIC, LXXX
        (October 3, 1934), 211.

2384   Wrigley, F. "The Centenary of Sartor Resartus," CONGRE-
        GATIONAL QUARTERLY, XII (January, 1934), 53-56.

2385   Young, Filson. "Round Carlyle's House (Chelsea)," LISTEN-
        ER, XI (June 20, 1934), 1057-1058.

                                1935

2386   Anon. "Letters of Thomas Carlyle--Gift to Scottish Library,"
        TIMES (March 16, 1935), 15.

2387   _____. "Tracing a Quotation [from Sartor Resartus]," NEW
        YORK TIMES (June 5, 1935), 18.

2388   _____. "Thomas Carlyle at Home: A Page of Pictures Honoring

the Philosopher's 140th Birthday," WILSON LIBRARY BULLE-
TIN, X (December, 1935), 276.

2389   Armstrong, T. Percy. "Carlyle and Uhland: Parallel Passages,"
NOTES AND QUERIES, CLXIX (September 28, 1935), 221.

2390   Drew, Elizabeth A. GENIUS AT HOME: A PLAY IN THREE
ACTS. London: H. F. W. Dane, n.d. [1935].

2391   Goldberg, Maxwell H. "Carlyle and Ruskin," TIMES LITER-
ARY SUPPLEMENT (May 16, 1935), 313.

2392   Gray, W. Forbes. "Dickens's Debt to Scotland," DICKEN-
SIAN, XXXI (Summer, 1935), 177-191.

2393   Harrold, Charles F. "Carlyle and the Mystical Tradition,"
CATHOLIC WORLD, CXLII (October, 1935), 45-49.

2394   Hicks, Granville. "Literature and Revolution," ENGLISH
JOURNAL, XXIV (March, 1935), 219-239.

2395   Howe, Susanne. GERALDINE JEWSBURY. London: George
Allen, 1935.

2396   Keith, C. "Where the Carlyles Lived," SMT MAGAZINE,
XV (September, 1935), 30-32.

2397   Morris, G. I. "Divine Hitler," NEW STATESMAN AND
NATION, IX (February 2, 1935), 139.

2398   Scudder, Townsend. "Thomas Carlyle Receives a Friend,"
SATURDAY REVIEW OF LITERATURE, XII (September 14, 1935),
9.

2399   Shine, Hill. "Carlyle and the German Philosophy Problem
During the Year 1826-1827," PUBLICATIONS OF THE MODERN
LANGUAGE ASSOCIATION, L (September, 1935), 807-827.

2400   Sunderland, J. T. "Thomas Carlyle," MODERN REVIEW,
LVIII (December, 1935), 619-625.

2401   Towne, Jackson E. "Carlyle and Oedipus," PSYCHOANA-
LYTIC REVIEW, XXII (July, 1935), 297-305.

2402   Woolf, Leonard. QUACK, QUACK! London: Hogarth Press, 1935.

1936

2403   Anon. "Carlyle at Edinburgh University--Diligence at Greek and Mathematics," TIMES (February 8, 1936), 14.

2404   _____. "The Sage of Silence," TIMES (April 21, 1936), 15.

2405   _____. "No. 6. Cheyne Row: Carlyle and His Next-Door Neighbors," TIMES (April 21, 1936), 17.

2406   _____. "Many Voluble Caesars," NEW YORK TIMES (May 20, 1936), 14.

2407   _____. "Carlyle's House: Gift to the Nation," TIMES (May 29, 1936), 11.

2408   Beach, Joseph W. THE CONCEPT OF NATURE IN NINE-TEENTH- CENTURY ENGLISH POETRY. New York: Mac-millan, 1936.

2409   Blackstone, B. "Carlyle and Little Gidding," TIMES LITERARY SUPPLEMENT (March 28, 1936), 278.

2410   Burke, Thomas. MURDER AT ELSTREE; OR, MR. THURTELL AND HIS GIG. London: Longmans, Green, 1936.

2411   Coleman, A. M. "A Carlyle Episode," NOTES AND QUER-IES, CLXXI (October 17, 1936), 286.

2412   Dwyer, J. J. "A French Catholic Among Eminent Victorians: Francois Rio," CATHOLIC WORLD, CXLII (February, 1936), 593-597.

2413   Ericson, Eston E. "A Scotch Dialect Contraction," ANGLIA, XLVII (November, 1936), 346.

2414   Harrold, Charles F. "The Nature of Carlyle's Calvinism," STUDIES IN PHILOLOGY, XXXIII (July, 1936), 475-486.

2415   Kummer, George. "Anonymity and Carlyle's Early Reputation in America," AMERICAN LITERATURE, VIII (November, 1936), 297-299.

2416 Linscheid, John E. CARLYLE'S TRANSLATIONS OF THE GERMAN ROMANCES INCLUDED IN "GERMAN ROMANCE." Kansas: Bethel College, 1936.

2417 Mead, George H. MOVEMENTS OF THOUGHT IN THE NINETEENTH CENTURY. Chicago: University of Chicago Press, 1936.

2418 Murphy, Ella M. "Carlyle and the Saint-Simonians," STUDIES IN PHILOLOGY, XXXIII (January, 1936), 93-118.

2419 Sayers, Dorothy L. GAUDY NIGHT. New York: Harcourt, Brace, 1936.

2420 Scudder, Townsend. THE LONELY WAYFARING MAN: EMERSON AND SOME ENGLISHMEN. London: Oxford University Press, 1936.

2421 Shine, Hill. "Carlyle's Views on the Relation between Religion and Poetry Up to 1832," STUDIES IN PHILOLOGY, XXXIII (January, 1936), 57-92.

2422 _____. "Articles in Fraser's Magazine Attributed to Carlyle," MODERN LANGUAGE NOTES, LI (March, 1936), 142-145.

2423 _____. "Carlyle's Views on the Relation between Poetry and History Up to Early 1832," STUDIES IN PHILOLOGY, XXXIII (July, 1936), 487-506.

2424 _____. "Carlyle and Fraser's 'Letter on the Doctrine of St. Simon,'" NOTES AND QUERIES, CLXXI (October 24, 1936), 291-293.

2425 Skipton, H. P. Kennedy. "Carlyle and Little Gidding," TIMES LITERARY SUPPLEMENT (April 11, 1936), 316.

2426 Smith, Logan P. REPERUSALS AND RECOLLECTIONS. London: Constable, 1936.

2427 Vance, William S. "Carlyle in America Before Sartor

Resartus," AMERICAN LITERATURE, VII (January, 1936),
363-375.

2428   White, Frederic C. "A Carlyle Episode, " NOTES AND QUER-
IES, CLXXI (October 3, 1936), 243.

1937

2429   Anon. "[Carlyle's Distrust of Majorities], " NEW YORK
TIMES (March 14, 1937), 9, Section IV.

2430   Baker, H. Kendra. "Carlyle and the Stratford Legend, "
BACONIANA, XXII (October, 1937), 331-338.

2431   Carr, Samuel. "Carlyle on Coronations, " NEW STATESMAN
AND NATION, n.s. XIII (April 10, 1937), 589-590.

2432   Drummond, Andrew L. EDWARD IRVING AND HIS CIRCLE.
London: James Clarke, n.d. [1937].

2433   Flower, R. "Letters of William Somerville and Thomas
Carlyle, " BRITISH MUSEUM QUARTERLY, XI (March, 1937),
66-68.

2434   Gray, W. Forbes. "Carlyle and John Forster: An Unpublished
Correspondence, " QUARTERLY REVIEW, CCLXVIII (April,
1937), 271-287.

2435   Harrold, Charles F. "Remembering Carlyle: A Visit with
His Nephew, July 27, August 5 and 14, 1931, " SOUTH ATLAN-
TIC QUARTERLY, XXXVI (October, 1937), 376-384.

2436   Klenze, Camillo von. CHARLES TIMOTHY BROOKS. London: Oxford University Press, 1937.

2437   Miller, Frank. POEMS FROM THE CARLYLE COUNTRY.
Glasgow: Jackson, 1937.

2438   Parsons, Coleman O. "Carlyle's Gropings about Montrose, "
ENGLISCHE STUDIEN, LXXI (1937), 360-371.

2439   Shine, Hill. "Carlyle's Fusion of Poetry, History, and

Religion by 1834," STUDIES IN PHILOLOGY, XXXIV (July, 1937), 438-466.

1938

2440 Anon. "[Sale of Mary R. Chrystal Carlyleiana]," TIMES (April 13, 1938), 16.

2441 Baker, H. Kendra. "Carlyle's Dicta," NOTES AND QUERIES, CLXXV (November 12, 1938), 351.

2442 Batho, Edith C., and Bonamy Dobree. THE VICTORIANS AND AFTER. London: Cresset Press, 1938.

2443 Coleman, A. M. "Keble: A Phrase from Carlyle," NOTES AND QUERIES, CLXXV (September 3, 1938), 173.

2444 Hirst, W. A. "The Manuscript of Carlyle's French Revolution," NINETEENTH CENTURY AND AFTER, CXXIII (January, 1938), 93-98.

2445 Jeffrey, William. "Daffodils at Craigenputtock," SMT MAGAZINE, XX (April, 1938), 49-52.

2446 Jervis, H. "Carlyle and 'The Germ,'" TIMES LITERARY SUPPLEMENT (August 20, 1938), 544.

2447 Lippincott, Benjamin E. VICTORIAN CRITICS OF DEMO-CRACY. Minneapolis: University of Minnesota Press, 1938.

2448 Primrose, Hilda S. "Jane Welsh Carlyle: Her Chelsea Home and Her Music Books," MUSICAL TIMES, LXXIX (March, 1938), 176-177.

2449 Quare [pseud.]. "Grouse Ramadhan," NOTES AND QUERIES, CLXXV (September 10, 1938), 187.

2450 Rubin, Joseph J. "Whitman and Carlyle: 1846," MODERN LANGUAGE NOTES, LIII (May, 1938), 370-371.

2451 Shine, Hill. CARLYLE'S FUSION OF POETRY, HISTORY, AND RELIGION BY 1834. Chapel Hill: University of North

Carolina Press, 1938.

2452　Thornton-Cook, Elsie P. "Carlylean Courtship," CORNHILL MAGAZINE, CLVII (January-April, 1938), 1-41, 145-174, 289-322, 433-472.

2453　_____. SPEAKING DUST: THOMAS AND JANE CARLYLE. A BIOGRAPHICAL NOVEL. London: John Murray, 1938.

2454　White, A. "The Childhood of Jane Welsh Carlyle," CHAMBERS'S JOURNAL, 8 sers., VII (July, 1938), 523-528.

1939

2455　Anon. "Carlyle Speaking," TIMES (September 6, 1939), 4.

2456　_____. "[Carlyle House Closed]," TIMES (October 26, 1939), 5.

2457　Beatty, Richmond C. "Macaulay and Carlyle," PHILOLO-GICAL QUARTERLY, XVIII (January, 1939), 25-34.

2458　Hartwig, George H. "An Immortal Friendship (Carlyle and Emerson)," HIBBERT JOURNAL, XXXVIII (October, 1939), 102-114.

2459　Paine, Gregory. "The Literary Relations of Whitman and Carlyle, with Especial Reference to Their Contrasting Views on Democracy," STUDIES IN PHILOLOGY, XXXVI (July, 1939), 550-563.

2460　Pike, James S. "Dickens, Carlyle, and Tennyson," ATLAN-TIC MONTHLY, CLXIV (December, 1939), 810-819.

2461　Scudder, Townsend. JANE WELSH CARLYLE. New York: Macmillan, 1939.

2462　Spivey, Herbert E. "Poe and Lewis Gaylord Clark," PUBLI-CATIONS OF THE MODERN LANGUAGE ASSOCIATION, LIV (December, 1939), 1124-1132.

2463　Tuell, Anne K. "Carlyle's Marginalia in Sterling's Essays and Tales," PUBLICATIONS OF THE MODERN LANGUAGE ASSOCIATION, LIV (September, 1939), 815-824.

2464 Wagner, Albert M. "Goethe, Carlyle, Nietzsche and the German Middle Class," MONATSCHEFTE FÜR DEUTSCHEN UNTERRICHT, DUETSCHE SPRACHE UND LITERATUR, XXXI (1939), 161-174, 235-242.

2465 Young, Louise M. CARLYLE AND THE ART OF HISTORY. Philadelphia: University of Pennsylvania Press, 1939.

1940

2466 Anon. "Founding of London Library: Carlyle's Speech," TIMES (June 24, 1940), 4.

2467 A[dams], E[lizabeth] L. "Carlyle and the Franklin Tithe-Book," MORE BOOKS, XV (May, 1940), 198.

2468 Baillie, J. B. "Jane Welsh Carlyle," TIMES LITERARY SUP-PLEMENT (April 20, 1940), 195.

2469 Cook, Henry. "Has Carlyle Still a Message?" BAPTIST QUARTERLY, n.s. X (1940), 134-138.

2470 Grierson, Herbert J. C. "Thomas Carlyle," PROCEEDINGS OF THE BRITISH ACADEMY, XXVI (1940), 301-325. Rpt. THOMAS CARLYLE. London: Humphrey Milford, 1940.

2471 _____. "The Hero and the Führer," ABERDEEN UNIVERSITY REVIEW, XXVII (March, 1940), 99-105.

2472 Kimball, LeRoy E. "Thomas Carlyle and Charles Butler of Wall Street," ESSAYS AND STUDIES IN HONOR OF CARLETON BROWN (New York: New York University Press, 1940), 281-295.

2473 Moore, Carlisle. "Thomas Carlyle and Fiction: 1822-1834," NINETEENTH CENTURY STUDIES (Ithaca: Cornell University Press, 1940), 131-177.

2474 Phelps, William L. "Books That Have Changed My Mind,"

ROTARIAN (March, 1940), 38.

2475 Rudman, Harry W. ITALIAN NATIONALISM AND ENGLISH LETTERS. New York: Columbia University Press, 1940.

2476 Shaskolskaya, T. "Dickens and Carlyle," TRANSACTIONS OF THE HERZEN STATE PEDAGOGICAL INSTITUTE (Leningrad), XXIX (1940), 113-120.

2477 Smith, Fred M. "Whitman's Poet-Prophet and Carlyle's Hero," PUBLICATIONS OF THE MODERN LANGUAGE ASSOCIATION, LV (December, 1940), 1146-1164.

2478 Virtue, John. "Carlyle's 'Mr. Symmons,'" STUDIES IN ENGLISH IN HONOR OF R. D. O'LEARY AND S. L. WHITCOMB (Lawrence: University of Kansas Press, 1940), 44-49.

2479 Walker, N. W. G. "Carlyle and the London Library," CHAMBERS'S JOURNAL, 8 sers., IX (December, 1940), 873-875.

1941

2480 Anon. "Carlyle's Sofa--Centenary Gift to London Library," TIMES (January 4, 1941), 6.

2481 _____. "A Century of Book Service. Learning's Debt to the London Library. Thomas Carlyle and Hagberg Wright," TIMES LITERARY SUPPLEMENT (May 3, 1941), 214-215.

2482 Goldberg, Maxwell H. "Jeffrey: Mutilator of Carlyle's 'Burns?'" PUBLICATIONS OF THE MODERN LANGUAGE ASSOCIATION, LVI (June, 1941), 466-471.

2483 Kavanagh, J. "Tales of My Grandfather," ASIATIC REVIEW, n.s. XXXVII (April, 1941), 325-331.

2484 Lea, Frank A. "Carlyle and the French Revolution," ADELPHI, n.s. XVIII (November-December, 1941), 20-24, 36-38.

2485 McGovern, William M. FROM LUTHER TO HITLER: THE HISTORY OF FACIST-NAZI POLITICAL PHILOSOPHY. Boston:

Houghton Mifflin, 1941.

2486 Nevinson, Henry W. "Carlyle and the London Library," NEW STATESMAN AND NATION, n.s. XXI (May 31, 1941), 556.

2487 Pritchett, Victor S. "Books in General," NEW STATESMAN AND NATION, n.s. XXII (December 6, 1941), 476.

2488 Reilly, Joseph J. "Some Immortal Letters," CATHOLIC WORLD, CLIII (May, 1941), 162-166.

2489 Roberts, W. W. "English Autograph Letters in the John Rylands Library," BULLETIN OF THE JOHN RYLANDS LIBRARY, XXV (1941), 119-136.

2490 Shine, Hill. CARLYLE AND THE SAINT-SIMONIANS: THE CONCEPT OF HISTORICAL PERIODICITY. Baltimore: Johns Hopkins Press, 1941.

2491 Tuell, Anne K. JOHN STERLING: A REPRESENTATIVE VICTORIAN. New York: Macmillan, 1941.

2492 Wentworth, Harold. "The Allegedly Dead Suffix -dom in Modern English," PUBLICATIONS OF THE MODERN LANG-UAGE ASSOCIATION, LVI (March, 1941), 280-306.

2493 Young, Karl. "The Uses of Rare Books and Manuscripts," YALE UNIVERSITY LIBRARY GAZETTE, XVI (October, 1941), 26-38.

1942

2494 Anon. "[Carlyle and Johnson]," NOTES AND QUERIES, CLXXXIII (December 19, 1942), 361.

2495 Page, Frederick. "'Balder Dead (1855),'" ESSAYS AND STUDIES, XXVIII (1942), 60-68.

2496 Rubin, Joseph J. "Carlyle on Contemporary Style," MOD-ERN LANGUAGE NOTES, LVII (May, 1942), 362-363.

2497   Sanders, Charles R. COLERIDGE AND THE BROAD CHURCH MOVEMENT. Durham: Duke University Press, 1942.

2498   Smith, Fred M. "Whitman's Debt to Carlyle's Sartor Resartus," MODERN LANGUAGE QUARTERLY, III (March, 1942), 51-65.

2499   Thompson, James W., and Bernard J. Holm. A HISTORY OF HISTORICAL WRITING. New York: Macmillan, 1942.

2500   Witte, William. "Carlyle as a Critic of German Literature," ABERDEEN UNIVERSITY REVIEW, XXIX (Spring, 1942), 105-113. Rpt. SCHILLER AND BURNS AND OTHER ESSAYS. Oxford: Blackwell, 1959.

2501   Young, Fredk S. "Carlyle and the Constellations," NOTES AND QUERIES, CLXXXII (April 11, 1942), 207.

1943

2502   Anon. "[Emerson, Thoreau, and Lowell on Carlyle]," NOTES AND QUERIES, CLXXXV (September 25, 1943), 181.

2503   ____. "[Carlyle's Genius]," NOTES AND QUERIES, CLXXXV (October 23, 1943), 241.

2504   ____. "The Lost Prophet," TIMES LITERARY SUPPLEMENT (November 27, 1943), 571.

2505   ____. "[Carlyle's Temper]," NOTES AND QUERIES, CLXXXV (December 18, 1943), 361-362.

2506   Barzun, Jacques. ROMANTICISM AND THE MODERN EGO. Boston: Little Brown, 1943. See also CLASSIC, ROMANTIC AND MODERN. Boston: Little Brown, 1961.

2507   Fiedler, H. G. "The Friendship of Thomas Carlyle and Varnhagen von Ense, with a Letter Hitherto Unknown," MODERN LANGUAGE REVIEW, XXXVIII (January, 1943), 32-37.

2508   Lea, Frank A. CARLYLE: PROPHET OF TO-DAY. London: Routledge, 1943.

2509   Mais, Stuart P. B. "The Scotland of Thomas Carlyle," SMT
        MAGAZINE, XXXI (March, 1943), 11-13, 42, 45.

2510   McKeehan, Irene P. "Carlyle, Hitler, and Emerson: A
        Comparison of Political Theories," UNIVERSITY OF COLORA-
        DO STUDIES, SERIES B. STUDIES IN THE HUMANITIES, II
        (May, 1943), 1-29.

2511   MEMORABILIST [pseud.]. "Richard Holt Hutton and Carlyle,"
        NOTES AND QUERIES, CLXXXV (July 31, 1943), 76.

2512   _____. "Carlyle and Indian Corn," NOTES AND QUERIES,
        CLXXXV (September 11, 1943), 164.

2513   _____. "Tennyson and Carlyle," NOTES AND QUERIES,
        CLXXXV (September 11, 1943), 166-167.

2514   _____. "Browning as Carlyle's Boswell," NOTES AND
        QUERIES, CLXXXV (December 18, 1943), 374-375.

2515   Moore, Carlisle. "Carlyle's 'Diamond Necklace' and Poetic
        History," PUBLICATIONS OF THE MODERN LANGUAGE
        ASSOCIATION, LVIII (June, 1943), 537-557.

2516   Price, Fanny. "Jowett on Carlyle," NOTES AND QUERIES,
        CLXXXV (July 17, 1943), 45-46.

2517   Rowse, A. L. "The Message of Past and Present," NEW
        STATESMAN AND NATION, XXV (June 5, 1943), 370.

2518   Salomon, Richard. "Notes and Carlyle's Journey to Germany,
        Autumn 1858," MODERN LANGUAGE NOTES, LVIII (Janu-
        ary, 1943), 67-69.

2519   Schreiber, Carl F. "Carlyle's Goethe Mask," YALE UNIVER-
        SITY LIBRARY GAZETTE, XVIII (October, 1943), 26-29.

2520   Stark, Werner. "Saint-Simon as a Realist," JOURNAL OF
        ECONOMIC HISTORY, III (May, 1943), 42-55.

2521   T., C. "Professor Galbraith on Universities," NOTES AND
        QUERIES, CLXXXV (July 17, 1943), 56.

2522   White, Freda. "The Philistine Scot," NEW STATESMAN AND NATION, XXV (June 12, 1943), 386.

2523   Wright, Cuthbert. "Carlyle and the Present Crisis," COMMONWEAL, XXXVIII (June 18, 1943), 219-221.

1944

2524   Anon. "[Dr. Hensley and Carlyle]," NOTES AND QUERIES, CLXXXVI (February 26, 1944), 105.

2525   ____. "[Browning and Carlyle]," NOTES AND QUERIES, CLXXXVI (May 6, 1944), 215.

2526   ____. "John Sterling as Hero," TIMES LITERARY SUPPLEMENT (September 23, 1944), 463.

2527   B., E. "Wordsworth in Italy," NOTES AND QUERIES, CLXXXVI (January 15, 1944), 48.

2528   Bentley, Eric R. "Modern Hero-Worship: Notes on Carlyle, Nietzsche, and Stefan George," SEWANEE REVIEW, LII (Summer, 1944), 441-456.

2529   ____. A CENTURY OF HERO-WORSHIP. Philadelphia: J. B. Lippincott, 1944. See also THE CULT OF THE SUPERMAN. London: Robert Hale, 1947.

2530   Deaton, Mary B. "Thomas Carlyle's Use of Metaphor," COLLEGE ENGLISH, V (March, 1944), 314-318.

2531   Parry, John J. "A Plea for Better Anthologies," COLLEGE ENGLISH, V (March, 1944), 318-324.

2532   Reilly, Joseph J. "Jane Carlyle Appraises Her Contemporaries," CATHOLIC WORLD, CLVIII (February, 1944), 443-451.

2533   Strout, Alan L. "Some Unpublished Letters of John Gibson Lockhart to John Wilson Croker," NOTES AND QUERIES, CLXXXVII (November 18, 1944), 225-227.

2534   T., C. "G. F. Watts and Carlyle," NOTES AND QUERIES,
       CLXXXVI (February 26, 1944), 114-115.

2535   Wellek, René. "Carlyle and the Philosophy of History,"
       PHILOLOGICAL QUARTERLY, XXIII (January, 1944), 55-
       76. Rpt. CONFRONTATIONS. Princeton: Princeton Uni-
       versity Press, 1965.

1945

2536   Ballard, A. E. "Carlyle's Birthplace," SMT MAGAZINE,
       XXXVI (December, 1945), 35-36.

2537   Bentley, Eric R. "The Premature Death of Thomas Carlyle
       (1795-1945): An Obituary and a Footnote," AMERICAN
       SCHOLAR, XV (Winter, 1945), 69-76.

2538   Ethlinger, L. "Carlyle on the Portraits of Frederick the
       Great. An Unpublished Letter," MODERN LANGUAGE
       REVIEW, XL (October, 1945), 259-265.

2539   G[rantham], E[velyn]. "A Gift from Carlyle to Boston,"
       MORE BOOKS, XX (September, 1945), 318.

2540   James, Lionel. A FORGOTTEN GENIUS: SEWELL OF ST.
       COLUMBA'S AND RADLEY. London: Faber and Faber,
       1945.

2541   Molony, J. Chartres. "The Fall of an Idol: Effect on
       Carlyle's Fame of His Reminiscences and Froude's Biography,"
       BLACKWOOD'S MAGAZINE, CCLVII (June, 1945), 411-420.

2542   Schapiro, J. Salwyn. "Thomas Carlyle: Prophet of
       Fascism," JOURNAL OF MODERN HISTORY, XVII (June,
       1945), 97-115.

2543   W., L. B. "Is Thy Servant a Dog," NOTES AND QUERIES,
       CLXXXVIII (May 19, 1945), 212.

1946

2544   Anon. "[Carlyle on His Contemporaries]," NEW YORK TIMES
       (June 16, 1946), 2, Section VII.

2545   . "[Carlyle on Voting]," NEW YORK TIMES (October 27, 1946), 35, Section VI.

2546   Cassirer, Ernst. THE MYTH OF THE STATE. New Haven: Yale University Press, 1946.

2547   Crow, Martin M. "The Hero as Desperado," LIBRARY CHRONICLE OF THE UNIVERSITY OF TEXAS, II (Spring, 1946), 3-16.

2548   Foot, Isaac. MICHAEL VERRAN AND THOMAS CARLYLE. London: Epworth Press, 1946.

2549   Goldberg, Maxwell H. "Carlyle, Pictet, and Jeffrey," MODERN LANGUAGE QUARTERLY, VII (September, 1946), 291-296.

2550   Kiely, Benedict. "Comment on Carlyle," IRISH ECCLESI-ASTICAL RECORD, LXVII (April, 1946), 223-231.

2551   Kirby, Thomas A. "Carlyle on Chaucer," MODERN LANG-UAGE NOTES, LXI (March, 1946), 184-185.

2552   . "Carlyle and Irving," JOURNAL OF ENGLISH LITERARY HISTORY, XIII (March, 1946), 59-63.

2553   Munford, W. A. "Carlyle and the Twentieth Century," LIBRARY REVIEW, no. 79 (Autumn, 1946), 157-159.

2554   Schilling, Bernard N. HUMAN DIGNITY AND THE GREAT VICTORIANS. New York: Columbia University Press, 1946.

1947

2555   Anon. "[Henry James and Carlyle]," NOTES AND QUER-IES, CXCII (April 5, 1947), 133.

2556   Blackburn, William. "Carlyle and the Composition of The Life of John Sterling," STUDIES IN PHILOLOGY, XLIV (October, 1947), 672-687.

2557   Carr, C. T. "Carlyle's Translations from German," MODERN LANGUAGE REVIEW, XLII (April, 1947), 223-232.

2558   Christian, Mildred G. "Carlyle's Influence Upon the Social
       Theory of Dickens," TROLLOPIAN, I (March, 1947), 27-
       35; II (June, 1948), 11-26.

2559   Esher. "'Nie Pozwalam,'" TIMES (September 3, 1947), 5.

2560   Kirby, Thomas A. "Carlyle, Fitzgerald, and the Naseby
       Project," MODERN LANGUAGE QUARTERLY, VIII (Sept-
       ember, 1947), 364-366.

2561   T[inker], C[hauncey] B. "Gabriel Wells," YALE UNIVER-
       SITY GAZETTE, XXI (April, 1947), 53-54.

                              1948

2562   Anon. "With Admiration and Love," COLBY LIBRARY
       QUARTERLY, sers. 2, no. 6 (May, 1948), 85-108.

2563   Brown, Theressa W. "Froude's Life of Thomas Carlyle,"
       IF BY YOUR ART: TESTAMENT TO PERCIVAL HUNT. Ed.
       Agnes L. Starrett (Pittsburgh: University of Pittsburgh Press,
       1948), 110-116.

2564   Bryant, Arthur. "[Latter-Day Pamphlets]," ILLUSTRATED
       LONDON NEWS, CCXII (June 26, 1948), 706.

2565   Chew, Samuel C. "Thomas Carlyle," A LITERARY HISTORY
       OF ENGLAND. Ed. Albert C. Baugh (New York: Appleton-
       Century-Crofts, 1948), 1309-1321.

2566   D., T. C. "Carlyle and 'Pickwick,'" NOTES AND QUER-
       IES, CXCIII (January 24, 1948), 40.

2567   Ford, George H. "The Governor Eyre Case in England,"
       UNIVERSITY OF TORONTO QUARTERLY, XVII (April,
       1948), 219-233.

2568   Jackson, Holbrook. DREAMERS OF DREAMS: THE RISE AND
       FALL OF 19th CENTURY IDEALISM. New York: Farrar,
       Straus, 1948.

2569   Kuhn, Helmut. "Carlyle, Ally and Critic of Emerson," EMORY
       UNIVERSITY QUARTERLY, IV (October, 1948), 171-180.

2570   Marchand, Leslie. "The Symington Collection," RUTGERS
UNIVERSITY LIBRARY JOURNAL, XII (December, 1948), 1-15.

2571   Obertello, Alfredo. CARLYLE'S CRITICAL THEORIES: THEIR
ORIGIN AND PRACTICE. Genova: Edizioni L. U. P. A.,
1948.

1949

2572   Anon. "The Two Carlyles," TIMES LITERARY SUPPLEMENT
(December 30, 1949), 857.

2573   Altick, Richard D. "Dickens and America: Some Unpublished
Letters," PENNSYLVANIA MAGAZINE OF HISTORY AND
BIOGRAPHY, LXXIII (July, 1949), 326-336.

2574   Calder, Grace J. THE WRITING OF PAST AND PRESENT.
New Haven: Yale University Press, 1949.

2575   Chillingworth, H. R. "Thomas Carlyle," HERMATHENA,
no. LXXIII (Mary, 1949), 25-32.

2576   Gallup, Donald. "Two Old Letters," YALE UNIVERSITY
LIBRARY GAZETTE, XXIV (July, 1949), 21-24.

2577   Halliday, James L. MR. CARLYLE MY PATIENT: A PSY-
CHOSOMATIC BIOGRAPHY. London: William Heinemann,
1949.

2578   Lindsay, Jack. "A Tale of Two Cities," LIFE AND LETTERS
TODAY, LXII (September, 1949), 191-204.

2579   Meikle, Henry W. "Two Letters of Jane Welsh Carlyle,"
SCOTTISH HISTORICAL REVIEW, XXVIII (April, 1949), 55-
58.

2580   Parish, Clement W. "Mrs. Carlyle Discovers Rottingdean,"
SUSSEX COUNTY MAGAZINE, XXIII (March, 1949), 86-88.

2581   Willey, Basil. NINETEENTH CENTURY STUDIES. New York:
Columbia University Press, 1949.

1950

2582 Anon. "[Lady Ashburton and Carlyle]," NOTES AND QUER-
IES, CXCV (December 9, 1950), 529.

2583 Baker, Joseph E. THE REINTERPRETATION OF VICTORIAN
LITERATURE. Princeton: Princeton University Press, 1950.

2584 Burke, Kenneth. A RHETORIC OF MOTIVES. New York:
Prentice-Hall, 1950.

2585 Gray, J. "Ordeal of a Difficult Marriage," SATURDAY RE-
VIEW OF LITERATURE, XXXIII (July 8, 1950), 15.

2586 Hughes, Glenn. MRS. CARLYLE: A HISTORICAL PLAY.
Seattle: University of Washington Press, 1950.

2587 Irving, William. "Carlyle and T. H. Huxley," BOOKER
MEMORIAL STUDIES (Chapel Hill: University of North Carolina Press, 1950), 104-121.

2588 Kent, William. "Names Inscribed on Window Glass,"
NOTES AND QUERIES, CXCV (August 19, 1950), 371.

2589 Origo, Iris. "The Carlyles and the Ashburtons: A Victorian
Friendship," CORNHILL MAGAZINE, CLXIV (Autumn, 1950),
441-483. Rpt. A MEASURE OF LOVE. London: Jonathan
Cape, 1957.

2590 Pritchett, Victor S. "[Jane Welsh Carlyle as Letter Writer],"
NEW STATESMAN AND NATION, XXXIX (February 4,
1950), 134.

2591 Shine, Hill. "Carlyle's Early Writings and Herder's Ideen:
The Concept of History," BOOKER MEMORIAL STUDIES
(Chapel Hill: University of North Carolina Press, 1950), 3-33.

2592 Templeman, William D. "Tennyson's 'Locksley Hall' and
Thomas Carlyle," BOOKER MEMORIAL STUDIES (Chapel Hill:
University of North Carolina Press, 1950), 34-59.

2593 Warren, Alba H. ENGLISH POETIC THEORY: 1825-1865.
Princeton: Princeton University Press, 1950.

1951

2594   Buckley, Jerome H. THE VICTORIAN TEMPER. Cambridge: Harvard University Press, 1951.

2595   Flournoy, F. R. "Thomas Carlyle, 1795-1881," SOME MODERN HISTORIANS OF BRITAIN: ESSAYS IN HONOR OF R. L. SCHUYLER. Ed. Herman Ausubel et al. (New York: Dryden Press, 1951), 35-48.

2596   House, Humphrey. "The Sage Who Despised Politicians," LISTENER, XLVI (December 13, 1951), 1009-1010.

2597   Lloyd, J. E. "Victorian Writers and the Great Exhibition," NOTES AND QUERIES, CXCVI (December 22, 1951), 565-566.

2598   Peckham, Morse. "Toward a Theory of Romanticism," PUBLICATIONS OF THE MODERN LANGUAGE ASSOCIATION, LXVI (March, 1951), 5-23.

2599   Short, Clarice. "Edward Fitzgerald on Some Fellow Victorians," WESTERN HUMANITIES REVIEW, V (Autumn, 1951), 373-378.

2600   Stark, Lewis M., and Robert W. Hill. "The Bequest of Mary Stillman Harkness," BULLETIN OF THE NEW YORK PUBLIC LIBRARY, LV (May, 1951), 213-224.

1952

2601   Anon. "The Carlyles," TIMES LITERARY SUPPLEMENT (February 15, 1952), 124.

2602   Adrian, Arthur A. "Dickens on American Slavery: A Carlylean Slant," PUBLICATIONS OF THE MODERN LANGUAGE ASSOCIATION, LXVII (June, 1952), 315-329.

2603   Annan, Noel. "Historians Reconsidered: IX. Carlyle," HISTORY TODAY, II (October, 1952), 659-665.

2604   Bett, W. R. THE INFIRMITIES OF GENIUS. New York: Philosophical Library, 1952.

2605   Burtis, Mary E. MONCURE CONWAY, 1832-1907. New Brunswick: Rutgers University Press, 1952.

2606   Estrich, Robert M., and Hans Sperber. THREE KEYS TO LANGUAGE. New York: Rinehart, 1952.

2607   Filler, Louis. "Parrington and Carlyle: Cross-Currents in History and Belles-Lettres," ANTIOCH REVIEW, XII (Summer, 1952), 203-216.

2608   Gascoyne, David. THOMAS CARLYLE. London: Longmans, Green, 1952.

2609   Hanson, Lawrence and Elisabeth. NECESSARY EVIL: THE LIFE OF JANE WELSH CARLYLE. London: Constable, 1952.

2610   Hayek, Frederick A. von. THE COUNTER-REVOLUTION OF SCIENCES: STUDIES ON THE ABUSE OF REASON. Glencoe, Illinois: Free Press, 1952.

2611   Himmelfarb, Gertrude. "The Carlyles at Home," AMERICAN MERCURY, LXXV (August, 1952), 116-119.

2612   Martin, Robert B. "Coventry Patmore," PRINCETON UNIVERSITY LIBRARY CHRONICLE, XIV (1952), 47-49.

2613   Maynard, T. "Sartor Resartus," COMMONWEAL, LVII (October 17, 1952), 43-44.

2614   Morrison, M. Brysson. "When Thomas Carlyle Met Jane Welsh," SCOTS MAGAZINE, LVI (March, 1952), 480-485.

2615   Reynolds, M. M. "A New Letter of Jane Welsh Carlyle," TIMES LITERARY SUPPLEMENT (March 28, 1952), 221.

2616   Rogers, William H. "A Study in Contrasts: Carlyle and Macaulay as Book Reviewers," FLORIDA STATE UNIVERSITY STUDIES, V (1952), 1-9.

2617   Slater, Joseph L. "George Ripley and Thomas Carlyle," PUBLICATIONS OF THE MODERN LANGUAGE ASSOCIATION, LXVII (June, 1952), 341-349.

2618   Stebbins, Lucy P. LONDON LADIES. New York: Columbia

University Press, 1952.

2619   Symons, Julian A. THOMAS CARLYLE: THE LIFE AND IDEAS OF A PROPHET. New York: Oxford University Press, 1952.

1953

2620   Anon. "To Goodykin, from a Genius," TIME MAGAZINE, LXII (July 13, 1953), 98.

2621   ____. "Carlyle's House in Chelsea--Pilgrimage Small But Steady," TIMES (September 1, 1953), 8.

2622   ____. "The People Next Door," TIMES (October 6, 1953), 9.

2623   Abrams, Meyer H. THE MIRROR AND THE LAMP. New York: Oxford University Press, 1953.

2624   Brooks, Elmer L. "B. W. Procter and the Genius of Carlyle's Frederick the Great," HARVARD LIBRARY BULLE-TIN, VII (Winter, 1953), 134-136.

2625   Burchell, Samuel C. "The Approaching Darkness: A Victorian Father to His Son," YALE UNIVERSITY LIBRARY GAZETTE, XXVIII (July, 1953), 27-32.

2626   Davies, W. R. "Can Carlyle Be Resurrected?" SATURDAY NIGHT, LXIX (October 31, 1953), 16-17.

2627   Holloway, John. THE VICTORIAN SAGE. London: Macmillan, 1953.

2628   LeRoy, Gaylord C. PERPLEXED PROPHETS: SIX NINETEENTH-CENTURY BRITISH AUTHORS. Philadelphia: University of Pennsylvania Press, 1953.

2629   Majut, R. "Georg Büchner and Some English Thinkers," MODERN LANGUAGE REVIEW, XLVIII (July, 1953), 310-322.

2630   Paul, Leslie. THE ENGLISH PHILOSOPHERS. London: Faber and Faber, 1953.

2631   Pritchett, Victor S. "[Carlyle's Letters]," NEW STATES-
MAN AND NATION, n.s. XLV (January 24, 1953), 96-97.

2632   _____. BOOKS IN GENERAL. London: Chatto and Windus, 1953.

2633   Rinehart, Keith. "Carlyle's Sartor Resartus," EXPLICATOR,
XI (March, 1953), item 32.

2634   Sanders, Charles R. THE STRACHEY FAMILY. Durham:
Duke University Press, 1953.

2635   Shine, Hill. CARLYLE'S EARLY READING TO 1834. Lexing-
ton: University of Kentucky Libraries, 1953.

2636   T., C. "Carlyle and Swinburne," NOTES AND QUERIES,
CXCVIII (February, 1953), 85.

2637   Taylor, Alan J. P. "The Art of Writing History," LISTENER,
L (July 16, 1953), 108-109.

2638   _____. "[Carlyle as Writer]," NEW STATESMAN AND
NATION, XLV (April 18, 1953), 459-460.

2639   Williams, Raymond. "The Idea of Culture," ESSAYS IN
CRITICISM, III (July, 1953), 239-266.

1954

2640   Anon. "[Carlyle Letter]," NOTES AND QUERIES, CXCIX
(September, 1954), 369.

2641   Briggs, Asa. VICTORIAN PEOPLE. London: Odhams Press,
1954.

2642   Calder, Grace J. "Carlyle and 'Irving's London Circle':
Some Unpublished Letters by Thomas Carlyle and Mrs. Edward
Strachey," PUBLICATIONS OF THE MODERN LANGUAGE
ASSOCIATION, LXIX (December, 1954), 1135-1149.

2643   Eidson, John O. "Charles Stearns Wheeler: Emerson's 'Good

Grecian,'" NEW ENGLAND QUARTERLY, XXVII (December, 1954), 472-483.

2644 Fielding, Kenneth J. "Carlyle, Charles Dickens, and William Maccall," NOTES AND QUERIES, CXCIX (November, 1954), 488-490.

2645 King, Marjorie P. "'Illudo Chartis': An Initial Study in Carlyle's Mode of Composition," MODERN LANGUAGE REVIEW, XLIX (April, 1954), 164-175.

2646 Liptzin, Solomon. THE ENGLISH LEGEND OF HEINRICH HEINE. New York: Bloch, 1954.

2647 Rinehart, Keith. "The Victorian Approach to Autobiography," MODERN PHILOLOGY, LI (February, 1954), 177-186.

2648 Sanders, Charles R. "Carlyle's Letters," VICTORIAN NEWSLETTER, no. 5 (April, 1954), 6.

2649 Strout, Alan L. "Writers on German Literature in Blackwood's Magazine, With a Footnote on Thomas Carlyle," LIBRARY, sers. 5, IX (March, 1954), 35-44.

2650 Tillotson, Kathleen. NOVELS OF THE EIGHTEEN-FORTIES. Oxford: Clarendon Press, 1954.

1955

2651 Fain, John T. "Word Echoes in Past and Present," VICTORIAN NEWSLETTER, no. 8 (Autumn, 1955), 5-6.

2652 Fish, Howard M. "Five Emerson Letters," AMERICAN LITERATURE, XXVII (March, 1955), 25-30.

2653 Geyl, Pieter. USE AND ABUSE OF HISTORY. New Haven: Yale University Press, 1955. See also DEBATES WITH HISTORIANS. Groningen: J. B. Wolters, 1955.

2654 Moore, Carlisle. "Sartor Resartus and the Problem of Carlyle's 'Conversion,'" PUBLICATIONS OF THE MODERN LANGUAGE ASSOCIATION, LXX (September, 1955), 662-681.

2655   Nobbe, Susanne H. "Four Unpublished Letters of Thomas
Carlyle," PUBLICATIONS OF THE MODERN LANGUAGE
ASSOCIATION, LXX (September, 1955), 876-884.

2656   Parker, W. M. "Dean Milman and The Quarterly Review,"
QUARTERLY REVIEW, CCXCIII (January, 1955), 30-43.

2657   Sanders, Charles R. "Carlyle's Letters," BULLETIN OF THE
JOHN RYLANDS LIBRARY, XXXVIII (September, 1955),
199-224.

2658   Simpson, Dwight J. "Carlyle and Natural Law," HISTORY
OF IDEAS NEWS LETTER, I (June, 1955), 10-12.

2659   Tillotson, Kathleen. "Arnold and Carlyle," NOTES AND
QUERIES, CC (March, 1955), 126.

2660   Watt, W. Montgomery. "Carlyle on Muhammad," HIBBERT
JOURNAL, LIII (April, 1955), 247-254.

2661   Wellek, René. A HISTORY OF MODERN CRITICISM. Vol.
III. New Haven: Yale University Press, 1955.

1956

2662   Anon. "The Carlylean Vision," TIMES LITERARY SUPPLE-
MENT (February 3, 1956), 61-62.

2663   _____. "Matthew Arnold and Carlyle," TIMES (May 24,
1956), 12.

2664   Allott, Kenneth. "An Arnold-Clough Letter: References to
Carlyle and Tennyson," NOTES AND QUERIES, CCI (June,
1956), 267.

2665   Duckett, Margaret. "Carlyle, 'Columbus' and Joaquin
Miller," PHILOLOGICAL QUARTERLY, XXXV (October,
1956), 443-447.

2666   Dunn, Waldo H. "Carlyle's Last Letters to Froude," TWEN-
TIETH CENTURY, CLIX (January-June, 1956), 44-53, 255-
263, 591-597; CLX (September, 1956), 241-246.

2667 Gooch, George P. "Some Great English Historians," CONTEMPORARY REVIEW, CXC (December, 1956), 344-349; CXCI (January, 1957), 19-24.

2668 Greenberg, Robert A. "A Possible Source of Tennyson's 'Tooth and Claw,'" MODERN LANGUAGE NOTES, LXXI (November, 1956), 491-492.

2669 Kegel, Charles H. "An Uncertain Biographical Fact," VICTORIAN NEWSLETTER, no. 10 (Autumn, 1956), 19.

2670 Krause, Anna. "Unamuno and Tennyson," COMPARATIVE LITERATURE, VIII (Spring, 1956), 122-135.

2671 Pearsall, Ronald. "Carlyle and Emerson: Horses and Revolutions," SOUTH ATLANTIC QUARTERLY, LV (April, 1956), 179-191.

2672 Quennell, Peter. "Noble Savage," SPECTATOR, CXCVI (February 10, 1956), 188-189.

2673 S., C. E. "Frederick's Grenadiers," NOTES AND QUERIES, CCI (June, 1956), 270.

2674 Sanders, Charles R. "The Question of Carlyle's 'Conversion,'" VISTORIAN NEWSLETTER, no. 10 (Autumn, 1956), 10-12.

2675 Symons, Julian A. "The Carlylean Vision," TIMES LITERARY SUPPLEMENT (February 10, 1956), 85.

2676 Taylor, Alan J. P. ENGLISHMEN AND OTHERS. London: H. Hamilton, 1956.

2677 Tillotson, Kathleen. "Matthew Arnold and Carlyle," PROCEEDINGS OF THE BRITISH ACADEMY, XLII (1956), 133-153.

2678 Worth, George C. "Three Carlyle Documents," PUBLICATIONS OF THE MODERN LANGUAGE ASSOCIATION, LXXI (June, 1956), 542-544.

1957

CARLYLE BIBLIOGRAPHY

2679 Anon. "Letters of Ruskin and Carlyle," BULLETIN OF THE
      JOHN RYLANDS LIBRARY, XL (September, 1957), 3-4.

2680 Adrian, Arthur A. "Dean Stanley's Report of Conversations
      with Carlyle," VICTORIAN STUDIES, I (September, 1957),
      72-74.

2681 Altick, Richard D. THE ENGLISH COMMON READER.
      Chicago: University of Chicago Press, 1957.

2682 Blair, Walter. "The French Revolution and Huckleberry Finn,"
      MODERN PHILOLOGY, LV (August, 1957), 21-35.

2683 Burd, Van Akin. "Ruskin's Antidote for Carlyle's Purges,"
      BOSTON UNIVERSITY STUDIES IN ENGLISH, III (Spring,
      1957), 51-57.

2684 Cecil, David. THE FINE ART OF READING, AND OTHER
      LITERARY STUDIES. Indianapolis: Bobbs-Merrill, 1957.

2685 Dickins, Louis G. "The Friendship of Dickens and Carlyle,"
      DICKENSIAN, LIII (May, 1957), 98-106.

2686 Gordon, Robert C. "A Victorian Anticipation of Recent
      Scott Criticism," PHILOLOGICAL QUARTERLY, XXXVI
      (April, 1957), 272-275.

2687 Houghton, Walter. THE VICTORIAN FRAME OF MIND. New
      Haven: Yale University Press, 1957.

2688 Langbaum, Robert W. THE POETRY OF EXPERIENCE. London:
      Chatto and Windus, 1957.

2689 Moore, Carlisle. "The Persistence of Carlyle's 'Everlasting
      Yea,'" MODERN PHILOLOGY, LIV (February, 1957), 187-
      196.

2690 _____. "Carlyle's Resartus," VICTORIAN NEWSLETTER, no.
      12 (Autumn, 1957), 11-13.

2691 Pankhurst, Richard K. P. THE SAINT SIMONIANS: MILL
      AND CARLYLE. London: Sidgwick and Jackson, 1957.

212

2692 Roellinger, Francis X. "The Early Development of Carlyle's Style," PUBLICATIONS OF THE MODERN LANGUAGE ASSOCIATION, LXXII (December, 1957), 936-951.

2693 Sanders, Charles R. "The Victorian Rembrandt: Carlyle's Portraits of His Contemporaries," BULLETIN OF THE JOHN RYLANDS LIBRARY, XXXIX (March, 1957), 521-557.

2694 Straka, Gerald M. "The Spirit of Carlyle in the Old South," HISTORIAN, XX (November, 1957), 39-57.

2695 Sutherland, James R. ON ENGLISH PROSE. Toronto: University of Toronto Press, 1957.

1958

2696 Anon. "Visit to Mrs. Carlyle--A Victorian Lady Who Knew All About Do-It-Yourself," TIMES (May 24, 1958), 8.

2697 Ben-Israel, Hedva. "Carlyle and the French Revolution," HISTORICAL JOURNAL, I (1958), 115-135.

2698 Clark, Alexander. "The Manuscript Collections of the Princeton University Library," PRINCETON UNIVERSITY LIBRARY CHRONICLE, XIX (Spring-Summer, 1958), 159-160.

2699 Cooke, Alice L. "Whitman as a Critic: Democratic Vistas with Special Reference to Carlyle," WALT WHITMAN NEWS-LETTER, IV (June, 1958), 91-95.

2700 Cooper, Berenice. "A Comparison of Quintus Fixlein and Sartor Resartus," TRANSACTIONS OF THE WISCONSIN ACADEMY OF SCIENCES, ARTS, AND LETTERS, XLVIII (1958), 253-272.

2701 Fraser, Russell A. "Shooting Niagara in the Novels of Thackeray and Trollope," MODERN LANGUAGE QUARTERLY, XIX (June, 1958), 141-146.

2702 Gragg, Wilson B. "Trollope and Carlyle," NINETEENTH-CENTURY FICTION, XIII (December, 1958), 266-270.

2703   Kaye, Julian B. BERNARD SHAW AND THE NINETEENTH
        CENTURY TRADITION. Norman: University of Oklahoma
        Press, 1958.

2704   Kegel, Charles H. "William Cobbett and Malthusianism,"
        JOURNAL OF THE HISTORY OF IDEAS, XIX (June, 1958),
        348-362.

2705   Kennedy, William F. HUMANIST VERSUS ECONOMIST:
        THE ECONOMIC THOUGHT OF SAMUEL TAYLOR COLE-
        RIDGE. Berkeley: University of California Press, 1958.

2706   Mackerness, E. D. "The Voice of Prophecy: Carlyle and
        Ruskin," FROM DICKENS TO HARDY. Ed. Boris Ford
        (Harmondsworth, England: Penguin Books, 1958), 294-308.

2707   Nowell-Smith, Simon, et al. ENGLISH LIBRARIES: 1800-
        1850. London: H. K. Lewis, 1958.

2708   Pennington, D. H. "Cromwell and the Historians,"
        HISTORY TODAY, VIII (September, 1958), 598-605.

2709   Rollins, Hyder E. "Charles Eliot Norton and Froude,"
        JOURNAL OF ENGLISH AND GERMANIC PHILOLOGY,
        LVII (October, 1958), 651-664.

2710   Sanders, Charles R. "Carlyle's Letters to Ruskin: A Finding
        List with Some Unpublished Letters and Comments," BULLE-
        TIN OF THE JOHN RYLANDS LIBRARY, XLI (September,
        1958), 208-238.

2711   Shine, Hill. "Thomas Carlyle," VICTORIAN NEWSLETTER,
        no. 13 (Spring, 1958), 22.

2712   Slater, Joseph L. "Goethe, Carlyle, and the Open Secret,"
        ANGLIA, LXXVI (1958), 422-426.

2713   Welsh, Alexander. "A Melville Debt to Carlyle," MODERN
        LANGUAGE NOTES, LXXIII (November, 1958), 489-491.

2714   Williams, Raymond. CULTURE AND SOCIETY: 1780-1950.
        New York: Columbia University Press, 1958.

1959

2715   Altick, Richard D. "Browning's 'Transcendentalism,'" JOURNAL OF ENGLISH AND GERMANIC PHILOLOGY, LVIII (January, 1959), 24-28.

2716   Bell, Richard. CARLYLE'S RELIGIOUS INFLUENCE (Edinburgh: Carlyle Society, 1959), 1-8.

2717   Calder, Grace J. "Erasmus A. Darwin: Friend of Thomas and Jane Carlyle," MODERN LANGUAGE QUARTERLY, XX (March, 1959), 36-48.

2718   Crocker, Stephen F. "Watson Doctors the Venerable Bede," BAKER STREET JOURNAL, IX (July, 1959), 157-164.

2719   Ericson, Eston E. "An American Indebtedness to Carlyle," NOTES AND QUERIES, CCIV (December, 1959), 456-457.

2720   Faverty, Frederic E. YOUR LITERARY HERITAGE. Philadelphia: J. B. Lippincott, 1959.

2721   Jacobs, Willis D. "Carlyle and Mill," CEA CRITIC, XXI (February, 1959), 5.

2722   Marshall, George O. "An Incident from Carlyle in Tennyson's 'Maude,'" NOTES AND QUERIES, CCIV (February, 1959), 77-78.

2723   Maurer, Oscar. "'My Squeamish Public': Some Problems of Victorian Magazine Publishers and Editors," STUDIES IN BIBLIOGRAPHY, XII (1959), 21-40.

2724   Peters, Robert L. "Some Illustrations of Carlyle's Symbolist Imagery," VICTORIAN NEWSLETTER, no. 16 (Fall, 1959), 31-34.

2725   Saunders, Beatrice. PORTRAITS OF GENIUS. London: John Murray, 1959.

2726   Timko, Michael. "Arthur Hugh Clough: A Portrait Retouched," VICTORIAN NEWSLETTER, no. 15 (Spring, 1959), 24-27.

2727   Toole, William B. "Carlyle's Sartor Resartus, II, ix,"
EXPLICATOR, XVII (June, 1959), item 65.

2728   Witte, William. "Carlyle's Conversion," THE ERA OF
GOETHE: ESSAYS PRESENTED TO JAMES BOYD (Oxford:
Blackwell, 1959), 179-193.

2729   _____. SCHILLER AND BURNS AND OTHER ESSAYS. Oxford: Blackwell, 1959.

1960

2730   Anon. "Carlyle's House in Cheyne Row," TIMES (February
25, 1960), 8.

2731   _____. "[Carlyle and His Wife]," TIMES (February 27, 1960),
7.

2732   Ausubel, Herman. IN HARD TIMES: REFORMERS AMONG
THE LATE VICTORIANS. New York: Columbia University
Press, 1960.

2733   Deneau, Daniel P. "Relationship of Style and Device in
Sartor Resartus," VICTORIAN NEWSLETTER, no. 17 (Spring,
1960), 17-20.

2734   Hart, Francis R. "Boswell and the Romantics: A Chapter in
the History of Biographical Theory," JOURNAL OF ENGLISH
LITERARY HISTORY, XXVII (March, 1960), 44-65.

2735   Hendrick, George. "William Sloane Kennedy Stalks
Carlyle," EMERSON SOCIETY QUARTERLY, no. 19 (II
Quarter, 1960), 19-20.

2736   Jones, Joseph. "Carlyle, Whitman, and The Democratic
Dilemma," ENGLISH STUDIES IN AFRICA, III (September,
1960), 179-197.

2737   Lindberg, John. "The Artistic Unity of Sartor Resartus,"
VICTORIAN NEWSLETTER, no. 17 (Spring, 1960), 20-23.

2738   Lochhead, Marion. "Jane Welsh Carlyle," QUARTERLY

REVIEW, CCXCVIII (July, 1960), 321-332.

2739 Moers, Ellen. THE DANDY: BRUMMELL TO BEERBOHM.
London: Secker and Warburg, 1960.

2740 Richardson, Joanna. "The Carlyles of Cheyne Row," LIS-
TENER, LXIII (March 24, 1960), 548.

2741 Sanders, Charles R. "Carlyle, Browning, and the Nature of
a Poet," EMORY UNIVERSITY QUARTERLY, XVI (Winter,
1960), 197-209.

1961

2742 Agnihotri, Surendra H. "The Philosophy of Carlyle as
Revealed in Sartor Resartus," ARYAN PATH, XXXII (May,
1961), 219-224.

2743 Dunn, Waldo H. JAMES ANTHONY FROUDE: A BIOGRA-
PHY. 2 vols. Oxford: Clarendon Press, 1961-1963.

2744 Finlayson, C. P. "Thomas Carlyle's Borrowings from Edinburgh
University Library, 1819-1820," BIBLIOTHECK, III (1961),
138-143.

2745 Kegel, Charles H. "Lord John Manners and the Young England Movement: Romanticism in Politics," WESTERN POLI-
TICAL QUARTERLY, XIV (September, 1961), 691-697.

2746 Malin, James C. "Carlyle's Philosophy of Clothes and
Swendenborg's," SCANDINAVIAN STUDIES, XXXIII (August, 1961), 155-168.

2747 Metzger, Lore. "Sartor Resartus: A Victorian Faust," COM-
PARATIVE LITERATURE, XIII (Fall, 1961), 316-331.

2748 Morris, John W. "Beauchamp's Career: Meredith's Acknow-
ledgement of His Debt to Carlyle," STUDIES IN HONOR OF
JOHN C. HODGES AND ALWIN THALER (Knoxville: University of Tennessee Press, 1961), 101-108.

2749 Ota, Saburo. "Thomas Carlyle's Relation with Modern

Japanese Literature, " STUDIES IN ENGLISH LITERATURE (Tokyo), English Number (1961), 83-95.

2750   Sanders, Charles R. "Retracing Carlyle's Irish Journey (1849)," STUDIES: AN IRISH QUARTERLY REVIEW, L (Spring, 1961), 38-50.

2751   _____. "Carlyle and Tennyson," PUBLICATIONS OF THE MODERN LANGUAGE ASSOCIATION, LXXVI (March, 1961), 82-97.

1962

2752   Anon. "An Evening with Thomas Carlyle's Heroes," TIMES (February 2, 1962), 13.

2753   Kim, Suk-Joo. "A Comparative Study of Emerson and Carlyle," ENGLISH LANGUAGE AND LITERATURE (Korea), XI (June, 1962), 66-75.

2754   Marrs, Edwin W. "Discovery of Some New Carlyle Letters," THOTH, III (Winter, 1962), 3-12.

2755   Peckham, Morse. BEYOND THE TRAGIC VISION. New York: George Braziller, 1962.

2756   Ryals, Clyde De L. "The 'Heavenly Friend': The 'New Mythus' of In Memoriam," PERSONALIST, XLIII (Summer, 1962), 383-402.

2757   Sanders, Charles R. "Carlyle, Poetry, and the Music of Humanity," WESTERN HUMANITIES REVIEW, XVI (Winter, 1962), 53-66.

2758   Semmel, Bernard. JAMAICAN BLOOD AND VICTORIAN CONSCIENCE: THE GOVERNOR EYRE CONTROVERSY. London: Macgibbon and Kee, 1962.

2759   Swart, Koenraad W. "'Individualism' in the Mid-Nineteenth Century (1826-1860)," JOURNAL OF THE HISTORY OF IDEAS, XXIII (January-March, 1962), 77-90.

2760   Weintraub, Wiktor. "Carlyle and Mickiewicz," STUDI
       IN ONORE DI ETIONE LO GATTO E GIOVANNI MAVER
       (Rome: Sansoni, 1962), 719-728.

2761   West, Paul. "Carlyle's Creative Disregard," MELBOURNE
       CRITICAL REVIEW, no. 5 (1962), 16-26.

                              1963

2762   Berger, Harold L. "Carlyle and Emerson--Stylists at Odds,"
       EMERSON SOCIETY QUARTERLY, no. 33 (IV Quarter,
       1963), 61-65.

2763   Brown, T. J. "English Literary Autographs XLVII: Thomas
       Carlyle, 1795-1881," BOOK COLLECTOR, XII (Autumn,
       1963), 339.

2764   Cameron, Kenneth W. "Emerson's Nature and British Swe-
       denborgianism (1840-1841)," EMERSON SOCIETY QUAR-
       TERLY, no. 30 (I Quarter, 1963), 11-89.

2765   Carter, Ray C. "Margaret Fuller and Two Sages," COLBY
       LIBRARY QUARTERLY, sers. 6, no. 5 (March, 1963), 198-
       201.

2766   Cobban, Alfred. "Carlyle's French Revolution," HISTORY,
       XLVIII (October, 1963), 306-316.

2767   Daiches, David. CARLYLE AND THE VICTORIAN DILEM-
       MA (Edinburgh: Carlyle Society, 1963), 1-19. Rpt. MORE
       LITERARY ESSAYS. Edinburgh: Oliver and Boyd, 1968.

2768   Deen, Leonard W. "Irrational Form in Sartor Resartus,"
       TEXAS STUDIES IN LITERATURE AND LANGUAGE, V
       (Autumn, 1963), 438-451.

2769   Frye, Northrup. "The Problem of Spiritual Authority in the
       Nineteenth Century," ESSAYS IN ENGLISH LITERATURE
       FROM THE RENAISSANCE TO THE VICTORIAN AGE PRE-
       SENTED TO A. S. P. WOODHOUSE. Ed. M. Maclure and
       F. W. Watt (Toronto: University of Toronto Press, 1964),
       304-319.

2770   Johnson, Wendell S. "Swinburne and Carlyle," ENGLISH LANGUAGE NOTES, I (December, 1963), 117-121.

2771   Peyre, Henri M. LITERATURE AND SINCERITY. New Haven: Yale University Press, 1963.

2772   Pritchard, John P. LITERARY WISE MEN OF GOTHAM. Baton Rouge: Louisiana State University Press, 1963.

2773   Ryan, Alvan S. "The Attitude Towards the Reader in Carlyle's Sartor Resartus," VICTORIAN NEWSLETTER, no. 23 (Spring, 1963), 15-16.

2774   Sanders, Charles R. "Some Lost and Unpublished Carlyle-Browning Correspondence," JOURNAL OF ENGLISH AND GERMANIC PHILOLOGY, LXII (April, 1963), 323-335.

2775   _____. "The Correspondence and Friendship of Thomas Carlyle and Leigh Hunt: The Early Years," BULLETIN OF THE JOHN RYLANDS LIBRARY, XLV (March, 1963), 439-485.

2776   _____. "The Correspondence and Friendship of Thomas Carlyle and Leigh Hunt: The Later Years," BULLETIN OF THE JOHN RYLANDS LIBRARY, XLVI (September, 1963), 179-216.

2777   Tener, Robert H. "Sources of Hutton's 'Modern Guides' Essay on Carlyle," NOTES AND QUERIES, CCVIII (December, 1963), 463-464.

2778   Tennyson, G. B. "Carlyle's Poetry to 1840: A Checklist and Discussion, a New Attribution, and Six Unpublished Poems," VICTORIAN POETRY, I (August, 1963), 161-181.

2779   _____. "Unnoted Encyclopaedia Articles by Carlyle," ENGLISH LANGUAGE NOTES, I (December, 1963), 108-112.

1964

2780   Ball, Patricia M. "Sincerity: The Rise and Fall of a Critical

Term," MODERN LANGUAGE REVIEW, LIX (January, 1964), I-II.

2781 Cameron, Kenneth W. "New Japanese Translations of Carlyle's Works," EMERSON SOCIETY QUARTERLY, no. 35 (II Quarter, 1964), 86-89.

2782 Crossman, R. H. S. "Carlyle and Froude," NEW STATES-MAN AND NATION, n.s. LXVII (January 17, 1964), 81-82.

2783 DeLaura, David J. "Arnold and Carlyle," PUBLICATIONS OF THE MODERN LANGUAGE ASSOCIATION, LXXIX (March, 1964), 104-129.

2784 Drew, Elizabeth A. THE LITERATURE OF GOSSIP: NINE ENGLISH WRITERS. New York: W. W. Norton, 1964.

2785 Earle, Peter G. "Unamuno and the Theme of History," HIS-PANIC REVIEW, XXXII (October, 1964), 319-339.

2786 Hertz, Robert N. "Victory and the Consciousness of Battle: Emerson and Carlyle," PERSONALIST, XLV (Winter, 1964), 60-71.

2787 Kegel, Charles H. "Carlyle and Ruskin: An Influential Friendship," BRIGHAM YOUNG UNIVERSITY STUDIES, V (Spring, 1964), 219-229.

2788 Lea, Frank A. "Carlyle and the French Revolution," LIS-TENER, LXXII (September 17, 1964), 421-423.

2789 Levine, George. "Sartor Resartus and the Balance of Fiction," VICTORIAN STUDIES, VIII (December, 1964), 131-160.

2790 Levine, Richard A. "Carlyle as a Poet: The Phoenix Image in 'Organic Filaments,'" VICTORIAN NEWSLETTER, no. 25 (Spring, 1964), 18-20.

2791 Lindberg, John. "The Decadence of Style: Symbolic Structure in Carlyle's Later Prose," STUDIES IN SCOTTISH LIT-ERATURE, I (January, 1964), 183-195.

2792   Sanders, Charles R. "Carlyle as Editor and Critic of Literary Letters," EMORY UNIVERSITY QUARTERLY, XX
(Summer, 1964), 108-120.

2793   _____. "The Byron Closed in Sartor Resartus," STUDIES IN
ROMANTICISM, III (Winter, 1964), 77-108.

2794   Smeed, J. W. "Thomas Carlyle and Jean Paul Richter,"
COMPARATIVE LITERATURE, XVI (Summer, 1964), 226-
253.

2795   _____. GERMAN INFLUENCE ON THOMAS CARLYLE
(Edinburgh: Carlyle Society, 1964), 1-19.

2796   Strauch, Carl F. "The Problem of Time and the Romantic
Mode in Hawthorne, Melville, and Emerson," EMERSON
SOCIETY QUARTERLY, no. 35 (2nd Quarter, 1964), 50-60.

2797   Tennyson, G. B. "Carlyle's Earliest German Translation,"
AMERICAN NOTES AND QUERIES, III (December, 1964),
51-54.

2798   _____. "'The true Shekinah is man,'" AMERICAN NOTES
AND QUERIES, III (December, 1964), 58.

2799   Watkins, Charlotte C. "Browning's 'Red Cotton Night-Cap
Country' and Carlyle," VICTORIAN STUDIES, VII (June,
1964), 359-374.

1965

2800   Berger, Harold L. "Emerson and Carlyle: The Dissenting
Believers," EMERSON SOCIETY QUARTERLY, no. 38 (1
Quarter, 1965), 87-90.

2801   Hayter, Alethea. A SULTRY MONTH: SCENES OF LON-
DON LITERARY LIFE IN 1846. London: Faber and Faber,
1965.

2802   Holme, Thea. THE CARLYLES AT HOME. London: Oxford
University Press, 1965.

2803   Little, W. A. "Walt Whitman and the Nibelungenlied,"
        PUBLICATIONS OF THE MODERN LANGUAGE ASSOCI-
        ATION, LXXX (December, 1965), 562-570.

2804   Martin, Peter E. "Carlyle and Mill: The 'Anti-Self-
        Consciousness' Theory," THOTH, VI (Winter, 1965), 20-
        34.

2805   Mill, Anna J. CARLYLE AND MILL: TWO SCOTTISH
        UNIVERSITY RECTORS (Edinburgh: Carlyle Society, 1965),
        I-15.

2806   Ryan, Alvan S. "Carlyle, Jeffrey, and the 'Helotage'
        Chapter of Sartor Resartus," VICTORIAN NEWSLETTER, no.
        27 (Spring, 1965), 30-32.

2807   Sankey, Benjamin. "Henchard and Faust," ENGLISH
        LANGUAGE NOTES, III (December, 1965), 123-125.

2808   Tennyson, G. B. 'SARTOR' CALLED 'RESARTUS.' Prince-
        ton: Princeton University Press, 1965.

2809   Waller, John O. "Thomas Carlyle and His Nutshell Iliad,"
        BULLETIN OF THE NEW YORK PUBLIC LIBRARY, LXIX
        (January, 1965), 17-30.

2810   Wolff, Michael. "The Uses of Context: Aspects of the
        1860's," VICTORIAN STUDIES, IX (September, 1965), 47-
        63. Rejoinder by Harold J. Harris, "The Failure to Use
        Context," X (September, 1966), 82-85, and "The Uses of
        Context: A Reply," 85-86.

                              1966

2811   Anon. "Bluestockings with a Difference," TIMES (April 21,
        1966), 15.

2812   ____. "Chelsea to Ecclefechan," TIMES (June 3, 1966),
        13.

2813   ____. "Grapes in Cheyne Row," TIMES (October 6, 1966),
        13.

2814   Castan, C. "Clough's 'Epi-Strauss-ium' and Carlyle,"
        VICTORIAN POETRY, IV (Winter, 1966), 54-56.

2815   Ebel, Henry. "'The Primaeval Fountain of Human Nature':
        Mill, Carlyle, and the French Revolution," VICTORIAN
        NEWSLETTER, no. 30 (Fall, 1966), 13-18.

2816   Ehrlich, H. "The Origin of Lowell's 'Miss Fooler,'"
        AMERICAN LITERATURE, XXXVII (January, 1966), 473-
        475.

2817   Ferguson, William. CARLYLE AS HISTORIAN (Edinburgh:
        Carlyle Society, 1966), 1-13.

2818   Holme, Thea. CARLYLE'S HOUSE CHELSEA. London:
        National Trust, 1966.

2819   Irwin, Raymond. THE ENGLISH LIBRARY: SOURCES AND
        HISTORY. London: Allen and Unwin, 1966.

2820   Jenkins, William D. "Who Might Thomas Carlyle Be?"
        BAKER STREET JOURNAL, XVI (December, 1966), 222-230.

2821   Moore, Carlisle. "Thomas Carlyle," ENGLISH ROMANTIC
        POETS AND ESSAYISTS. Rev. ed. Ed. Carolyn W. Hout-
        chens and Lawrence H. Houtchens (New York: New York
        University Press, 1966), 333-378.

2822   Pearsall, Ronald. "The Death of Jane Welsh Carlyle," HIS-
        TORY TODAY, XVI (April, 1966), 270-275.

2823   Reed, Joseph W. ENGLISH BIOGRAPHY IN THE EARLY
        NINETEENTH CENTURY: 1801-1838. New Haven: Yale
        University Press, 1966.

2824   Rutherford, Andrew. "Carlyle and Kipling," KIPLING
        JOURNAL, XXXIII (June-December, 1966), 10-19, 11-19,
        11-16.

2825   Sharrock, Roger. "Carlyle and the Sense of History,"
        ESSAYS AND STUDIES, XIX (1966), 74-91.

2826   Sowder, William J. EMERSON'S IMPACT ON THE BRITISH

ISLES AND CANADA. Charlottesville: University of Virginia Press, 1966.

2827 Sutton, Max K. "'Inverse Sublimity' in Victorian Humor," VICTORIAN STUDIES, X (December, 1966), 177-192.

2828 Wursthorn, Peter A. "The Position of Thomas Carlyle in the History of Mathematics," MATHEMATICS TEACHER, LIX (December, 1966), 755-770.

1967

2829 Anon. "Tree of Heaven Falls on House--Planted by Carlyle," TIMES (August 5, 1967), 12.

2830 Adrian, Arthur A. "Carlyle on Editing Letters," VICTORIAN NEWSLETTER, no. 31 (Spring, 1967), 45-46.

2831 Baumgarten, Murray. "The Ideas of History of Thomas Carlyle and John Stuart Mill," MILL NEWSLETTER, III (Fall, 1967), 8-9.

2832 Bertolotti, D. S. "Mark Twain Revisits the Tailor," MARK TWAIN JOURNAL, XIII (Summer, 1967), 18-19.

2833 Feltes, Norman N. "Bentham and Coleridge: Mill's Competing Counterparts," MILL NEWSLETTER, II (Spring, 1967), 2-7.

2834 Harding, Walter. "Delugeous or Detergeous or?" THOREAU SOCIETY BULLETIN, no. 101 (Fall, 1967), 5.

2835 Hirsch, David. "Melville's Ishmaelite," AMERICAN NOTES AND QUERIES, V (April, 1967), 115-116.

2836 Jones, Iva G. "Trollope, Carlyle and Mill on the Negro: An Episode in the History of Ideas," JOURNAL OF NEGRO HISTORY, LII (July, 1967), 185-199.

2837 Keith, W. J. "An Interview with Carlyle," NOTES AND QUERIES, XIV (October, 1967), 371-372.

2838 Kocmanova, J. "The Aesthetic Opinions of William

Morris," COMPARATIVE LITERATURE STUDIES, IV (1967), 409-429.

2839 Mansell, Darrell. "George Eliot's Conception of Tragedy," NINETEENTH-CENTURY FICTION, XXII (September, 1967), 155-171.

2840 Marrs, Edwin W. "Reminiscences of a Visit with Carlyle in 1878 by His Nephew and Namesake," THOTH, VIII (Spring, 1967), 66-83.

2841 _____. "Dating the Writings of Past and Present," NOTES AND QUERIES, XIV (October, 1967), 370-371.

2842 Mendel, Sydney. "Carlyle: Notes Toward a Revaluation," ENGLISH STUDIES IN AFRICA, X (March, 1967), 11-21.

2843 Preston, Anthony, and John Major. SEND A GUNBOAT! London: Longmans, Green, 1967.

2844 Sanders, Charles R. "Editing the Carlyle Letters: Problems and Opportunities," EDITING NINETEENTH-CENTURY TEXTS. Ed. John M. Robson (Toronto: University of Toronto Press, 1967), 77-95.

2845 Swanson, Donald R. "Ruskin and His 'Master,'" VICTORIAN NEWSLETTER, no. 31 (Spring, 1967), 56-59.

1968

2846 Alexander, Edward. "Thomas Carlyle and D. H. Lawrence: A Parallel," UNIVERSITY OF TORONTO QUARTERLY, XXXVII (April, 1968), 248-267.

2847 Baumgarten, Murray. "Carlyle and 'Spiritual Optics,'" VICTORIAN STUDIES, XI (June, 1968), 503-522.

2848 Ben-Israel, Hedva. ENGLISH HISTORIANS ON THE FRENCH REVOLUTION. London: Cambridge University Press, 1968.

2849 Casale, O. M. "Poe on Transcendentalism," EMERSON

SOCIETY QUARTERLY, no. 50 (1st Quarter, 1968), 85-97.

2850   Chapman, Raymond. THE VICTORIAN DEBATE: ENGLISH
       LITERATURE AND SOCIETY, 1832-1901. London: Weiden-
       feld and Nicolson, 1968.

2851   Clarke, Alexander F. "[Frederick the Great Ms]," MANU-
       SCRIPTS, XX (Winter, 1968), 41-44.

2852   Curran, Eileen M. "Carlyle's First Contribution to the
       Foreign Quarterly Review: A Small Identification," VIC-
       TORIAN PERIODICALS NEWSLETTER, no. 2 (June, 1968),
       25-27.

2853   D'Avanzo, Mario L. "'The Cassock' and Carlyle's 'Church-
       Clothes,'" EMERSON SOCIETY QUARTERLY, no. 50 (1st
       Quarter, 1968), 74-76.

2854   De Bellis, J. "Sidney Lanier and German Romance: An
       Important Qualification," COMPARATIVE LITERATURE, 11
       (1968), 145-155.

2855   Eidson, John O. "Charles Stearns Wheeler: Friend of
       Emerson," EMERSON SOCIETY QUARTERLY, no. 52 (3rd
       Quarter, 1968), 13-75.

2856   Fielding, Kenneth J., and Alec W. Brice. "Charles Dick-
       ens on 'The Exclusion of Evidence,'" DICKENSIAN, LXIV
       (September, 1968), 131-140.

2857   Gilbert, Elliot L. "Kipling's Imperialism: A Point of De-
       parture," KIPLING JOURNAL, XXXV (June, 1968), 15-
       19.

2858   Goodheart, Eugene. THE CULT OF THE EGO: THE SELF
       IN MODERN LITERATURE. Chicago: University of Chicago
       Press, 1968.

2859   Harding, Walter. "Delugeous or Detergeous or?" CENTER
       FOR THE EDITIONS OF AMERICAN AUTHORS NEWSLET-
       TER, no. 1 (March, 1968), 5-6.

2860   Himmelfarb, Gertrude. VICTORIAN MINDS. London:

Weidenfeld and Nicolson, 1968.

2861 Honan, Park. "The Murder Poem for Elizabeth," VICTORI-
AN POETRY, VI (Autumn-Winter, 1968), 215-230.

2862 LaValley, Albert J. CARLYLE AND THE IDEA OF THE
MODERN. New Haven: Yale University Press, 1968.

2863 Levine, George. THE BOUNDARIES OF FICTION. Princeton: Princeton University Press, 1968.

2864 _____. "The Uses and Abuses of Carlylese," THE ART OF
VICTORIAN PROSE. Ed. George Levine and William
Madden (New York: Oxford University Press, 1968), 101-
126.

2865 Marrs, Edwin W. "Carlyle, Bernardin de Saint-Pierre,
and Madame Cottin," VICTORIAN NEWSLETTER, no. 33
(Spring, 1968), 43-45.

2866 Marwick, William H. "Carlyle and Quakerism," FRIENDS'
QUARTERLY, XVI (January, 1968), 37-45.

2867 McMaster, Rowland D. "Criticism of Civilization in the
Structure of Sartor Resartus," UNIVERSITY OF TORONTO
QUARTERLY, XXXVII (April, 1968), 268-280.

2868 Merritt, James D. "The Novelist St. Barbe in Disraeli's
Endymion: Revenge on Whom?" NINETEENTH-CENTURY
FICTION, XXIII (June, 1968), 85-88.

2869 Mitford, Nancy. "Tam and Fritz: Carlyle and Frederick
the Great," HISTORY TODAY, XVIII (1968), 3-13.

2870 Roberts, Mark. "Carlyle and the Rhetoric of Unreason,"
ESSAYS IN CRITICISM, XVIII (October, 1968), 397-419.

2871 Shipley, John B. "A New Carlyle Letter," ENGLISH
STUDIES, XLIX (October, 1968), 441-444.

2872 Stewart, Jack F. "Romantic Theories of Humor Relating to
Sterne," PERSONALIST, XLIX (Autumn, 1968), 459-473.

2873   Stratford, J.   "'Eminent Victorians,'" BRITISH MUSEUM
        QUARTERLY, XXXII (Spring, 1968), 93-95.

2874   Sussman, Herbert L.   VICTORIANS AND THE MACHINE.
        Cambridge: Harvard University Press, 1968.

2875   Tarr, Rodger L.   "Thomas Carlyle and Henry M'Cormac:
        Two Letters on the Condition of Ireland in 1848," STUDIES
        IN SCOTTISH LITERATURE, V (April, 1968), 253-256.

2876   Tennyson, G. B.   "The Bildungsroman in Nineteenth-Century
        English Literature," MEDIEVAL EPIC TO THE "EPIC
        THEATER" in UNIVERSITY OF SOUTHERN CALIFORNIA
        STUDIES IN COMPARATIVE LITERATURE, no. 1 (1968), 135-
        146.

2877   Trowbridge, Ronald L.   "Carlyle's Illudo Chartis as Prophe-
        tic Exercise in the Manner of Swift and Sterne," STUDIES
        IN SCOTTISH LITERATURE, VI (October, 1968), 115-122.

2878   Woodson, Thomas.   "The Two Beginnings of Walden: A
        Distinction of Styles," JOURNAL OF ENGLISH LITERARY
        HISTORY, XXXV (September, 1968), 440-473.

2879   Woodwell, Roland H.   "Whittier and Carlyle," EMERSON
        SOCIETY QUARTERLY, no. 50 (1st Quarter, 1968), 42-46.

                              1969

2880   Alexander, Edward.   "Mill's Marginal Notes on Carlyle's
        'Hudson Statue,'" ENGLISH LANGUAGE NOTES, VII
        (December, 1969), 120-123.

2881   Brantlinger, Patrick.   "The Case Against Trade Unions in
        Early Victorian Fiction," VICTORIAN STUDIES, XIII (Sept-
        ember, 1969), 37-52.

2882   Burnett, T. A. J.   "Swinburne's The Ballad of Bulgarie,"
        MODERN LANGUAGE REVIEW, LXIV (April, 1969), 276-
        282.

2883   Burwick, Frederick L.   "Stylistic Continuity and Change in the Prose of Thomas Carlyle, " STATISTICS AND STYLE (New York: American Elsevier, 1969), 178-196.

2884   Campbell, Ian. "Carlyle's Borrowings from the Theological Library of Edinburgh University," BIBLIOTHECK, V (1969), 165-168.

2885   DeLaura, David J. "Ishmael as Prophet: Heroes and Hero-Worship and the Self-Expressive Basis of Carlyle's Art," TEXAS STUDIES IN LITERATURE AND LANGUAGE, XI (Spring, 1969), 705-732.

2886   Gridgeman, Norman. "Thomas Carlyle, geometer," NEW SCIENCE, XLIV (November 27, 1969), 466-467.

2887   Gross, John J. THE RISE AND FALL OF THE MAN OF LETTERS. London: Weidenfeld and Nicolson, 1969.

2888   Havens, Elmer A. "Lanier's Critical Theory," EMERSON SOCIETY QUARTERLY, no. 55 (2nd Quarter, 1969), 83-89.

2889   Kirk, Russell. ENEMIES OF THE PERMANENT THINGS: OBSERVATIONS OF ABNORMALITY IN LITERATURE AND POLITICS. New Rochelle, New York: Arlington House, 1969.

2890   Kusch, Robert W. "Carlyle and the Milieu of 'Spontaneous Combustion,'" NEUPHILOLOGISCHE MITTEILUNGEN, LXX (1969), 339-344.

2891   _____. "Pattern and Paradox in Heroes and Hero-Worship," STUDIES IN SCOTTISH LITERATURE, VI (January, 1969), 146-155.

2892   McGhee, Richard D. "'Blank Misgivings': Arthur Hugh Clough's Search for Poetic Form," VICTORIAN POETRY, VII (Summer, 1969), 105-115.

2893   Miyoshi, Masao. THE DIVIDED SELF: A PERSPECTIVE ON THE LITERATURE OF THE VICTORIANS. New York: New York University Press, 1969.

2894   Monteiro, George. "'Delugeous' or 'Detergeous'?--A Contextual Argument," CENTER FOR THE EDITIONS OF AMERICAN AUTHORS NEWSLETTER, no. 2 (July, 1969), 4-5.

2895   Omans, Glen. "Browning's 'Fra Lippo Lippi,'" VICTORIAN POETRY, VII (Spring, 1969), 56-62.

2896   Pritchett, Victor S. "Heroes and Potboilers," NEW STATESMAN AND NATION, LXXVII (May 23, 1969), 733-734.

2897   Sharples, Edward. "Carlyle's 'Christopher North,'" NOTES AND QUERIES, XVI (January, 1969), 34-35.

2898   Strauch, Carl F. "Emerson's Use of the Organic Method," EMERSON SOCIETY QUARTERLY, no. 55 (2nd Quarter, 1969), 18-24.

2899   Swanson, Donald R. "Carlyle and the English Romantic Poets," LOCK HAVEN REVIEW, XI (1969), 25-32.

2900   Walton, William G. "Carlyle--Forgotten Prophet," AMERICAN MERCURY, CV (Summer, 1969), 31-33.

2901   Wyllie, John C. "Delugeous or Detergeous or?" CENTER FOR THE EDITIONS OF AMERICAN AUTHORS NEWSLETTER, no. 2 (July, 1969), 3.

1970

2902   Baetzhold, Howard G. MARK TWAIN AND JOHN BULL: THE BRITISH CONNECTION. Bloomington: Indiana University Press, 1970.

2903   Beaty, Jerome. "All Victoria's Horses and All Victoria's Men," NEW LITERARY HISTORY, I (Winter, 1970), 271-292.

2904   Cameron, Kenneth W. "Literary News in the American Renaissance Newspapers: Carlyle Evaluated and Criticized," AMERICAN TRANSCENDENTAL QUARTERLY, no. 5 (1st Quarter, 1970), 70-71.

2905   . "American and British Authors in F. B. Sanborn's Papers," AMERICAN TRANSCENDENTAL QUARTERLY, no. 6 (2nd Quarter, 1970), 2-53.

2906   Campbell, Ian. "Carlyle, Cromwell and Kimbolton," BIBLIOTHECK, V (1970), 246-252.

2907   . "James Barrett and Carlyle's Journal," NOTES AND QUERIES, XVII (January, 1970), 19-21.

2908   Chandler, Alice K. A DREAM OF ORDER: THE MEDIE-VAL IDEAL IN NINETEENTH CENTURY ENGLISH LITERATURE. Lincoln: University of Nebraska Press, 1970.

2909   Coulling, Sidney M. B. "Carlyle and Swift," STUDIES IN ENGLISH LITERATURE, X (Autumn, 1970), 741-758.

2910   Domelen, John E. Van. "A Note on the Reading of Conrad's Characters," CONRADIANA, III (1970-1971), 87-89.

2911   Dunn, Richard J. "David Copperfield's Carlylean Retailoring," DICKENS THE CRAFTSMAN. Ed. Robert Partlow (Carbondale: Southern Illinois University Press, 1970), 95-114.

2912   . "'Inverse Sublimity': Carlyle's Theory of Humour," UNIVERSITY OF TORONTO QUARTERLY, XL (Fall, 1970), 41-57.

2913   Hook, Andrew. CARLYLE AND AMERICA (Edinburgh: Carlyle Society, 1970), 1-22.

2914   John, Brian. "Yeats and Carlyle," NOTES AND QUERIES, XVII (December, 1970), 455.

2915   Johnson, Richard C., and G. Thomas Tanselle. "The Haldemann-Julius 'Little Blue Books' as a Bibliographical Problem," PAPERS OF THE BIBLIOGRAPHICAL SOCIETY OF AMERICA, LXIV (1st Quarter, 1970), 63-64.

2916   Kenny, Blair G. "Carlyle and Bleak House," DICKENSIAN, LXVI (January, 1970), 36-41.

2917   Kirkham, E. Bruce. "The Iron Crown of Lombardy in Moby Dick," EMERSON SOCIETY QUARTERLY, no. 58 (1st Quarter, 1970), 127-219.

2918   McCullen, J. T. "Tobacco and Victorian Literature," FORUM (Houston), VIII (Summer, 1970), 20-26.

2919   Morgan, P. "Carlyle, Jeffrey, and the Edinburgh Review," NEOPHILOLOGUS, LIV (July, 1970), 297-310.

2920   Morgan, Peter F. "Carlyle and Macaulay as Critics of Literature and Life in the Edinburgh Review," STUDIA GERMANICA GANDENSIA, XII (1970), 131-144.

2921   Peckham, Morse. VICTORIAN REVOLUTIONARIES. New York: George Braziller, 1970.

2922   Ross, Donald. "Composition as a Stylistic Feature," STYLE, IV (Winter, 1970), 1-10.

2923   Slater, Michael. "Dicken's Tract for the Times," DICKENS: 1970 (London: Chapman and Hall, 1970), 99-123.

2924   ____. "Carlyle and Jerrold into Dickens: A Study of The Chimes," NINETEENTH-CENTURY FICTION, XXIV (March, 1970), 506-526.

2925   Smith, Sheila M. "Blue Books and Victorian Novelists," REVIEW OF ENGLISH STUDIES, XXI (February, 1970), 23-40.

2926   Sparrow, W. Keats. "The Work Theme in Kipling's Novels," KIPLING JOURNAL, XXXVII (March, 1970), 10-19.

2927   Spivey, Herbert E. "'Here is a New Mystic,'" MILL NEWSLETTER, V (Spring, 1970), 5-6.

2928   Starzyk, Lawrence J. "Arnold and Carlyle," CRITICISM, XII (Fall, 1970), 281-300.

2929   Tarr, Rodger L. "Emerson's Transcendentalism in L. M. Child's Letter to Carlyle," EMERSON SOCIETY QUARTERLY, no. 58 (1st Quarter, 1970), 112-115.

2930 ____ . "'A Sentimental Journey': Carlyle's Final Visit to The Grange," NOTES AND QUERIES, CCXV (January, 1970), 21-22.

2931 Trowbridge, Ronald L. "Thomas Carlyle's Masks of Humor," MICHIGAN ACADEMICIAN, III (Fall, 1970), 57-66.

1971

2932 Brown, Herbert. "Carlyle," TIMES LITERARY SUPPLEMENT (December 3, 1971), 1525.

2933 Campbell, Ian. "Edward Irving, Carlyle and the Stage," STUDIES IN SCOTTISH LITERATURE, VIII (January, 1971), 166-173.

2934 ____ . "Thomas Carlyle and George Cron," NOTES AND QUERIES, XVIII (May, 1971), 183-185.

2935 ____ . "Carlyle and the Negro Question Again," CRITICISM, XIII (Summer, 1971), 279-290.

2936 ____ . "The Duke and Edinburgh Edition of the Carlyle Letters," SCOTTISH LITERARY NEWS, I (August, 1971), 84-88.

2937 ____ . "Carlyle Letters, Thomas and Jane," UNIVERSITY OF EDINBURGH JOURNAL, XXV (December, 1971), 120-122.

2938 Chalmers, E. B. "Mrs. Carlyle's Letters to John Stodart," TIMES LITERARY SUPPLEMENT (June 25, 1971), 739-741.

2939 Christensen, Allan C. "A Dickensian Hero Retailored: The Carlylean Apprenticeship of Martin Chuzzlewit," STUDIES IN THE NOVEL, III (Spring, 1971), 18-25.

2940 Clarke, Margaret. "Dickens and Carlyle," TIMES LITERARY SUPPLEMENT (April 16, 1971), 449.

2941 Clubbe, John. "John Carlyle in Germany and the Genesis of Sartor Resartus," ROMANTIC AND VICTORIAN: STUDIES

IN MEMORY OF WILLIAM H. MARSHALL (Rutherford, N. J.: Fairleigh Dickinson University Press, 1971), 264-289.

2942   Collins, Philip. "Dickens and Carlyle," TIMES LITERARY SUPPLEMENT (March 19, 1971), 325.

2943   Collis, John S. THE CARLYLES. London: Sidgwick and Jackson, 1971.

2944   Dunn, Richard J. "Dickens, Carlyle, and the Hard Times Dedication," DICKENS STUDIES NEWSLETTER, II (September, 1971), 90-92.

2945   Fulford, Roger. "Ruskin's Notes on Carlyle," TIMES LITERARY SUPPLEMENT (April 16, 1971), 453.

2946   Hilles, Frederick W. "Tom Carlyle and His Mocking Bonny Jane," YALE REVIEW, LX (Summer, 1971), 569-576.

2947   Kusch, Robert W. "The Eighteenth Century as 'Decaying Organism' in Carlyle's The French Revolution," ANGLIA, LXXXIX (1971), 456-470.

2948   Lane, Lauriat. "Dickens and Melville: Our Mutual Friends," DALHOUSIE REVIEW, LI (Autumn, 1971), 315-331.

2949   Leicester, H. M. "The Dialectic of Romantic Historiography: Prospect and Retrospect in The French Revolution," VICTORIAN STUDIES, XV (September, 1971), 5-17.

2950   McCarthy, Patrick J. "Reading Victorian Prose: Arnold's 'Culture and Its Enemies,'" UNIVERSITY OF TORONTO QUARTERLY, XL (Winter, 1971), 119-135.

2951   Morse, J. M. "The Coach with the Six Insides," A WAKE NEWSLITTER, VIII (June, 1971), 46-47.

2952   Rawson, C. J. "Matthew Arnold to Henry Reeve: An Unpublished Letter," NOTES AND QUERIES, XVIII (July, 1971), 251.

2953   Reed, Walter J. "The Pattern of Conversion in Sartor Resartus," JOURNAL OF ENGLISH LITERARY HISTORY,

XXXVIII (September, 1971), 411-431.

2954   Seigel, Jules P. THOMAS CARLYLE: THE CRITICAL HERI-
TAGE. London: Routledge and Kegan Paul, 1971.

2955   Smith, A. Helen. "Origin and Interpretation of Song of
Myself," WALT WHITMAN REVIEW, XVII (June, 1971), 45-
54.

2956   Starzyk, Lawrence J. "Towards a Reassessment of Early
Victorian Aesthetics," BRITISH JOURNAL OF AESTHETICS,
XI (Spring, 1971), 167-177.

2957   Stuart, Donald C. "Swinburne: The Composition of a Self-
Portrait," VICTORIAN POETRY, IX (Spring, 1971), 111-128.

2958   Tarr, Rodger L. "Carlyle's Answer to the 'Libussa Riddle,'"
AMERICAN NOTES AND QUERIES, IX (May, 1971), 133-
134.

2959   _____. "Mary Aitken Carlyle: An Unpublished Letter to Her
Son," ENGLISH LANGUAGE NOTES, VIII (June, 1971),
281-283.

2960   _____. "The 'Foreign Philanthropy Question' in Bleak House:
A Carlylean Influence," STUDIES IN THE NOVEL, III (Fall,
1971), 275-281.

2961   _____, and Ian Campbell. "Carlyle's Early Study of German, 1819-1821," ILLINOIS QUARTERLY, XXXIV (December,
1971), 19-27.

2962   Tennyson, G. B. CARLYLE AND THE MODERN WORLD
(Edinburgh: Carlyle Society, 1971), 1-26.

2963   Wogeler, Martha S. "'Ruskin's Notes on Carlyle,'" TIMES
LITERARY SUPPLEMENT (May 7, 1971), 536.

2964   Wilkinson, D. R. M. "Carlyle, Arnold, and Literary Justice," PUBLICATIONS OF THE MODERN LANGUAGE
ASSOCIATION, LXXXVI (March, 1971), 225-235. See
replies: Arthur H. Nethercot, "Carlyle and Arnold," LXXXVII

(January, 1972), 102-103; and Rodger L. Tarr, "Carlyle, Tennyson, and 'Sincere' Literary Justice, " LXXXVIII (January, 1973), 136-138.

1972

2965 Brantlinger, Patrick. "'Teufelsdröckh' Resartus, " ENGLISH LANGUAGE NOTES, IX (March, 1972), 191-193.

2966 Brock, D. Heyward. "The Portrait of Abbot Sampson in Past and Present: Carlyle and Jocelin of Brakelond, " ENGLISH MISCELLANY, XXIII (1972), 149-165.

2967 Brookes, Gerry H. THE RHETORICAL FORM OF CARLYLE'S "SARTOR RESARTUS." Berkeley: University of California Press, 1972.

2968 Bufano, Randolph J. "Emerson's Apprenticeship to Carlyle, 1827-1848, " AMERICAN TRANSCENDENTALIST QUARTERLY, no. 13 (1st Quarter, 1972), 17-25.

2969 Cameron, Kenneth W. "Literary News in American Renaissance Newspapers, " AMERICAN TRANSCENDENTAL QUARTERLY, no. 14 (1st Quarter, 1972), 112-125.

2970 Campbell, Ian. "Carlyle and the Secession, " RECORDS OF THE SCOTTISH CHURCH HISTORY SOCIETY, XVIII (1972), 48-64.

2971 _____ . "Carlyle and Sir Gideon Dunn, " ENGLISH LANGUAGE NOTES, IX (March, 1972), 185-191.

2972 Clark, Lord. "Mandarin English, " TRANSACTIONS OF THE ROYAL SOCIETY OF LITERATURE, sers. 3, XXXVII (1972), 31-46.

2973 Dilthey, Wilhelm. (Trans. Murray Baumgarten and Evelyn Kanes). "Sartor Resartus: Philosophical Conflict, Positive and Negative Eras, and Personal Resolution, " CLIO, I (June, 1972), 40-60. See "Thomas Carlyle, " ARCHIV FÜR GESCHICHTE DER PHILOSOPHIE, IV (1891), 260-285.

2974 Dunn, Richard J. "Carlyle and that Hard Times Dedication, "

CARLYLE BIBLIOGRAPHY

DICKENS STUDIES NEWSLETTER, III (June, 1972), 60-61.

2975 Faulkner, Peter. "Carlyle's Letters to Charles Redwood," YEARBOOK OF ENGLISH STUDIES, II (1972), 139-180.

2976 Frykman, Erik. "Some Notes on the Theme of Self-Realization in English and Scandinavian Literature of the Nineteenth and Twentieth Centuries," ABERDEEN UNIVERSITY REVIEW, XLIV (Spring, 1972), 241-255.

2977 Gilbert, Elliot L. "'A Wondrous Contiguity': Anachronism in Carlyle's Prophecy and Art," PUBLICATIONS OF THE MODERN LANGUAGE ASSOCIATION, LXXXVII (May, 1972), 432-442.

2978 Goldberg, Michael. "From Bentham to Carlyle: Dickens' Political Development," JOURNAL OF THE HISTORY OF IDEAS, XXXIII (January, 1972), 61-76.

2979 _____. CARLYLE AND DICKENS. Athens: University of Georgia Press, 1972.

2980 Gozzi, Raymond D. "Walden and a Carlyle Letter," THOREAU SOCIETY BULLETIN, no. 118 (Winter, 1972), 4.

2981 Hall, N. John. "Trollope and Carlyle," NINETEENTH-CENTURY FICTION, XXVII (September, 1972), 197-205.

2982 Hardwick, Elizabeth. "Amateurs: Dorothy Wordsworth and Jane Carlyle," NEW YORK REVIEW OF BOOKS, XXX (November, 1972), 3-4.

2983 Hopwood, Alison L. "Carlyle and Conrad: Past and Present and Heart of Darkness," REVIEW OF ENGLISH STUDIES, XXIII (May, 1972), 162-172.

2984 Ikeler, A. Abbott. PURITAN TEMPER AND TRANSCENDENTAL FAITH: CARLYLE'S LITERARY VISION. Columbus: Ohio State University Press, 1972.

2985 Oddie, William. "Dickens and the Indian Mutiny," DICKENSIAN, LXVIII (January, 1972), 3-15.

CARLYLE BIBLIOGRAPHY

2986 _____ . DICKENS AND CARLYLE: THE QUESTION OF INFLUENCE. London: Centenary Press, 1972.

2987 Sigman, Joseph. "'Diabolico-angelical Indifference': The Imagery of Polarity in Sartor Resartus," SOUTHERN REVIEW (Australia), V (September, 1972), 207-224.

2988 Tarr, Rodger L. A BIBLIOGRAPHY OF ENGLISH LANG-UAGE ARTICLES ON THOMAS CARLYLE, 1900-1965. Bibliographical Series No. 7. University of South Carolina, 1972.

2989 _____ . "Carlyle and the Problem of the Hard Times Dedica-tion," DICKENS STUDIES NEWSLETTER, III (March, 1972), 25-27.

2990 _____ . "Dickens' Debt to Carlyle's 'Justice Metaphor' in The Chimes," NINETEENTH-CENTURY FICTION, XXVII (September, 1972), 208-215.

2991 Thurman, William R. "Carlyle, Browning, and Ruskin on One Purpose of Art," SOUTH ATLANTIC BULLETIN, XXXVII (May, 1972), 52-57.

2992 West, Paul. "Carlyle's Bravura Prophetics," COSTERUS, V (1972), 153-195.

2993 Wilson, John R. "'Signs of the Times' and 'The Present Age': Essays of Crisis," WESTERN HUMANITIES REVIEW, XXVI (Autumn, 1972), 369-374.

2994 Witte, William. CARLYLE AND GOETHE (Edinburgh: Carlyle Society, 1972), 1-18.

2995 Young, Kenneth. "The Literature of Politics," TRANSAC-TIONS OF THE ROYAL SOCIETY OF LITERATURE, sers. 3, XXXVII (1972), 134-152.

1973

2996 Anon. "Thomas Carlyle to Charles T. Brooks," AMERICAN TRANSCENDENTAL QUARTERLY, no. 17 (1st Quarter, 1973), 29.

239

2997 _____. "Carlyle and Emerson," AMERICAN TRANSCEN-
DENTAL QUARTERLY, no. 17 (1st Quarter, 1973), 45.

2998 Altick, Richard D. VICTORIAN PEOPLE AND IDEAS. New
York: W. W. Norton, 1973.

2999 Brantlinger, Patrick. "'Romance,' 'Biography,' and the
Making of Sartor Resartus," PHILOLOGICAL QUARTERLY,
LII (January, 1973), 108-118.

3000 Cazamian, Louis. THE SOCIAL NOVEL IN ENGLAND:
1830-1850. Trans. Martin Fido. London: Routledge, 1973.

3001 Cline, C. L. "Meredith's Meeting with the Carlyles,"
TIMES LITERARY SUPPLEMENT (November 9, 1973), 1380.

3002 C[onway], M[oncure] D. "A Visit to Thomas Carlyle,"
AMERICAN TRANSCENDENTAL QUARTERLY, no. 17 (1st
Quarter, 1973), 30-31.

3003 Coustillas, Pierre. "Meredith and the Carlyles," TIMES
LITERARY SUPPLEMENT (November 23, 1973), 1449.

3004 Donovan, Robert A. "Carlyle and the Climate of Hero-
Worship," UNIVERSITY OF TORONTO QUARTERLY, XLII
(Winter, 1973), 122-141.

3005 Hughs, J. J., and Peter M. Horowitz. "Organic Biography: The Death of Art," JOURNAL OF BRITISH STUDIES,
XII (May, 1973), 86-104.

3006 Nicholson, Frederick J. THOMAS CARLYLE AND HUGH
MACDIARMID (Edinburgh: Carlyle Society, 1973), 1-22.

3007 Roberts, Mark. THE TRADITION OF ROMANTIC MORAL-
ITY. London: Macmillan, 1973.

3008 Sanders, Charles R. "The Background of Carlyle's Portrait
of Coleridge in The Life of John Sterling," BULLETIN OF
THE JOHN RYLANDS LIBRARY, LV (Spring, 1973), 434-
458.

3009 Tarr, Rodger L. "Some Unpublished Letters of Varnhagen

von Ense to Thomas Carlyle," MODERN LANGUAGE RE-
VIEW, LXVIII (January, 1973), 22-27.

3010   Tennyson, G. B. "The Carlyles," VICTORIAN PROSE:
A GUIDE TO RESEARCH. Ed. David J. DeLaura (New York:
Modern Language Association, 1973), 31-111.

3011   Tierney, Frank M. "The Causes of the Revival of the Ron-
deau in Nineteenth Century England," REVUE DE L'UNI-
VERSITÉ D'OTTAWA, XLIII (1973), 96-113.

1974

3012   Anon. "Emerson and Carlyle Compared in the Pall Mall
Gazette (1867)," AMERICAN TRANSCENDENTAL QUAR-
TERLY, no. 22 (1st Quarter, 1974), 130.

3013   ____. "The Dickens Forum: Thomas Carlyle," DICKENS
STUDIES NEWSLETTER, V (December, 1974), 98-102.

3014   August, Eugene R. "Mill as Sage: The Essay on Bentham,"
PUBLICATIONS OF THE MODERN LANGUAGE ASSOCI-
ATION, LXXXIX (January, 1974), 142-153.

3015   Campbell, Ian. "Carlyle, Pictet and Jeffrey Again,"
BIBLIOTHECK, VII (1974), 1-15.

3016   ____. "Carlyle in the 1830's," NOTES AND QUERIES,
XXI (September, 1974), 336-339.

3017   ____. THOMAS CARLYLE. London: Hamish Hamilton,
1974.

3018   Cheever, Leonard A. "A Concept of Freedom: Carlyle's
and B. F. Skinner's," STUDIES IN RELEVANCE: ROMAN-
TIC AND VICTORIAN WRITERS IN 1972. Ed. Thomas M.
Harwell (Salzburg: University of Salzburg, 1974), 98-113.

3019   Cockshut, A. O. J. TRUTH TO LIFE: THE ART OF BIO-
GRAPHY IN THE 19th CENTURY. London: Collins, 1974.

3020   Davis, Frank. "[Carlyle Portrait by Walter Greaves in

1870]," COUNTRY LIFE, CLV (1974), 1352-1353.

3021   Dibble, Jerry A. "Carlyle's 'British Reader' and the Structure of Sartor Resartus," TEXAS STUDIES IN LITERATURE AND LANGUAGE, XVI (Summer, 1974), 293-304.

3022   Faverty, Frederic E. "The Brownings and Their Contemporaries," BROWNING INSTITUTE STUDIES. Ed. William S. Peterson (New York: Browning Institute, 1974), 161-180.

3023   Franke, Wolfgang. "Another Derivation of 'Teufelsdröckh,'" NOTES AND QUERIES, XXI (September, 1974), 339-340.

3024   Goreau, Eloise K. "Carlyle and Ruskin: The Private Side of the Public Coin," VICTORIAN NEWSLETTER, no. 46 (Fall, 1974), 15-19.

3025   Hardwick, Elizabeth. SEDUCTION AND BETRAYAL: WOMEN AND LITERATURE. New York: Random House, 1974.

3026   Morrison, N. Brysson. TRUE MINDS: THE MARRIAGE OF THOMAS AND JANE CARLYLE. London: J. M. Dent, 1974.

3027   Rhodes, Joseph. "[Carlyle and Mill]," DAEDALUS, CIII (Fall, 1974), 302-310.

3028   Rosenberg, Philip. THE SEVENTH HERO: THOMAS CARLYLE AND THE THEORY OF RADICAL ACTIVISM. Cambridge: Harvard University Press, 1974.

3029   Sanders, Charles R. "The Carlyles and Thackeray," NINETEENTH-CENTURY LITERARY PERSPECTIVES: ESSAYS IN HONOR OF LIONEL STEVENSON. Ed. Clyde de L. Ryals (Durham: Duke University Press, 1974), 161-200.

3030   Sigman, Joseph. "Adam-Kadmon, Nifl, Muspel, and the Biblical Symbolism of Sartor Resartus," JOURNAL OF ENGLISH LITERARY HISTORY, XLI (Summer, 1974), 233-256.

3031   Smith, Shelia M. "'Captain Swing' Explained," NOTES AND QUERIES, XXI (January, 1974), 13-15.

3032   Tarr, Rodger L. "Thomas Carlyle's Libraries at Chelsea and Ecclefechan," STUDIES IN BIBLIOGRAPHY, XXVII (1974), 249-266.

3033   _____ . "Thomas Carlyle's Growing Radicalism: The Social Context of The French Revolution," COSTERUS, n.s. I (1974), 113-126.

3034   Tennyson, G. B. "The Carlyles" in "A Guide to Year's Work in Victorian Poetry and Prose. 1973," VICTORIAN POETRY, Supplement. Ed. Richard Robias (Autumn, 1974), 235-238, 252-255.

3035   Wáite, William. "Whitman on Carlyle: A New Letter," WALT WHITMAN REVIEW, XX (June, 1974), 74.

3036   Wilson, John R. "Sartor Resartus: A Study in the Paradox of Despair," CHRISTIANITY AND LITERATURE, XXIII (Winter, 1974), 9-27.

3037   Workman, Gillian. "Thomas Carlyle and the Governor Eyre Controversy: An Account with Some New Material," VICTORIAN STUDIES, XVIII (September, 1974), 77-102.

APPENDIX

Journals

and

Newspapers Cited

APPENDIX

Note: an asterisk is used to indicate journals and newspapers that contain, in the nineteenth century, material on Carlyle.

A WAKE NEWSLITTER
ABERDEEN UNIVERSITY REVIEW
* ACADEMY
ADELPHI
* ALBION
* ALL THE YEAR ROUND
* AMERICAN
* AMERICAN ARCHITECT
* AMERICAN BIBLICAL REPOSITORY
AMERICAN BOOK COLLECTOR
* AMERICAN CATHOLIC QUARTERLY
AMERICAN FEDERATIONIST
AMERICAN JOURNAL OF THE-
   OLOGY
AMERICAN LITERATURE
AMERICAN MERCURY
* AMERICAN MONTHLY MAGA-
   ZINE
AMERICAN NOTES AND QUERIES
* AMERICAN PRESBYTERIAN REVIEW
* AMERICAN QUARTERLY OBSERVER
* AMERICAN QUARTERLY REVIEW
AMERICAN SCHOLAR
AMERICAN TRANSCENDENTAL
   QUARTERLY
* AMERICAN WHIG REVIEW
ANCESTOR
* ANDOVER REVIEW
ANGLIA
* ANNUAL REGISTER
ANTIOCH REVIEW
* ANTIQUARY
* APPLETON'S JOURNAL
* ARCHIV FÜR DAS STUDIUM DER
   NEUEREN SPRACHEN UND
   LITERATUREN
* ARCTURUS
* ARENA

* ARGOSY
* ART JOURNAL
* ARTHUR'S ILLUSTRATED
   HOME MAGAZINE
ARYAN PATH
ASIATIC REVIEW
* ATALANTA
* ATHENAEUM
* ATLANTIC MONTHLY
* AUTOGRAPHIC MIRROR

BACONIANA
BAKER STREET JOURNAL
* BALLOU'S PICTORIAL
   DRAWING-ROOM COM-
   PANION
* BALTIMORE AMERICAN AND
   COMMERCIAL ADVER-
   TISER
* BALTIMORE GAZETTE
* BALTIMORE SUN
BAPTIST QUARTERLY
* BAPTIST REVIEW
* BENTLEY'S MISCELLANY
* BIBLICAL REVIEW
BIBLIOTHECK
* BIOGRAPH AND REVIEW
* BIOGRAPHICAL MAGAZINE
* BLACKWOOD'S EDINBURGH
   MAGAZINE
* BOOKBUYER
* BOOK-LORE
BOOK-LOVER'S MAGAZINE
* BOOKMAN (London)
* BOOKMAN (New York)
* BOOK-WORM
BOOK COLLECTOR
BORDER MAGAZINE

*BOSTON DAILY ADVERTISER
*BOSTON EVENING STAR
*BOSTON EVENING TRANSCRIPT
*BOSTON EVENING TRAVELLER
*BOSTON HERALD
*BOSTON LIBERATOR
*BOSTON QUARTERLY REVIEW
BOSTON UNIVERSITY STUDIES
  IN ENGLISH
BRIGHAM YOUNG UNIVERSITY
  STUDIES
*BRITISH AND FOREIGN REVIEW
BRITISH JOURNAL OF AESTHETICS
BRITISH MEDICAL JOURNAL
BRITISH MUSEUM QUARTERLY
*BRITISH QUARTERLY REVIEW
*BRITISH WEEKLY
*BROADWAY JOURNAL
BULLETIN OF THE JOHN RYLANDS
  LIBRARY
BULLETIN OF THE NEW YORK PUBLIC
  LIBRARY

*CALCUTTA REVIEW
*CALIFORNIAN
*CANADIAN MAGAZINE
*CANADIAN MONTHLY
CATHOLIC BULLETIN
*CATHOLIC PRESBYTERIAN
*CATHOLIC WORLD
CEA CRITIC
CENTER FOR THE EDITIONS OF
  AMERICAN AUTHORS NEWS-
  LETTER
*CENTURY MAGAZINE
*CHAMBERS'S EDINBURGH JOUR-
  NAL
*CHAMBERS'S REPOSITORY OF
  TRACTS
*CHARLESTON COURIER (South
  Carolina)
*CHARLESTON MERCURY
  (South Carolina)

*CHARLESTON NEWS (South
  Carolina)
*CHARLESTON NEWS AND
  COURIER (South Carolina)
*CHICAGO DAILY NEWS
*CHICAGO EVENING JOURNAL
*CHICAGO INTER-OCEAN
*CHICAGO TIMES
*CHICAGO TRIBUNE
*CHOICE LITERATURE
*CHRISTIAN EXAMINER
*CHRISTIAN MONTHLY
*CHRISTIAN OBSERVATORY
*CHRISTIAN OBSERVER
*CHRISTIAN QUARTERLY RE-
  VIEW
*CHRISTIAN REGISTER
*CHRISTIAN REMEMBRANCER
*CHRISTIAN REVIEW
*CHRISTIAN WORLD MAGAZINE
CHRISTIANITY AND LITERATURE
*CHURCHMAN
*CHURCHMAN'S SHILLING
  MAGAZINE
*CITIZEN
*CLASSIC; OR, COLLEGE
  MONTHLY
CLASSICAL JOURNAL
CLIO
COLBY LIBRARY QUARTERLY
*COLLECTOR
COLLEGE ENGLISH
COMMONWEAL
COMPARATIVE LITERATURE
COMPARATIVE LITERATURE
  STUDIES
*CONGREGATIONAL MAGA-
  ZINE
CONGREGATIONAL QUAR-
  TERLY
*CONGREGATIONAL REVIEW
*CONGREGATIONALIST
CONRADIANA

* CONTEMPORARY REVIEW
* CORNHILL MAGAZINE
  COSTERUS
  COUNTRY LIFE
  CRAFTSMAN
* CRITIC (London)
* CRITIC (New York)
  CRITICISM
  CURRENT LITERATURE
  CURRENT OPINION

  DAEDALUS
  DALHOUSIE REVIEW
* DARTMOUTH
* DE BOW'S REVIEW
* DEMOCRATIC REVIEW
* DIAL (Boston)
* DIAL (Chicago)
  DICKENS STUDIES NEWS-
    LETTER
  DICKENSIAN
  DIE LITERATUR
* DIOGENES HYS LANTERNE
* DOUGHLAS JERROLD'S SHILLING
    MAGAZINE
* DUBLIN REVIEW
* DUBLIN UNIVERSITY MAGAZINE
* DUMFRIES MONTHLY MAGAZINE
* DUMFRIESSHIRE AND GALLOWAY
    HERALD AND ADVERTISER
* DUMFRIESSHIRE AND GALLOWAY
    STANDARD AND ADVERTISER

* ECHO
* ECLECTIC MAGAZINE
* ECLECTIC REVIEW
* EDINBURGH DAILY REVIEW
* EDINBURGH REVIEW
  EDUCATION
* ELEPHANT
* ELIZA COOK'S JOURNAL
  EMERSON SOCIETY QUARTERLY

  EMORY UNIVERSITY QUAR-
    TERLY
  ENGLISCHE STUDIEN
* ENGLISH HISTORICAL REVIEW
* ENGLISH ILLUSTRATED MAGA-
    ZINE
  ENGLISH JOURNAL
  ENGLISH LANGUAGE AND
    LITERATURE (Korea)
  ENGLISH LANGUAGE NOTES
  ENGLISH MISCELLANY
  ENGLISH REVIEW
  ENGLISH STUDIES
  ENGLISH STUDIES IN AFRICA
  ESSAYS AND STUDIES
  ESSAYS IN CRITICISM
* EXAMINER
  EXPLICATOR
  EXPOSITORY TIMES

  FLORIDA STATE UNIVERSITY
    STUDIES
* FORTNIGHTLY REVIEW
* FORUM
  FORUM (Houston)
* FRANK LESLIE'S POPULAR
    MAGAZINE
* FRASER'S MAGAZINE
* FRIEND'S INTELLIGENCER
  FRIENDS' QUARTERLY

* GALAXY
* GENTLEMAN'S MAGAZINE
* GLASGOW HERALD
* GLOBE QUARTERLY REVIEW
* GODEY'S LADY'S BOOK
  GOETHE JAHRBUCH
  GOLDEN BOOK MAGAZINE
  GOOD HOUSEKEEPING
* GOOD WORDS
* GRAHAM'S MAGAZINE
* GRAPHIC

* GREEN BAG

* HAMILTON SPECTATOR
* HARPER'S MAGAZINE
* HARPER'S WEEKLY
  HARVARD LIBRARY BULLETIN
  HARVARD LIBRARY NOTES
* HARVARD MONTHLY
* HARVARD UNIVERSITY
    BULLETIN
  HERMATHENA
* HESPERIAN
* HESPERIAN (Nebraska)
* HIBERNIA (Ireland)
  HIBBERT JOURNAL
  HISPANIC REVIEW
  HISTORIAN
  HISTORICAL JOURNAL
* HISTORICAL MAGAZINE
  HISTORY
  HISTORY OF IDEAS NEWS
    LETTER
  HISTORY TODAY
* HOGG'S WEEKLY INSTRUCTOR
* HOLDEN'S DOLLAR MAGAZINE
* HOME CHIMES
* HOURS AT HOME

* IGDRASIL
  ILLINOIS QUARTERLY
* ILLUSTRATED LONDON NEWS
* INDEPENDENT
* INQUIRER (London)
  INTERNATIONAL JOURNAL OF
    ETHICS
* INTERNATIONAL MONTHLY
    MAGAZINE
* INTERNATIONAL REVIEW
* IRIS
  IRISH BOOK LOVER
* IRISH ECCLESIASTICAL RECORD
* IRISH MONTHLY

JOURNAL OF BRITISH STUDIES
JOURNAL OF ECONOMIC
  HISTORY
JOURNAL OF EDUCATION
JOURNAL OF ENGLISH AND
  GERMANIC PHILOLOGY
JOURNAL OF ENGLISH
  LITERARY HISTORY
JOURNAL OF MODERN HISTORY
JOURNAL OF NEGRO HISTORY
JOURNAL OF THE FRIENDS
  HISTORICAL SOCIETY
JOURNAL OF THE HISTORY OF
  IDEAS
* JOURNAL OF SCIENCE

KIPLING JOURNAL
* KNICKERBOCKER MAGAZINE
* KNIGHT'S PENNY MAGAZINE

* LADIES' HOME JOURNAL
* LADIES' REPOSITORY
  LAMP
  LANDMARK
  LANTERN
* LEADER
* LEISURE HOUR
* LIBRARY
  LIBRARY CHRONICLE OF THE
    UNIVERSITY OF TEXAS
* LIBRARY JOURNAL
* LIBRARY MAGAZINE OF
    FOREIGN THOUGHT
  LIBRARY REVIEW
  LIFE AND LETTERS TODAY
* LIPPINCOTT'S MAGAZINE
  LISTENER
  LITERARY DIGEST
* LITERARY EXAMINER AND
    WESTERN MONTHLY REVIEW
* LITERARY GAZETTE
* LITERARY WORLD (Boston)

*LITERARY WORLD (London)
*LITTELL'S LIVING AGE
*LITTELL'S MUSEUM OF FOREIGN
   LITERATURE
 LOCK HAVEN REVIEW
*LONDON AND WESTMINSTER
   REVIEW
*LONDON MAGAZINE
 LONDON MERCURY
*LONDON QUARTERLY REVIEW
*LONDON REVIEW
*LONDON SOCIETY
 LONGMAN'S MAGAZINE

*MACMILLAN'S MAGAZINE
*MAGAZINE OF ART
*MAGAZINE OF DOMESTIC
   ECONOMY AND FAMILY REVIEW
*MAGNOLIA; OR SOUTHERN AP-
   PALACHIAN
 MARK TWAIN JOURNAL
*MANHATTAN
 MATHEMATICS TEACHER
 McCALL'S MAGAZINE
 MELBOURNE CRITICAL REVIEW
*MELORIA
 MENTOR
*METHODIST QUARTERLY REVIEW
 METHODIST REVIEW
*METROPOLITAN MAGAZINE
 MICHIGAN ACADEMICIAN
 MILL NEWSLETTER
 MODERN CHURCHMAN
 MODERN LANGUAGE NOTES
 MODERN LANGUAGE QUARTERLY
 MODERN LANGUAGE REVIEW
 MODERN PHILOLOGY
*MODERN REVIEW
 MONATSCHEFTE FÜR DEUTSCHEN
   UNTERRICHT, DUETSCHE
   SPRACHE UND LITERATUR
 MONIST

*MONTH
*MONTHLY CHRONICLE
*MONTHLY MAGAZINE
*MONTHLY REPOSITORY
*MONTHLY RELIGIOUS MAGA-
   ZINE
*MONTHLY REVIEW
*MOOKERJEE'S MAGAZINE
 MORE BOOKS
*MORNING CHRONICLE
 MUNSEY'S MAGAZINE
 MUSICAL TIMES

*NATION
*NATIONAL MAGAZINE
*NATIONAL REVIEW
*NEBRASKA STATE JOURNAL
 NEOPHILOLOGUS
 NEUPHILOLOGISCHE MIT-
   TEILUNGEN
*NEW ECLECTIC
*NEW ENGLAND MAGAZINE
 NEW ENGLAND QUARTERLY
*NEW ENGLANDER
 NEW LITERARY HISTORY
*NEW MONTHLY MAGAZINE
*NEW PRINCETON REVIEW
 NEW QUARTERLY
*NEW QUARTERLY REVIEW
 NEW REPUBLIC
*NEW REVIEW
 NEW SCIENTIST
 NEW STATESMAN AND
   NATION
*NEW YORK DAILY GRAPHIC
*NEW YORK EVENING POST
*NEW YORK REVIEW
*NEW YORK REVIEW OF
   BOOKS
*NEW YORK SUN
*NEW YORK TIMES
*NEW YORK TRIBUNE

*NEW YORK WORLD
*NEW YORKER
*NINETEENTH CENTURY
  NINETEENTH CENTURY AND
    AFTER
  NINETEENTH-CENTURY FICTION
*NORTH AMERICAN REVIEW
*NORTH BRITISH REVIEW
*NOTES AND QUERIES

*OBERLIN QUARTERLY REVIEW
*OLD AND NEW
*ONCE A WEEK
*OPEN COURT
  OUTLOOK
*OXFORD AND CAMBRIDGE MAG-
    AZINE
  OXFORD AND CAMBRIDGE REVIEW

  PALAESTRIA
*PALL MALL GAZETTE
*PALLADIUM
  PAPERS OF THE BIBLIOGRAPHICAL
    SOCIETY OF AMERICA
*PATERNOSTER REVIEW
*PENN MONTHLY
  PENNSYLVANIA MAGAZINE OF
    HISTORY AND BIOGRAPHY
  PEOPLE'S AND HOWITT'S JOURNAL
  PERSONALIST
*PETERSON'S MAGAZINE
*PHILADELPHIA EVENING BULLETIN
*PHILADELPHIA INQUIRER
*PHILADELPHIA PRESS
*PHILADELPHIA PUBLIC LEDGER
*PHILADELPHIA RECORD
*PHILADELPHIA UNITED STATES
    GAZETTE AND NORTH AMERI-
    CAN
  PHILOLOGICAL QUARTERLY
*PHRENOLOGICAL MAGAZINE
*POET-LORE

  POLITICAL SCIENCE QUAR-
    TERLY
*POPULAR SCIENCE MONTHLY
*POTTER'S AMERICAN MONTH-
    LY
*PRINCETON REVIEW
  PRINCETON UNIVERSITY
    LIBRARY CHRONICLE
  PROCEEDINGS OF THE
    BRITISH ACADEMY
*PROCEEDINGS OF THE MAS-
    SACHUSETTS HISTORICAL
    SOCIETY
*PROCEEDINGS OF THE
    SOCIETY OF ANTIQUARIES
    OF SCOTLAND
*PROGRESS
*PROSPECTIVE REVIEW
  PSYCHOANALYTIC REVIEW
  PUBLICATIONS OF THE
    DUMFRIESSHIRE AND
    GALLOWAY NATURAL
    HISTORY AND ANTIQUAR-
    IAN SOCIETY
  PUBLICATIONS OF THE ENG-
    LISH GOETHE SOCIETY
  PUBLICATIONS OF THE
    MODERN LANGUAGE
    ASSOCIATION
  PUBLISHER'S CIRCULAR
*PUNCH
*PUTNAM'S MONTHLY
    MAGAZINE

*QUARTERLY REVIEW
*QUEEN
  QUEEN'S QUARTERLY

*RAMBLER
  RECORDS OF THE SCOTTISH
    CHURCH HISTORY SOCIETY
*RED DRAGON MAGAZINE

*RELIGIOUS MAGAZINE AND
   MONTHLY REVIEW
REVIEW OF ENGLISH STUDIES
*REVIEW OF REVIEWS
REVUE DE L'UNIVERSITE
   D'OTTAWA
*RICHMOND CENTRAL PRESBY-
   TERIAN
*RICHMOND DISPATCH
*RICHMOND ENQUIRER
*RICHMOND RECORD
*RICHMOND STANDARD
*RICHMOND STATE
*RICHMOND TIMES
*RICHMOND WHIG
ROTARIAN
*RUSKIN READING GUILD
   JOURNAL
RUTGERS UNIVERSITY LIBRARY
   JOURNAL

*SAINT PAUL'S MONTHLY MAG-
   AZINE
*SAN FRANCISCO EVENING
   BULLETIN
*SARTAIN'S UNION MAGAZINE
SATURDAY NIGHT
*SATURDAY REVIEW
SATURDAY REVIEW OF LITERATURE
SCANDINAVIAN STUDIES
SCHOOL AND SOCIETY
SCOTIA
*SCOTS MAGAZINE
SCOTTISH COUNTRY LIFE
SCOTTISH HISTORICAL REVIEW
SCOTTISH LITERARY NEWS
*SCOTTISH REVIEW
SCRAP BOOK
*SCRIBNER'S MAGAZINE
*SELECT JOURNAL OF FOREIGN
   PERIODICAL LITERATURE
SEWANEE REVIEW

*SHARPE'S LONDON MAGAZINE
*SKETCH
SMT MAGAZINE
SOUTH ATLANTIC QUARTERLY
*SOUTHERN LITERARY
   JOURNAL
*SOUTHERN LITERARY MES-
   SENGER
*SOUTHERN QUARTERLY REVIEW
*SOUTHERN REVIEW
SOUTHERN REVIEW (Australia)
*SOUTHERN ROSE
*SPEAKER
*SPECTATOR
*SPRINGFIELD MASSACHU-
   SETTS REPUBLICAN
*ST. JAMES GAZETTE
*ST. JAMES MAGAZINE
*ST. LOUIS GLOBE-DEMOCRAT
*ST. LOUIS MISSOURI
   DEMOCRAT
*ST. LOUIS POST DISPATCH
*ST. LOUIS REPUBLICAN
*STRAND MAGAZINE
STUDIA GERMANICA GAN-
   DENSIA
STUDIES: AN IRISH QUARTER-
   LY REVIEW
STUDIES IN BIBLIOGRAPHY
STUDIES IN ENGLISH LITER-
   ATURE
STUDIES IN ENGLISH LITER-
   ATURE (Tokyo)
STUDIES IN PHILOLOGY
STUDIES IN ROMANTICISM
STUDIES IN SCOTTISH LITER-
   ATURE
STUDIES IN THE NOVEL
STYLE
*SUN (London)
*SUNDAY MAGAZINE
SUSSEX COUNTY MAGAZINE

* SWORD AND THE TROWL

* TABLET (London)
* TAIT'S EDINBURGH MAGAZINE
* TEMPLE BAR
  TEXAS REVIEW
  TEXAS STUDIES IN LITERATURE
    AND LANGUAGE
  THOREAU SOCIETY BULLETIN
  THOTH
  TIME MAGAZINE
* TIMES (London)
* TIMES LITERARY SUPPLEMENT
  TRANSACTIONS OF THE HERZEN
    STATE PEDAGOGICAL INSTITUTE
* TRANSACTIONS OF THE ROYAL
    HISTORICAL SOCIETY
  TRANSACTIONS OF THE ROYAL
    SOCIETY OF CANADA
  TRANSACTIONS OF THE ROYAL
    SOCIETY OF LITERATURE
  TRANSACTIONS OF THE UNIVER-
    SITY OF WISCONSIN ACADEMY
    OF SCIENCES, ARTS, AND
    LETTERS
  TROLLOPIAN
* TRUTH-SEEKER
  TWENTIETH CENTURY

* UNITARIAN REVIEW
* UNIVERSALIST QUARTERLY REVIEW
* UNIVERSITY MAGAZINE (Dublin)
  UNIVERSITY OF CALIFORNIA
    CHRONICLE
  UNIVERSITY OF COLORADO
    STUDIES
  UNIVERSITY OF EDINBURGH
    JOURNAL
  UNIVERSITY OF SOUTHERN CALI-
    FORNIA STUDIES IN COMPAR-
    ATIVE LITERATURE
  UNIVERSITY OF TORONTO
    QUARTERLY

* UNIVERSITY QUARTERLY
    REVIEW
  UNPOPULAR REVIEW

  VICTORIAN NEWSLETTER
  VICTORIAN POETRY
  VICTORIAN STUDIES
  VILLAGER

  WALT WHITMAN NEWSLETTER
* WELDON'S REGISTER
* WESLEYAN METHODIST
    MAGAZINE
  WESTERN HUMANITIES
    REVIEW
* WESTERN MESSENGER
  WESTERN POLITICAL QUAR-
    TERLY
  WILSON LIBRARY BULLETIN
* WORLD (London)

  XENIA PRAGENSIA

* YALE LITERARY MAGAZINE
  YALE REVIEW
  YALE UNIVERSITY LIBRARY
    BULLETIN
  YALE UNIVERSITY LIBRARY
    GAZETTE
  YEARBOOK OF ENGLISH
    STUDIES
* YOUNG MAN

AUTHOR INDEX

AUTHOR INDEX

Barry, William F., 1259
Bartlett, David W., 364
Bartol, C. A., 74
Barzun, Jacques, 2506
Bates, William, 654
Bathhurst, Katharine, 2105
Batho, Edith C., 2442
Batt, Max, 1814
Battershall, W. W., 476
Baugh, Albert C., 2565
Baumgarten, Murray, 2831, 2847, 2973
Bayne, Peter, 391, 746, 747, 748, 749, 750, 751, 752
Bayne, Thomas, 775, 1348, 1457, 1458, 1514, 1724, 1846, 1974
Baynes, T. Spencer, 660, 1349
Beach, Joseph W., 2408
Beatty, Richmond C., 2457
Beaty, Jerome, 2903
Beckwith, Frank A., 731
Belben, Edward P., 1644
Bell, Charles D., 940
Bell, Elizabeth G., 2155
Bell, Richard, 2716
Ben-Israel, Hedva, 2697, 2848
Bennett, D. M., 709
Bensly, E., 1774, 1951, 2016, 2106
Benson, Arthur C., 2017
Bentley, Eric R., 2528, 2529, 2537
Bently, George, 941, 942
Benton, Jay, 1928, 1929
Berger, Harold L., 2762, 2800
Bernbaum, Ernest, 2286
Bertolotti, D. S., 2832
Besant, Walter, 1567
Bett, W. R., 2604
Bevan, Henry E. J., 1830
Beveridge, H., 1219
Bickley, F., 2264
Bicknell, Percy F., 1775, 1815, 1899

Binns, William, 943
Birch, W. J., 1308
Birrell, Augustine, 1220, 1280, 1776
Black, William, 1663
Blackburn, William, 2556
Blackstone, B., 2409
Blaikie, William G., 944
Blair, David, 542, 661
Blair, Walter, 2682
Blankenagel, John C., 2199
Blunt, Reginald, 945, 1591, 1738, 2032, 2107, 2108, 2332
Bodelsen, Carl A., 2174
Bolton, Sarah K., 1430
Boner, Charles, 629
Bonnard, G. A., 2265
Bouchier, Jonathan, 630, 710, 1350, 1459, 1515, 1592, 1725
Bowen, Clarence W., 691
Bowen, Francis, 48
Bower, George S., 946
Boyesen, H. H., 1516
Bradbrook, W., 1865
Bradley, Herbert D., 2126
Brand, C. Neville, 2087
Brantlinger, Patrick, 2881, 2965, 2999
Brewer, E. Cobham, 1221
Brice, Alec W., 2856
Briggs, Alsa, 2651
Brightwell, D. Barron, 947
Brimley, George, 345
Brinton, C. Crane, 2351
Britton, Norman, 1160
Broadbent, Henry, 2200
Brock, D. Heyward, 2966
Brookes, Gerry H., 2967
Brookfield, Charles, 1831
Brookfield, Frances, 1831, 1847
Brooks, Elmer L., 2624
Brooks, Richard, 2371
Brown, Frances, 1930

Cazamian, Louis, 1976, 2334, 3000
Cecil, David, 2684
Chadwick, John W., 956
Chalmers, E. B., 2938
Chamberlain, D. H., 1261
Chamberlin, Benjamin B., 2227
Chambers, Robert, 395
Chancellor, E. Beresford, 1593
Chandler, Alice K., 2908
Channing, W. H., 75
Chapman, Edward M., 1934
Chapman, J. A., 2129
Chapman, Raymond, 2850
Cheever, Leonard A., 3018
Chesterton, Gilbert K., 1750, 1751, 1780, 1977, 1997, 2141
Chew, Samuel C., 2565
Chillingworth, H. R., 2575
Chrisman, Lewis H., 2175, 2203
Christensen, Allan C., 2939
Christian, Mildred G., 2558
Clapp, Theodore, 409
Chapton, George T., 2335
Clare, Maurice, 1998
Clark, Alexander, 2698
Clark, Daniel, 652
Clark, Henry W., 2313
Clark, J. B. M., 2142
Clark, J. Scott, 1690
Clark, Lord, 2972
Clarke, Alexander F., 2851
Clarke, C., 1900
Clarke, James F., 76, 521
Clarke, Margaret, 2940
Clarke, William, 1549
Cline, C. L., 3001
Clubbe, John, 2941
Cobban, Alfred, 2766
Cochrane, Mary, 1594
Cochrane, Robert, 753, 767, 1381, 1594

Cochrane, William, 1351
Cocke, Zitella, 1431
Cockshut, A. O. J., 3019
Cofer, David B., 2314
Coffey, Robert S., 957
Coffin, Edward F., 2352
Coleman, A. M., 2411, 2443
Collier, William F., 478
Collins, John C., 1595
Collins, Philip, 2942
Collis, John S., 2943
"Common Sense," 958
Common, Thomas 1596
Congdon, Charles T., 1225
Conway, Moncure D., 959, 960, 961, 962, 1411, 1816, 3002
Cook, Davidson, 2075
Cook, Emily, 1781
Cook, Henry, 2469
Cooke, Alice L., 2699
Cooke, John E., 309, 379, 444
Coolidge, Susan, 1262
Cooper, Berenice, 2700
Copcott, Francis, 146
Copeland, Charles T., 1691, 1692
Cornwall, Barry, 740
Cosh, T. R., 1833
Coulling, Sidney M. B., 2909
Courthope, William J., 662, 1165, 1263
Courtney, William L., 768
Courtney, William P., 1954
Coustillas, Pierre, 3003
Cowell, Herbert, 1105
Craig, Robert S., 1883
Cramb, John A., 2020
Creek, H. L., 2187
Crichton-Browne, James, 1665, 1779, 1782, 2021, 2130, 2204, 2290
Cocker, Stephen F., 2718
Croker, D., 963

E., J. W., 713
E., M. B., 1413
E., R. B., 148
Earland, Ada, 1935
Earle, Peter G., 2785
Ebel, Henry, 2815
Edgar, A., 732
Edger, Samuel, 1314
Edinburgh Evening Post, 22
Editor, 697, 1166
Edmunds, A. J., 2337
Ehrlich, H., 2816
Eidson, John O., 2643, 2855
Eliot, George, 366, 392
Elliott, J. J., 2077
Ellis, George E., 77
Ellsworth, Erastus W., 312
Elton, Oliver, 1979, 2092
Emerson, George H., 1266, 1267
Emerson, Ralph W., 149, 396, 975
Ericson, Eston E., 2413, 2719
Ernle, Lord, 2158
Esher, 2559
Espinasse, Francis, 348, 1463
Estrich, Robert M., 2606
Ethlinger, L., 2538
Evans, T. C., 1382
Everett, Alexander H., 34
Ewing, Thomas J., 1464

F., A., 1268
F., A. J., 1353
F., A. L., 1955
F., A. R., 1269
F., C. L., 1851
Fain, John T., 2651
Falconer, J. A., 2110
Farrar, Frederick W., 1666
Faulkner, Peter, 2975
Faverty, Frederic E., 2720, 3022
Feltes, Norman N., 2833
Felton, C. C., 213

Ferguson, William, 2817
Ficulnus, 377
Fidelis, 976
Fido, Martin, 3000
Fiedler, H. G., 2507
Field, H. M., 313
Fielding, Kenneth J., 2644, 2856
Fields, James T., 698
Filler, Louis, 2607
Finlayson, C. P., 2744
Firkins, O. W., 2232
Fischer, Thomas A., 1754, 1784
Fish, Howard M., 2652
Fisher, W. J., 2206
Fitch, George H., 1980
FitzGerald, Percy, 1999
Fitzhugh, George, 410, 470
Fleming, George, 1597
Fletcher, J. B., 1834
Flint, Helen C., 1936
Flint, Thomas, 1868, 1869, 1870,
    1871, 1902, 1903, 1937, 1956,
    1981, 2000, 2022, 2078, 2159
Flournoy, F. R., 2595
Flower, R., 2433
Flügel, Ewald, 1465
Foot, Isaac, 2548
Forbes, H. M., 2233
Ford, Boris, 2706
Ford, George H., 2567
Forster, John, 438
Forster, Joseph, 1667
Foster, Fred W., 1167
Foster, J. K., 150
Foster, W. E., 977
Fox-Bourne, H. R., 978, 1107
Francis, John C., 979
Francison, Alfred, 1315
Francke, Kuno, 2207
Frank, Parson, 314
Franke, Wolfgang, 3023
Franklin, G. M., 1694

Jervis, H., 2446
Jessop, A., 1360
Jewett, Isaac, 78
John, Brian, 2914
Johnson, J. Ruddiman, 2095, 2115
Johnson, Lionel, 1526
Johnson, Richard C., 2915
Johnson, Wendell S., 2770
Johnson, William S., 1960
Jones, Iva G., 2836
Jones, Joseph, 2736
Jones, Philip L., 1002
Jones, Samuel A., 1791, 2080
Jones, William A., 411
Joynt, J. W., 2299

K., L. L., 1525
Kanes, Evelyn, 2973
Kavanagh, J., 2483
Kaye, Julian B., 2703
Kebbel, Thomas E., 523
Keeling, Annie E., 1003
Kegel, Charles H., 2669, 2704, 2745, 2787
Keith, C., 2396
Keith, W. J., 2837
Kelly, J. J., 1385
Kelly, Marshall, 2037
Kelman, John, 1983, 2162
Kelton, Mrs., 459
Kennard, Kate, 378
Kennedy, W. S., 1386, 1527
Kennedy, William F., 2705
Kenny, Blair G., 2916
Kent, William, 2588
Kerlin, Robert T., 1984
Kerr, James, 1361
Keys, D. R., 2341
Kiely, Benedict, 2550
Kim, Suk-Joo, 2753
Kimball, LeRoy E., 2472
King, Marjorie P., 2645

Kingsland, W. G., 1469
Kingsley, M. E., 1961
"Kingsmill, Hugh," 2342, 2358, 2359
Kirby, Thomas A., 2551, 2552, 2560
Kirk, J. F., 594, 595, 603
Kirk, Russell, 2889
Kirkham, E. Bruce, 2917
Klenze, Camillo von, 2436
Knickerbocker, Kenneth L., 2360
Knight, George, 2192
Knight, William, 1818
Knighton, William, 1004
Kocmanova, J., 2838
Krause, Anna, 2670
Kuhn, Helmut, 2569
Kummer, George, 2415
Kusch, Robert W., 2890, 2891, 2947

L., S., 499
L., W. P., 215
Laing, Samuel, 1274
Lancaster, Henry H., 548
Landreth, P., 482
Lane, Lauriat, 2948
Lane, William C., 1176, 1362
Lane-Poole, Stanley, 1363
Lang, Andrew, 1005, 1792
Langbaum, Robert W., 2688
Larkin, Henry, 758, 1006, 1320
Larminie, W., 1730
Laughlin, Clara E., 1839
Laun, Henri Van, 634, 1387
LaValley, Albert J., 2862
Lea, Frank A., 2484, 2508, 2788
Lecky, William E. H., 1470
Lee, Gerald S., 1604
Lee, Marian, 1418
Lee, Sydney, 1793
"Lee, Vernon," 1819

Martin, Peter E., 2804
Martin, Robert B., 2612
Martin, William, 1435
Martineau, Harriet, 737
Martineau, James, 399
Marwick, William, 1419
Marwick, William H., 2866
Marx, Olga, 2179
Mason, J., 1364
Masson, David, 323, 549, 641,
   1011, 1277, 1472, 1888
Masson, Flora, 2319
Masson, Rosaline, 2117, 2131
Masterman, C. F. G., 1841
Matheson, A., 1436
Matthew, G. A., 1796
Matthews, Brander, 1938
Matz, Bertram W., 1757, 2163
Maurer, Oscar, 2723
Maurice, Frederick D., 151
Maurois, Andrè, 2273
Maynard, T., 2613
Mayo, I. F., 1638
Mazzini, Joseph, 107, 162
McCarthy, D., 1910
McCarthy, Justin, 1012, 1797, 1911
McCarthy, Patrick J., 2950
McCosh, James, 1178
McCrie, George, 702
McCullen, J. T., 2918
McGhee, Richard D., 2892
McGovern, J. B., 1873, 2211
McGovern, William M., 2485
McKeehan, Irene P., 2510
McMahon, James, 2026
McMahon, Morgan, 1912, 1572
McMaster, Rowland D., 2867
McNeill, R., 1798
McNicoll, Thomas, 368
McPherson, J. G., 1437
McRobert, G., 1966
Mead, Edwin D., 1013, 1799

Mead, George H., 2417
Medico, 2050
Meikle, Henry W., 2579
Meiklejohn, J. M. D., 1821
Meldrum, David S., 1473
Mellish, J T., 1913
MEMORABILIST, 2511, 2512, 2513,
   2514
Mendel, Sydney, 2842
Mercer, Elizabeth A., 1573
Merivale, Herman, 108, 550
Merritt, James D., 2868
Metcalfe, William M., 1179, 1278
Metzger, Lore, 2747
Milburn, William H., 460
Mill, Anna J., 2805
Mill, John S., 47, 243, 310, 655
Millar, Moorhouse I. X., 2066
Miller, Frank, 1939, 2082, 2437
Milner, Gamaliel, 2376
Minnow in a Creek, 1553
Minto, William, 642, 666
Mitchell, Ellen M., 667
Mitford, A. B., 945
Mitford, Nancy, 2869
Miyoshi, Masao, 2893
Moers, Ellen, 2739
Molony, J. Chartres, 2541
Moncrieff, James, 216
Monkhouse, Cosmo, 1731
Monkshood, 400
Monteiro, George, 2894
Moody, John, 2212
Moody, William V., 1758
Moore, Carlisle, 2473, 2515, 2654,
   2689, 2690, 2821
Moore, T. V., 252
More, Paul E., 1842
Morgan, Lady Sydney, 49, 109, 152
Morgan, P., 2919
Morgan, Peter F., 2920
Morgan, W., 2051

Spalding, John L., 770
Sparke, Archibald, 1987
Sparrow, W. Keats, 2926
Sparrow, W. S., 2040
Speck, William A., 2196
Spence, Louis, 2134
Spence, R. M., 1192
Spencer, F. M., 1616
Sperber, Hans, 2606
Spivey, Herbert E., 2462, 2927
Spring-Rice, Thomas, 329
St., C. B., 1391
St. Helier, Mary J., 1942
St. John, Horace, 503
Stanley, Arthur P., 1122
Stark, Lewis M., 2600
Stark, Werner, 2520
Starnes, De Witt T., 2120
Starrett, Agnes L., 2563
Starzyk, Lawrence J., 2928, 2956
Stawell, F. Melian, 1968, 2247, 2248
Stearns, Frank P., 1617, 1677
Stebbins, Lucy P., 2618
Steggall, Julius, 1391
Stephen, James F., 442, 525, 526, 527, 552, 553, 1327, 1328
Stephen, Leslie, 668, 1040, 1041, 1369, 1618, 1760, 1943, 2167
Sterling, John, 90
Stevenson, G. H., 2379
Stewart, George, 759
Stewart, Herbert L., 2057, 2058, 2070, 2083, 2084, 2099, 2121
Stewart, Jack F., 2872
Stigand, William, 463
Stirling, James H., 307, 605
Stockley, V. A., 2277
Storrs, Margaret, 2278
Strachan, L. R. M., 1877, 1988, 1989, 1990, 2249, 2325

Strachey, Edward, 1579
Strachey, G., 1535, 1558
Straka, Gerald M., 2694
Stratford, J., 2873
Strauch, Carl F., 2796, 2898
Strout, Alan L., 2533, 2649
Stuart, Donald C., 2957
Sullivan, Margaret F., 1042, 1193
Summerfield, Charles, 232
Sunderland, J. T., 2400
Sussman, Herbert L., 2874
Sutherland, James R., 2695
Sutton, Max K., 2827
Swanson, Donald R., 2845, 2899
Swart, Koenraad W., 2759
Swinburne, Algernon C., 718, 719, 1043
Swithin, St., 1890
Sykes, W., 1804
Symington, Andrew J., 1044
Symonds, Emily M., 2346
Symons, Julian A., 2619, 2675
Synge, M. B., 1922

T., C., 2521, 2534, 2636
T., J. E., 1619
Tabor, Mary C., 1045
Taine, Hippolyte A., 634
Tanselle, G. Thomas 2915
Tarr, Rodger L., 2875, 2929, 2930, 2958, 2959, 2960, 2961, 2964, 2988, 2989, 2990, 3009, 3032, 3033
Tassin, Algernon, 2008
Tayler, John J., 220
Taylor, Alan J. P., 2637, 2738, 2676
Taylor, E. R., 1746
Taylor, Henry, 1046, 1287
Tebbutt, C. P., 1747
Templeman, William D., 2592
Tener, Robert H., 2777

SUBJECT INDEX

SUBJECT INDEX

Note: this index is designed to facilitate use of the bibliography proper, but is not intended to replace actual reference.

125, 160, 181, 229, 316, 321, 348,
364, 365, 383, 389, 390, 395,
396, 411, 434, 445, 478, 484,
546, 599, 613, 614, 616, 628,
637, 642, 652, 654, 667, 669,
670, 691, 697, 706, 721, 735,
802, 803, 851, 859, 880, 946,
954, 969, 974, 975, 983, 1006,
1008, 1026, 1050, 1059, 1177,
1182, 1240, 1277, 1286, 1353,
1364, 1369, 1381, 1430, 1448,
1528, 1530, 1568, 1570, 1580,
1642, 1643, 1665, 1668, 1735,
1737, 1751, 1757, 1793, 1827,
1829, 1884, 1911, 1943, 2117,
2145, 2167, 2197, 2522
Biographies, 611, 653, 727, 729,
730, 782, 953, 962, 965, 1039,
1062, 1108, 1197, 1226, 1354,
1379, 1433, 1435, 1529, 1594,
2287, 2303, 2328, 2382, 2461,
2577, 2608, 2609, 3017
"BIOGRAPHY," 2647
Birrens (Scotland), 1950
Birthday (C's), 638, 683, 684, 687,
704, 744, 1586, 1587, 1626, 1628
Bismark, Prince, 649, 687, 1346
BLACKWOOD'S EDINBURGH
MAGAZINE, 308, 2649
Blake, William, 2127, 2223, 2914
Blue Books, 2925
Blumine, 1535, 1573, 1733
Blunt, Reginald, 1588, 1629
Bolte, Amely, 1487
Bonhours, Père, 635
Bookplate (C's), 2061
Booksellers, 274, 2095, 2115
Boswell, James, 18, 757, 1614, 2514
Brooks, Charles T., 2436, 2996
Browning, Elizabeth B., 161, 1608,
1689, 3022
Browning, Robert, 605, 1337, 1429,

2033, 2514, 2525, 2715, 2741,
2774, 2799, 2861, 2895, 2991,
3022
Buchanan, George, 696
Büchner, Georg, 2629
Buckle, Henry T., 779
Bunsen, Christian C. J., Baron, 2196
"BURNS," 18, 244, 775, 1837,
1958, 1961, 2482
Burns, J., 1933
Burns, Robert, 17, 18, 700, 710, 714,
720, 764, 1636, 1639, 1699, 1709,
1722, 2091, 2136
Butler, Charles, 1680, 2472
Byron, George Gordon, Lord, 146,
1887, 1909, 2793
Cambridge Scholarship, 2349
Cameron, Julia M., 1659
Campan, Madame, 1181, 1185
Canada, 2121, 2305, 2754
Canadian Carlyles, 2112, 2341,
2754
Carlyle, Alexander (brother), 2754
Carlyle, Alexander (cousin), 225
Carlyle, Alexander (nephew), 763,
2308, 2435
Carlyle, James (father), 927, 971
Carlyle, Jane Welsh (wife), 566,
862, 930, 938, 1006, 1045, 1089,
1107, 1130, 1138, 1142, 1143, 1144,
1145, 1146, 1148, 1150, 1151, 1156,
1161, 1169, 1175, 1179, 1180, 1183,
1184, 1191, 1194, 1195, 1216, 1217,
1224, 1234, 1265, 1275, 1276,
1282, 1286, 1303, 1355, 1363,
1377, 1395, 1399, 1400, 1402,
1403, 1407, 1408, 1419, 1426,
1427, 1432, 1442, 1448, 1449,
1450, 1463, 1467, 1468, 1487,
1510, 1512, 1533, 1580, 1609,
1627, 1669, 1687, 1697, 1717,
1728, 1738, 1742, 1761, 1764,